Babylonia, the Gulf Region, and the Indus

Mesopotamian Civilizations

General Editor
Jerrold S. Cooper, *Johns Hopkins University*

Editorial Board

Walter Farber, *University of Chicago*
Piotr Michalowski, *University of Michigan*
Simo Parpola, *University of Helsinki*
Karen Radner, *Ludwig-Maximilians Universität, Munich*

Jack Sasson, *Vanderbilt University*
Piotr Steinkeller, *Harvard University*
Marten Stol, *Free University of Amsterdam*
Irene Winter, *Harvard University*

Babylonia, the Gulf Region, and the Indus

Archaeological and Textual Evidence for Contact in the Third and Early Second Millennia B.C.

Steffen Laursen and Piotr Steinkeller

Winona Lake, Indiana
EISENBRAUNS
2017

Library of Congress Cataloging-in-Publication Data

Names: Laursen, Steffen, author. | Steinkeller, Piotr, author.
Title: Babylonia, the Gulf Region, and the Indus : archaeological and textual evidence for contact in the third and early second millennia B.C. / Steffen Laursen and Piotr Steinkeller.
Description: Winona Lake, Indiana : Eisenbrauns, 2017. | Includes bibliographical references. | Description based on print version record and CIP data provided by publisher; resource not viewed.
Identifiers: LCCN 2017007318 (print) | LCCN 2017012647 (ebook) | ISBN 9781575067575 (ePDF) | ISBN 9781575067568 | ISBN 9781575067568 (hardback) : alk. paper)
Subjects: LCSH: Iraq—Civilization—To 634. | Iraq—Antiquities. | Babylonia—Civilization.
Classification: LCC DS69.5 (ebook) | LCC DS69.5 .L38 2017 (print) | DDC 935/.05—dc23
LC record available at https://lccn.loc.gov/2017007318

The story of life is quicker than the wink of an eye
— Jimi Hendrix

In fond memory of
Maurizio Tosi (1944–2017),
a colossus of Middle Asian archaeology and
a dear friend and colleague

Contents

Preface

This book is the product of a collaborative effort that began, almost accidentally, in 2008. Following many e-mail exchanges about various points related to the archaeology and history of the Persian Gulf region during the third millennium BC, we concluded that, because of the great accumulation of new data and the persistence of some misconceptions, there was a pressing need to produce an up-to-date synthetic evaluation of this subject. Conceived originally as an article, this project gradually expanded, eventually becoming a monograph.

The evidence bearing on the early Persian Gulf is enormous, and so the choice of data and topics explored in this book is of necessity selective. Because of our mutual interests, we focus primarily on the nature of cultural and commercial interactions that existed between Mesopotamia and the cultures of Tilmun (Bahrain), Makkan (Oman Peninsula), and Meluhha (Indus Valley). Although we reach back to the fourth millennium, the time-frame of our investigation is essentially the third and early second millennia BC.

It is our great pleasure to acknowledge the assistance this project received from various individuals and institutions. Laursen gives his special thanks to the Moesgaard Museum and its staff, who, over a period of many years, have enthusiastically supported his excavations on Bahrain and offered a perfect environment for his research. His work on this book was made possible by a grant from the Danish Council for Independent Research / Culture and Communication.[1]

We both offer our heartfelt thanks to Jim Eisenbraun for accepting our manuscript in his *Mesopotamian Civilizations* series, and to Jerrold Cooper, for reading it exceedingly carefully and suggesting many important improvements, both with regard to content and form. We also warmly acknowledge the editorial help provided by Ryan Winters. While all this assistance was essential, only we are responsible for this book's final shape.

There is yet another, more personal side to this project. Both of our interests in the ancient history of the Persian Gulf in no small measure grew from the work and inspiration of our teachers: Flemming Højlund and A. Leo Oppenheim and I. J. Gelb, respectively. Højlund has extensively published and excavated in Bahrain and on Failaka Island, producing some of the fundamental studies on Gulf archaeology (see the bibliography below, pp. 119ff., esp. p. 126). Oppenheim and Gelb wrote articles that were instrumental in putting Tilmun, Makkan, and Meluhha on the map.[2] Our debt to these three scholars is gratefully and affectionately acknowledged.

---

1. Project 0602-02482B "Collapse: The 'Eclipse of the East' and the Rise of Dilmun State in Bahrain, ca. 2000 BC."
2. "The Seafaring Merchants of Ur," *Journal of the American Oriental Society* (1954) 6–17; "Makkan and Meluhha in Early Mesopotamian Sources," *Revue d'Assyriologie* 64 (1970) 1–8.

As we were correcting the proofs, the news of the untimely passing of Maurizio Tosi reached us. More than any other scholar, Maurizio was responsible for the formulation of the concept of early Middle Asia as a highly interconnected entity, a notion that is central to this book. In recognition of Maurizio's enormous contributions to the history and archaeology of Middle Asia, and of the Ancient Near East more generally, we dedicate these pages to his memory.

Chapter 1

Introduction

Textual evidence of contact between Babylonia and the Persian Gulf [1] during the third and early second millennium BC has been extensively collected and analyzed by scholars in the past.[2] Together, these studies have established a fundamental understanding of the activities of Babylonia in the Lower Sea and provided valuable insight into the more-or-less exotic lands with which the Babylonians came into contact (see fig. 1, p. 2). It has, however, been a common characteristic of these principally textual studies to refrain from wholeheartedly integrating the archaeological evidence from the Gulf in their reconstructions. The consequent shortcomings have only been further accentuated by the dramatic increase of archaeological data, in particular on Tilmun and Makkan, in recent decades.

As a reflection of our respective professional interests and because of the extant historical and archaeological sources, in this study emphasis has been placed on the role of Babylonia and her interactions with Tilmun and Makkan. The relationships with other regions—for example, Marhaši and Meluhha—are also addressed but less systematically so and only when they serve to frame our reconstructions at the more general level. The main focus has been on developments through the third millennium BC, particularly its later half, and the first centuries of the second millennium BC, while the prehistoric background for international Gulf trade in earlier millennia is more briefly touched upon.

The intention of this contribution is by no means to deliver a fully exhaustive survey of the now staggering body of evidence for contact between Babylonia and the lands of the Gulf and beyond. Instead, we shall here attempt to blend the qualities of a kaleidoscopic overview with a number of selected micro-studies in which the combination of archaeology and texts offers new insights.

The main body of the book (chaps. 2–7) offers a chronologically organized discussion of the pertinent data, from the Prehistoric phase down to the post-Ur III period. Two additional chapters treat, respectively, the long-term function of the Lagaš town of Gu'abba as Babylonia's main seaport as well as its shipyard, caravanserai, and major textile production facility (chap. 8), and the question of the presence of Meluhhans in Babylonia and the data illustrating the contacts between Babylonia and Meluhha (chap. 9).

---

1. Hereafter: "the Gulf."
2. For example, Oppenheim 1954; Leemans 1960; Heimpel 1987; Glassner 2002.

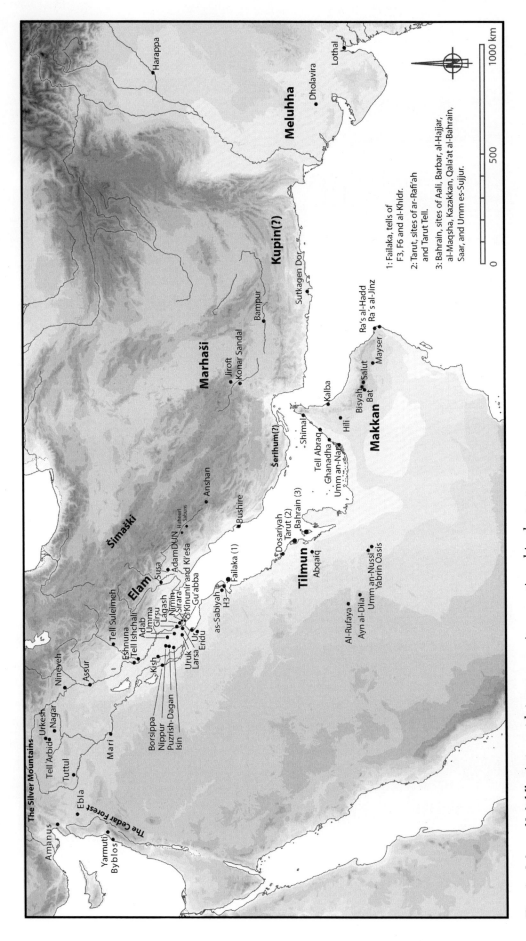

Fig. 1. Map of Middle Asia, with important sites mentioned in the text.

The book is completed by three appendixes, which offer supplementary data of relevance to both micro-studies and the overall case. Appendix 1 contains a selection of fourteen texts ranging in date from Gudea of Lagaš to Šu-ilišu of Isin, offering important information on the contacts between Babylonia and Makkan and Tilmun. Appendix 2 discusses Babylonia's seagoing fleet of the so-called "Makkan Ships" and "Big Ships" and presents a cylinder seal belonging to a "captain" of one of the big ships (ugula lu₂ ma₂-gal-gal), as well as two cylinder seals belonging to "big ship" personnel, all discovered at sites in Tilmun. Appendix 3 discusses two characteristic types of late third- and early second-millennium BC Babylonian import vessels, frequently used as grave goods in Tilmun, as evidence of systematic exchange.

Among the specific historical questions we address are the following:

- What conditioned the decline of Tilmun in the post Sargonic and Ur III periods?
- What caused the major population contraction on Bahrain Island ca. 2200 BC?
- Why did Makkan, Marhaši, and Meluhha disappear after the fall of the Ur III state?

Working Premise

Copious literature now exists dealing with the geography of the lands known by the ancient Babylonians as Tilmun, Makkan, Marhaši, and Meluhha. Even if the geographical locations of these lands remain to varying degrees the subject of controversy, we shall operate on the premise that:

- *Tilmun* includes present-day Kuwait, the Eastern province of Saudi Arabia, and Bahrain Island, and corresponds archaeologically to the "Barbar/Dilmun culture."
- *Makkan* encompasses present-day United Arab Emirates and Northern Oman and possibly the coastal region of Iran along the Strait of Hormuz, and the western section of Makran/Baluchistan. Archaeologically, Makkan corresponds to the Hafit, Umm an-Nar, and Wadi Suq Cultures.
- *Marhaši* roughly corresponds to the Iranian province of Kerman, in particular the Halid Rud river basin, and had its urban center at Konar Sandal. Archaeologically, Marhaši is identical to the "Jiroft Civilization," possibly also encompassing the "Bampur culture."[3]
- *Meluhha* broadly represents the Indus Valley and Gujarat. Archaeologically, Meluhha corresponds to the Harappan culture in its mature phase.

Confronting and Combining Archaeology and Texts

When working in a period and geographical area for which written sources are available, it is obvious that the archaeologist has no choice but to consider the evidence in his evaluation of the material data. Although this has been the standard practice in Near Eastern archaeology since the very beginning of the discipline, this procedure has not been free of certain ambiguity—and perhaps even resentment—on the part of archaeologists. Because they lack the philological and historical expertise that would permit them to evaluate written data independently, archaeologists usually need to rely on the findings and judgments of their philologically oriented colleagues. This dependence on

---

3. For reference, see Steinkeller 2006a: 1–2.

other authorities, which unavoidably imposes an element of restriction on the work of the archaeologist, has sometimes led to a sense of frustration if not outright deprivation. One frustrated archaeologist has even bitterly asked: "why have most archaeologists suffered so long from 'the tyranny of the text'?" (Kohl 2006: 335). To be sure, archaeology and philology are two independent disciplines, possessing completely different methodologies, and by their very nature they are suited to ask and to answer entirely different types of questions. Ideally, each of them should address specific issues from its own unique vantage point and through the use of its own data and methodology, without any recourse to the resources of the other field. However, since archaeology is a historical science, and since the ultimate questions it seeks to answer are historical ones, few would disagree that some sort of a synthesis between its findings and the data that is derived from written sources should be produced, at least at the very end of the process. As a matter of fact, the history of archaeological research shows that few of the essential findings about the "historical" Near Eastern periods have been made through the study of material data alone; more often than not, such findings rest primarily on the evidence of texts. This is particularly obvious in the area of periodization and the identification of discrete cultural and historical phenomena (such as, e.g., the Sargonic phenomenon, whose existence, if not for texts, would not be detectable in the material data).[4] Thus, whether he wishes or not, the archaeologist cannot escape texts. What he can do, however, is to approach texts knowlegably and professionally—and this can only be achieved through close cooperation with a qualified philologist, ideally one with an interest in material culture and with at least some grasp of archaeological issues. Needless to say, such a cooperation will inform the thinking and the work of the philologist as well. And this is precisely the objective this study seeks to accomplish. The reader will be the judge.

Solutions to the problems of the floating third- and early second-millennium BC historical chronology[5] or the weaknesses in contemporary regional archaeological chronologies are not readily available. Consequently, when combining archaeological and textual evidence from the third and early second millennium BC within a single chronological framework, one is, because of the coarse-grained temporal resolution of both types of data, confronted with an obvious issue of cohesion.[6] In addition, the convergence of philological and archaeological data becomes increasingly difficult when a geographical distance exists between the sources of the two types of data.[7]

Since we inevitably cannot avoid (or resist) including in our interpretations both discussions of major historic trajectories and single events/isolated archaeological observations, caution will be exercised in order to avoid our historical reconstruction becoming "a house of cards" that will come tumbling down in the likely future event that one or more invalid arguments have to be removed.

Among the questions one wishes to address by comparing archaeology and texts, an effort should be made to distinguish between conclusions that are more-or-less sensitive to the problems of chronological resolution. As an example, the validity of conclusions about the causal relationship between historically documented single events temporally confined to a day, month, or year (e.g., the sacking

---

4. Archaeologists use texts all the time—and often very enthusiasically—though not always with good results. *Vide casus* Kohl, the self-declared "enemy" of texts, who has based his theories about economic exchanges in third millenium Western Asia partly on the doubtful evidence of Sumerian literary sources (Kohl 1978; 1979).

5. Hunger 2009.

6. Cleuziou and Méry 2002: 279.

7. Eidem and Højlund 1993: 441.

of Ur / the fall of the Third dynasty of Ur) and phenomena observed in the archaeological record (e.g., the change in material culture from the Umm an-Nar to Wadi Suq period on the Oman peninsula) are inherently challenged by the temporal resolution available for comparison. Conversely, on those occasions when one seeks to draw inference between a historically documented horizon lasting a century or more (e.g., the ca. 2250–2100 BC post Sargonic collapse of the Gulf trade) and lasting changes observed in the archaeological record, we expect the problem of chronological precision to be less pronounced.

Some Methodological Considerations

It is useful at this point to offer a few general observations about texts as a potential source of information about foreign trade and contacts with the outside world more generally. Almost as a rule, foreign trade is exceedingly rarely reflected in cuneiform documentation. While true of all the periods of ancient Mesopotamian history, this applies in particular to the third millennium BC. Two basic reasons are responsible for this situation. First, foreign commercial exchanges were conducted either through official/diplomatic channels or via the activities of private merchants (who acted as purchasing agents for public institutions), neither of which were recorded. More important here, however, are the general characteristics of administrative records. As a general principle, this kind of documentation is concerned overwhelmingly with the expenditures of goods produced or owned by a given agency. In contrast, deliveries of incoming goods—that is, those entering the agency from the outside—are usually not recorded in administrative texts (Steinkeller 2003). For this reason, records of foreign materials brought to Mesopotamia from abroad are exceedingly rare. Somewhat more common, but still very rare in comparison with the information bearing on other areas of economic activity, are records of goods that were issued to long-distance traders as merchandise. Usually, however, one learns about such exchanges only indirectly, from evidence such as references to the materials that were used to pack the outgoing merchandise, the provisioning and repair of sea-going boats, the issues of food to the sailors and other personnel that were associated with the ventures in question, and similar indications of accidental nature.

A good case in point is written documentation bearing on the exports of Babylonian textiles to Makkan and the Gulf region more generally. From the Ur III period, there survive only a handful of texts mentioning such exports. It can safely be conjectured, however, that shipments of this kind were extremely common, with the volume of textiles that were yearly exported to Makkan and other Gulf destinations running in the thousands, if not in the tens of thousands. As we argue in detail in chap. 8, this point is demonstrated by the fact that one of the principal centers of textile production in Ur III times was located in Gu'abba, a major town of the Girsu/ Lagaš province and the chief seaport of the Ur III state. The peripheral location of this important (possibly even the largest) center of Ur III textile production defies any explanation—*unless* one assumes that the vast majority of Gu'abba's textiles were produced for export in the Gulf region. But, of the hundreds of thousands of garments that had likely been shipped from Gu'abba to the various Gulf destinations over the century or so marking the existence of the Ur III state, only a few were recorded in cuneiform tablets. And, due to their perishable nature, none of them left any trace in the surviving archaeological record from the Gulf.

For the same reasons, it is equally difficult to trace—either in texts or archaeology—the movement of other perishables, such as cereals, oils, and spices—from Babylonia to the Gulf. In the case of oils and spices, however, the receptacles that were used to transport these commodities can occasionally be identified among the archaeological remains. As in the case of textiles, the volume of these exports may have been very substantial.

As already noted, materials that were imported from the Gulf region are even more rarely mentioned in Babylonian economic texts. Hence the importance of archaeology, since the archaeological record is an invaluable index of what had actually been imported from the Gulf to Mesopotamia (at least as far as non-perishables are concerned). These finds demonstrate that, at least since the Uruk period, the Gulf region was actively involved in the transshipment of a variety of luxury goods, among which lapis lazuli, carnelian, and decorated chlorite vases stand out. The case of chlorite vases is particularly instructive here, since these artifacts, which are archaeologically documented throughout the Gulf, Babylonia, and the neighboring regions, can ultimately be traced to workshops situated in southeastern Iran—in historical terms, the kingdom of Marhaši. Thus, even without textual corroboration, we may conclude that these objects were first carried overland from southeastern Iran to the Gulf, then to be shipped via various Gulf stops to Babylonia. Carnelian, a product obtained mainly (if not exclusively) from the Indus valley and Gujarat (Meluhha), was transported from the Indus valley over a very similar sea route. And it can be surmised that most of the lapis that came to Mesopotamia during the third millennium was likewise obtained via maritime connections, from the intermediary sources in southeastern Iran (Marhaši). The profusion of chlorite vessels in Mesopotamia and northern Syria, and that of lapis and carnelian in Old Kingdom Egypt, is proof enough that the volume of these materials that were shipped in the Gulf over the course of the third millennium must have been enormous. Although lapis, carnelian, and chlorite vases were undoubtedly also obtained by way of land routes, it is fair to think that, at least during the third millennium, because of logistical considerations, overland trade had considerably less importance than water transportation.

For all these reasons, written sources—both economic and historical—offer but a tiny reflection of what international trade was really like. At best, these texts provide us with an outline of the main patterns. But they certainly do not constitute a reliable record of the traded materials, the mechanisms of exchange, and, above all, the actual volume of traded wares.

Of equally limited and supect value is the information provided by texts, be they economic or historical, about foreign geography. Here it is particularly important to realize that geographical names such as Makkan, Meluhha, and Tilmun are *Babylonian* designations, which, even if identical with the native terms that the inhabitants of those lands used self-referentially, are broad and probably highly imprecise designations. It is safe to assume that the Babylonian scribes who used these terms usually had only a vague notion of where these places were situated and what exactly they represented in purely geographical terms (cf. the modern usage of terms such as "the Indies," "the Balkans," or "the Americas") and, even more so, of what they represented as *political* entities. To use Makkan as a specific example, it is likely that, in its basic and primary sense, this name indeed describes, from the Babylonian perspective, the Oman peninsula and the coastal area immediately to the west of it. This is strongly indicated by the fact that Makkan was consistently thought by the ancients to be a source of copper and diorite, both of which are found in Oman. At the same time, it is possible that Makkan also had a broader sense in which it designated the coastal region of Iran along the Strait of

Hormuz and perhaps even of the western section of Baluchistan as well. As shown by the later history, the two regions often were unified politically, with the center of power shifting back and forth between Iran and Oman, as did the respective populations and cultural traditions. Therefore, what precisely the "king of Makkan" who is mentioned in an Ur III source (Appendix 1 Text 1) ruled over at that particular point in time and where he resided is impossible to say. The term Meluhha is even more vague. Although it is certain that it denotes various manifestations of the Indus civilization, the safest assumption is that it describes everything to the east beyond Makkan: eastern Baluchistan, Gujarat, all the way to Sindh.

There is even more inherent uncertainty and ambiguity in the way Makkan and Meluhha are cited by ancient texts as sources of exotic woods, stones, animals, and plants. Obviously, the scribes who wrote them lacked the knowledge (and were not even interested in knowing) where precisely these items came from, beyond the fact that they originated far in the east, in the exotic and half-mythical Makkan-Meluhha complex. Moreover, since the merchandise originating in Meluhha necessarily reached Babylonia via Makkan, it is not surprising that much confusion existed in this matter, with the typical Meluhhan items often being attributed to Makkan and vice versa (see chap. 9.2). Cases of this sort of terminological confusion abound in our own time as well. Classic examples are the North American turkey bird, which is named after "Turkey" in English but after India/Indies in French (*dinde, dindon*) and Polish (*indyk*); and the semi-precious stone turquoise, which is named after Turkey, even though it comes from Iran.

Chapter 2

The Prehistoric Foundation (ca. 6000–2650 BC)

Without doubt, from the time when the Persian Gulf started to form at the end of the last glaciations, the emerging sea body already functioned as a channel for social interaction and exchange of material culture. As rising sea levels gradually flooded what was, during the last glacial maximum, a major river valley[1] with its estuary around the Strait of Hormuz,[2] the population in this so-called "Ur-Schatt River Valley" must have retreated up-slope, abandoning previous settlements as they became submerged.[3] Since the Gulf in this way has effectively inundated all traces of the basin's early post-glacial inhabitants,[4] it should be borne in mind that not until roughly 6000 BC, when present-day sea levels were reached, does archaeological evidence make it possible to detect the coastal population. Consequently, the flooding of the coastal settlements, where one should expect to find the most intense intercultural exchange, has created a substantial lacuna in the archaeological data on the earliest interactions in the Gulf.[5]

This notwithstanding, during the late sixth to late fifth millennium BC, the distinctly painted Ubaid Ware (Ubaid 3–4), with its associated repertoire of vessel shapes, filtered southward into the Gulf from Mesopotamia. Ubaid pottery was absorbed by the local Gulf populations at settlements ranging from the coast of Kuwait to the Straits of Hormuz.[6] The linguistic and ethnic relationships between the Ubaid culture proper in Mesopotamia and the "coastal Ubaid" of the lower Gulf coast is unknown, but the fundamental difference in subsistence economy is reflected by the contrasting lithic traditions, among other evidence.[7]

1. Teller et al. 2000; Glennie 2001: 18; Rose 2010.
2. Reade 2008: fig. 1.
3. Teller et al. 2000; Rose 2010: 854.
4. Reade 2008: 12; Cuttler 2013.
5. However, it appears almost certain that the societies that had populated the *terra incognita* of the "Ur-Schatt River Valley" continued to inhabit the Gulf costal basin after the "flood." This conclusion is supported by the observation of Crassard and Dreshler (2013) that the lithic technologies of the post-flood population appears to be rooted in indigenous development going back to the Pleistocene.
6. For a distribution map, see Carter and Crawford 2010a: fig. 1.2.
7. A recent discovery in Kuwait of an Ubaid period triangular barbed and tanged flint arrowhead in the chamber of burial mound SMQ 49 at Sabiyah (Makowski 2013) should certainly be understood to be an antique and should not be taken as indicating a Neolithic origin of the Gulf's burial mound tradition.

That the Gulf waters were already being navigated by this time in large reed boats caulked with bitumen is demonstrated by countless reed-impressed bitumen fragments, a clay boat model, and a sherd with a painted design of a boat with a two-footed mast found in the Ubaid site H3 in Kuwait.[8]

A local "Arabian Coarse Ware" appeared in the northwestern end of the Gulf,[9] but apart from this, all other pottery has been shown to be imported from Babylonia.[10] Consequently, we should already at this early stage envision some mechanism of long-distance exchange,[11] which, if we look at the ever-diminishing quantity of Ubaid pottery that can be observed as one moves eastward down the Gulf,[12] tentatively must be considered as resulting from a system of down-the-line exchange.[13] However, the presence of bitumen, which almost exclusively came from North Mesopotamia,[14] at the Ubaid site of Dosariyah might suggest the occasional long-distance seafaring expedition as well.

About 4000–3800 BC, much more arid conditions set in, as the Holocene Pluvial Phase came to an end[15] and the export of Babylonian pottery (Ubaid 5) to the Gulf stops.[16] For most of the fourth millennium BC, we are faced with a partial hiatus in the occupational record from the Gulf, which explains why it has been termed "the dark millennium."[17] During the late fourth millennium BC, the expansive Uruk phenomenon in Mesopotamia becomes the dominating engine of cultural and technological advance,[18] and although the relation between the hyper-inventive cultural phenomenon and the Gulf communities is of global social evolutionary interest, it regrettably cannot yet be correlated due to a limited body of evidence. However, a distant echo of Urukian urbanism may have resonated through the Gulf, as evinced by the appearance around 3100–3000 BC of the Gulf region's first major sociocultural formations. Specifically, the archeological record documents the advent of the Bronze Age and the first vague manifestations of two cultural complexes in Saudi Arabia and the Oman Peninsula (the Dilmun/Barbar culture and the Hafit/Umm an-Nar culture), whose respective territories subsequently were to be known as *Tilmun* and *Makkan* by the Babylonians.[19]

From the Tilmun region, archaeological evidence dating to before 2650 BC is limited, and its relation to the later cultural formations is poorly understood.

More than twenty years ago, the archaeological evidence from eastern Saudi Arabia dating from the sixth through early second millennium BC was thoroughly examined by J. Zarins,[20] who had to rely extensively on the work of C. Piesinger.[21] Unfortunately, during the years that have passed since, the archaeological record from eastern Saudi Arabia has increased only marginally.

---

8. Respectively, Carter 2010: 91–101, fig. 5.1, fig. 5.2.
9. Masry 1974: 123; Potts 2005: 71.
10. Oates et al. 1977: 232.
11. Carter 2010: 102–4.
12. Drechsler 2012: 491.
13. For this conclusion, see already Carter and Crawford 2010b: 208–9.
14. Van de Velde et al. 2015.
15. Uerpmann 2003; Parker 2009.
16. Mutin 2012: 163.
17. Uerpmann 2003; Parker and Goudie 2008; Parker 2009.
18. Algaze 1989; 1993.
19. Peyronel 2006.
20. Zarins 1989.
21. Piesinger 1983.

The evidence dating to the late fourth to early third millennium from the Eastern Province of Saudi Arabia suggests that a local ceramic tradition developed there under modest influence from Late Uruk and ED I period Babylonia.[22] Piesinger encountered Babylonian pottery dating to the Late Uruk–Early Dynastic I transition at a tell[23] that is associated with the vast Abqaiq Tumuli field near Sabkha Hammam. In the earliest burial mounds at Abqaiq, she recovered pottery that was tentatively dated to the late fourth millennium BC.[24] Excavation of burial mounds and survey in this tumuli field also produced substantial quantities of Babylonian pottery of Early Dynastic I and II date,[25] as did excavations and survey at a site in the Hofuf Oasis.[26] A "Jemdat Nasr styled" vessel, found in a burial mound in Kuwait provides evidence of exchange around 3000 BC, as well as the early introduction of the regional tumulus tradition.[27]

Judging from the Babylonian pottery of Early Dynastic I and II date found on Tarut,[28] this strategically located island must have already at this time assumed a position of some significance in the exchange networks. However, even if inscribed, sculpted chlorite vessels compatible to types found on Tarut (see below) are known to date from the Early Dynastic II period onward,[29] it appears more likely that the sculpted chlorite traded into Tarut date to the Early Dynastic III and Sargonic periods.

The evidence from Kuwait, Tarut Island, and the Saudi mainland is contrasted with the situation on Bahrain Island, where materials dating to the fourth through early third millennium BC only amount to a small Late Ubaid to Early Uruk campsite[30] and a few stray finds.[31] The only noteworthy evidence of early third-millennium BC occupation from Bahrain Island is a burial dated to ca. 3000 BC, accidentally discovered in the western edge of the early second-millennium BC Karzakkan Mound Cemetery; it contained two "Jemdat Nasr styled" vessels imported from Mesopotamia (fig. 2: nos. 1–2).[32]

As the above sketch illustrates, our understanding of the cultural formations of the western Gulf and its external relations during late fourth to the early third millennium BC remains clouded. Certainly, this situation stems to a large degree from the fact that, at this early point in time, the regional population was concentrated in the Eastern Province of Saudi Arabia where generally little fieldwork

22. Zarins (1989: 75) attributed deposits from Tell Ramad and Tell Umm an-Nussi in the Hofuf and Yabrin Oases to the Late Uruk period. He furthermore suggested that four now destroyed settlements from the Dammam Dome area were originally populated during the Late Uruk–ED I transition (1989: 74). The latter group includes a shell midden site originally reported by Cornwall (1946: 38).

23. In the upper levels of the settlement AS 27. See Piesinger 1983: 494–95, against Zarins 1989: 74.

24. Piesinger 1983: 482–83.

25. Piesinger 1983: 484; Zarins 1989: figs. 4–5.

26. For Tell Ramad, see Zarins 1989: 75.

27. For a sketch drawing of the vessel found in the otherwise unpublished Tomb SBH-17 at Sabiyah, see Carter 2013: fig. 30.4 right side.

28. Masry 1974; Piesinger 1983: 484–85; Zarins 1989: fig. 6 nos.1–5, 7–11, 13–15, 18–19; Franke 2011: 74, 84–85 obj. 34–37.

29. See Marchesi and Marchetti 2011: pl. 14:3 for a sculpted chlorite vase fragment inscribed with the name of Me-silim, an Early Dynastic II ruler.

30. For the Al-Markh site, see Roaf 1976.

31. For a polychrome "Jemdat Nasr" sherd and a spout found at the Barbar Temple, see Mortensen 1971: 395; Andersen and Højlund 2003: 219 figs. 392–93. Finally, sherds, of which at least one stems from an Uruk bevelled-rim bowl, have been found north of the Early Dilmun settlement at Saar, Bahrain (Jane Moon, personal communication).

32. Laursen 2013.

has been undertaken. Importantly, the introduction of a burial mound custom as witnessed at Abqaiq and Sabiyah and the coterminous appearance of a local ceramic tradition in the late fourth or early third millennium BC must be regarded as embryonic stages in the formation of the later "Dilmun culture." The distribution of sites from this phase documents that this "incipient Tilmun population," in addition to Tarut Island and Bahrain Island, also occupied the discontinuous stretch of semi-arable land and oases that ran between Qatif Bay and Al-Hasa, possibly with an extreme southern appendix in the Yabrin Oasis[33] and with its northernmost extent at Sabiyah, Kuwait.

The materials found on Tarut Island indicate that, during the first quarter of the third millennium BC, this sheltered natural harbor continually served as a node of some significance in the Gulf network.

In the region of ancient Makkan, the archaeological record dating to before 2650 BC is relatively substantial. The appearance around 3100 BC of the Hafit culture represents the most important development from this phase on the Oman peninsula. This cultural formation is best known from its characteristic stone-built tomb towers of the so-called "Hafit Type," tens of thousands of which loom on the horizon along mountain ridges all across the Oman peninsula.[34] Based on some exceptionally large Hafit tombs crowning a number of cemeteries at al-Barinah, Oman, Deadman and Kennet have convincingly argued for the existence of social stratification in this period.[35] However, it is unclear whether the extra investment of resources that went into these specific (collective!) tombs was intended to promote individuals of preeminent rank or to reflect assymetrical access to human resources between competing social groups.

The settlements are less well known, but mud-brick houses have been documented in the inland oasis of Bat, HD-6, and at Hili 8.[36] Carter has pointed out the striking fact that the houses at the eastern Oman settlement HD-6 exhibit the classic tripate construction known otherwise from Ubaid, Uruk, and ED period settlement in Babylonia.[37]

Although the Hafit Type tomb undeniably is a distinctly local innovation, imported artifacts from Mesopotamia that can be attributed to the late Uruk through Early Dynastic I period (ca. 3100–2700 BC) appear conspicuously frequently in what can be considered the "funerary kit" of the Hafit period.[38] Mesopotamian import is primarily evinced by a high number of polychrome "Jemdat Nasr style" pottery vessels, which were routinely deposited in the tombs from about 3100 BC onward (fig. 2: nos. 3–14).[39] Importantly, many of the vessels are of similar shape and size as the two abovementioned vessels found on Bahrain Island, and they probably all arrived at the Gulf containing the same Babylonian product. The characteristic everted rims indicate that a leather or cloth lid/cover was originally secured here with a string (see Appendix 3, fig. 13, p. 114). The small size of the

33. Potts 1983.
34. Frifelt 1971.
35. Deadman and Kennet 2015.
36. Respectively, Possehl et al. 2009; Azzarà 2009; Cleuziou and Tosi 1989: 33.
37. Carter 2010: 584 with references.
38. Frifelt 1980.
39. Frifelt 1971; 1980. For an extensive bibliography, see Potts 1986a; 1990a. For a petrographic analysis that confirms that all these vessels are of Mesopotamian manufacture, see Méry 2000: 169–89. It is now commonly believed that they had stopped circulating in Oman by 2700–2600 BC (see Cleuziou and Méry 2002: 286), even if their chronological range previously has been questioned by Potts (1986).

Figure	Location	References	Volume
2.1	Hamad Town, Bahrain	Laursen 2013: fig.8:1	0.82L
2.2	Hamad Town, Bahrain	Laursen 2013: fig.8:2	0.48L
2.3	Ibri 1141.A, Oman	Frifelt 1975: fig.1:4; Méry 2000: fig.106:3	0.52L
2.4	Hafit 1038.C, Abu Dhabi	Frifelt 1970: fig.18a:3; Méry 2000: fig.106:2	0.66L
2.5	Bida Bint Saʾud BS 138, Abu Dhabi	Méry 2000: fig.106:4	0.56L
2.6	Hafit 1031.A, Abu Dhabi	Frifelt 1970: fig.13.A.2; Méry 2000: fig.106:1	0.66L
2.7	Buraimi, Abu Dhabi	Méry 2000: fig.107:4	0.52L
2.8	Mazyad 1321.A, Oman	Frifelt 1975: fig.9:3; Méry 2000: fig.107:2	0.24L
2.9	Hafit 1051.C, Abu Dhabi	Frifelt 1970: fig.21c; Méry 2000: fig.107:1	0.52L
2.10	Hafit 1052.B, Abu Dhabi	Frifelt 1970: fig.2a; Méry 2000: fig.107:3	0.46L
2.11	Mazyad 1313.A, Oman	Méry 2000: fig.108:1	2.04L
2.12	Mazyad 1309.G, Oman	Frifelt 1979: fig.14:3; Méry 2000: fig.108:2	0.87L
2.13	Hafit Tomb B, Abu Dhabi	Méry 2000: fig.108:4	0.93L
2.14	Hafit 1051.C, Abu Dhabi	Frifelt 1970: fig.21a; Méry 2000: fig.106:5	4.45L
2.15	Umm an-Nar grave I	Frifelt 1991: fig.86	N/A
2.16	Umm an-Nar grave I	Frifelt 1991: fig.125	N/A
2.17	Umm an-Nar grave I	Frifelt 1991: fig.88	N/A
2.18	Umm an-Nar grave I	Frifelt 1991: fig.87	N/A
2.19	Umm an-Nar grave VII	Frifelt 1991: fig.207	N/A
2.20	Umm an-Nar "Test Trench"	Frifelt 1995: fig.170	N/A

vessels and their elusive contents may well echo a "provincial" assimilation in Makkan and Tilmun of consumer habits from "urban" Babylonia.[40]

The presence, albeit in small quantities, of a variety of other Babylonian vessel types in the settlements of the inland oases demonstrates that, in addition to the small jars found in the graves, other Babylonian products were occasionally traded deep into the interior of Oman.[41]

Aside from the above-mentioned data, there is at present little direct evidence of the commodities that the Babylonians or their (Tilmun) intermediaries received in return for these imports. Recent analysis of metal objects from Babylonia suggests that although, in the Uruk period, some of Babylonia's copper originated in Oman, alternative suppliers dominated the metal market in the Early Dynastic I and II periods.[42]

Needless to say, before ca. 2650 BC, written evidence from Babylonia bearing on interaction with the Gulf is practically nonexistent. There is a probable mention of Tilmun in a lexical text dating

40. For this suggestion, see already Peyronel 2006.

41. For example, at Hili 8 in the Al Ain Oasis, Abu Dhabi, more than 50% of the limited amount of pottery from the deposits of period 1 (ca. 3000–2750 BC) are of Mesopotamian manufacture (Cleuziou and Méry 2002: table 3). Further, Mesopotamian sherds of Jemdat Nasr to Early Dynastic date have been reported from a settlement layer below Tower 1147 in the Bat Oasis, Oman. See Possehl et al. 2009.

42. Begemann et al. 2010: 157–60.

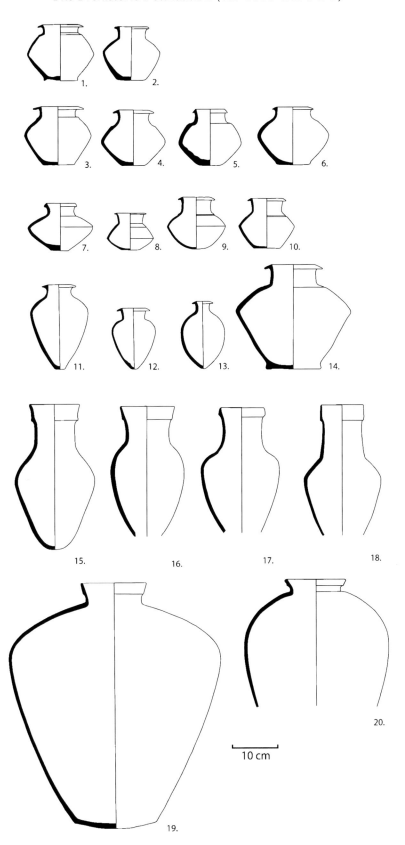

Fig. 2. Examples of Babylonian pottery from the first half of the 3rd millennium BC found in the Gulf. For details and references, see the description opposite.

to the Uruk III period.[43] In addition, in a number of Uruk III economic tablets, the sign DILMUN appears in connection with textiles.[44]

The relatively large quantities of contemporary Babylonian pottery reported from the Saudi mainland supports the notion of an ongoing trade between Tilmun and Sumer, which, judging from the evidence at hand, was facilitated by a commercial center on Tarut Island.

A function of Oman as a small-scale producer and supplier of copper potentially from as early as fourth millennium BC is a distinct possibility[45] and helps explain the appearance at ca. 3100 BC of substantial amounts of Babylonian pottery vessels in the burials of Hafit Type in Oman. Generally, this reconstruction corresponds equally well with the hypothesized explanation of the emergence of the Hafit culture as a response within Oman society to the increasing demand for metals within the emerging urban economies of Babylonia.[46]

43. See below, p. 21 n. 58.
44. Englund 1983, discussed below, p. 21 n. 58.
45. See above and Begemann et al. 2010: 157–60.
46. Cleuziou 1996: 159.

Chapter 3

The Pre-Sargonic Period
(ca. 2650–2350 BC)

Archaeology

From the middle of the third millennium BC onward, the archaeological and historical evidence generally becomes more substantial. However, given the chronological resolution of the archaeological data, artifacts are both as a rule and by necessity attributed to this period with varying degrees of certainty.

From the northwestern Gulf region encompassing the territories of Tilmun, the evidence dating to 2650–2350 BC once again concentrates on Tarut Island. If this island until this time had merely hosted an intermediate trading post, the evidence suggests that it was now emerging as one of the most important ports of trade on the southern Gulf coast. Situated approximately in the center of Tarut Island is a high tell, now crowned by a ruined Portuguese fort, but with walls of well-dressed ashlar masonry protruding from the remains.[1] Regrettably, this indisputably important site remains largely unexplored. However, with reference to materials recovered from two minor soundings carried out by A. Masry,[2] J. Zarins suggests that the Babylonian pottery recovered from the deepest levels should be attributed to the Early Dynastic III period.[3] Tentative as the evidence from the Tarut tell may be, it shows that the beginning of this island's most substantial prehistoric settlement site dates no later than the Early Dynastic III period.

The remains of a settlement mound dating from the Early Dynastic period were investigated by C. Piesinger at ar-Rafi'ah, Tarut Island.[4] The presence at this site of Babylonian pottery, fragments of carved chlorite vessels, and substantial quantities of unworked lapis lazuli imply that it was an important center of exchange on Tarut Island at this time.[5]

By far the most significant finds from Tarut Island are the more than 300 sculpted chlorite vessels and fragments, which were accidently recovered by local gardeners in what must have been disturbed

1. Bibby 1973: 28–31.
2. Masry 1974: 143–45.
3. Zarins 1989: 78.
4. Piesinger 1983: 176–90.
5. Piesinger 1983: 190.

burial contexts at ar-Rafi'ah.[6] Importantly, it has now been established that this class of vessels were produced in the Iranian province of Kerman,[7] within the kingdom of Marhaši.[8] It is possible that the bulk of these materials first arrived at Tarut during the Sargonic period (see below), but it is highly probable that trade in this Marhašian commodity had taken off already during the Early Dynastic III period (or perhaps even during Early Dynastic II).

Aside from the launch of trade between Tilmun and Marhaši as early as Early Dynastic III, as suggested by the chlorite vessels, there is ample additional evidence on Tarut Island of interaction with the lands of ancient Iran more generally. An Iranian origin is probable for, among others, a small lapis lazuli figurine[9] and a number of alabaster or calcite vessels,[10] all of which cautiously could be attributed to the late Pre-Sargonic period. That the sea route via Tilmun (Tarut) facilitated trade in alabaster or calcite vessels from Iran is suggested by an inscribed alabaster vessel found at Girsu.[11] What possibly connects the vessel in question with the Gulf trade, aside from it having been found in Girsu, is its dedicatory inscription to a ruler/goddess of Lagaš that identifies the donor of the vessel as a g a e š (*kaeššum*), "seafaring merchant."

On Tarut Island, exchange with Babylonia is attested by multiple artifacts, of which the limestone statue portraying a standing nude male with clasped hands in a traditional Sumerian devotional posture should be emphasized.[12] Suggested dates for this statue have ranged from the "Jemdat Nasr" (ca. 3000 BC)[13] to a more credible dating in the Early Dynastic period.[14] Additional artifacts from Tarut Island of Babylonian manufacture with a broad Early Dynastic I–III date include a marble macehead[15] and a copper bull's head roughly comparable to the classic examples mounted on lyres from the Royal Tombs of Ur.[16]

From the Abqaiq tumuli, some of the Babylonian pottery excavated probably dates from the Early Dynastic II to Early Sargonic periods.[17] Another noteworthy datum from the burial mounds of Abqaiq regards imports from the Oman Peninsula, roughly dating to the Early Dynastic III period. Here, in particular, black-on-red canisters[18] and biconical jars[19] are of interest, because these vessels are typical examples of the earliest indigenous fine ware tradition on the Oman Peninsula (ca. 2600–2400 BC) and thus represent the earliest direct testimony of exchange between Tilmun and Makkan. A substantial (semi-)pastoral population in the borderlands of Tilmun may be attested at

6. Bibby 1973; Masry 1974: 80; Zarins 1979; Potts 1989.

7. Lamberg-Karlovsky 1970; 1993: 283; Kohl 2001: 209–30.

8. Steinkeller 1982; 2006a: 2–7.

9. Golding 1974: 27 fig. 4 no. 11. For a color photograph, see Collins 2003: 324 fig. 223.

10. See Burkholder 1984: nos.16a–c and 29a; Franke 2011: 76 fig. 6. Note that the production of similar stone vessels among others have been documented at Shahr-i Sokhta (Iran) and Mundigak (Afghanistan). See Ciarla 1979.

11. Steible 1991: 409–10 and pl. XXII "Lagaš" 37.

12. Rashid 1972; T. F. Potts 1989: fig. 6.

13. Ippolitoni-Strika 1986: 311.

14. Rashid 1972; Collins 2003: 323.

15. Burkholder 1984: nos. 21b.

16. Potts 1989: 25–26 and fig. 21.

17. Piesinger 1983: figs. 48, 56, 58–59, and 61.

18. Piesinger 1983: fig. 50.

19. Piesinger 1983: fig. 55.

mound cemeteries such as al-Rufaya 1–3 and Ayn al-Dila in the Al-Kharj region, KSA,[20] and in the Al-Kharj region, Kuwait,[21] most of which are loosely attributable to the Bronze Age.

On Bahrain Island, the lack of evidence of occupation characteristically continues into the late pre-Sargonic period. However, even if nothing has yet materialized that can with certainty be ascribed to this time, it would be an overinterpretation to regard lush Bahrain as a deserted island. Nevertheless, the lack of data strongly indicates that until the post-Sargonic period Bahrain Island was, for still poorly understood reasons, of inferior importance compared to Tarut Island and the oasis communities on the Saudi mainland.[22]

From Makkan, the evidence dating to ca. 2650–2350 BC is relatively substantial. Most importantly, the archaeological record from the Oman peninsula incontestably demonstrates that the external orientation of Makkan radically shifted toward or consolidated on the lands in the north (Marhaši) and east (Meluhha). Concurrently, the taste for Babylonian products, as reflected in the "Jamdat Nasr" burial jars that had been prevalent in Hafit Type tombs ca. 3100 BC, faded away, and from around 2700–2600 BC, Babylonian artifacts more rarely reached the interior of the Oman peninsula.

Coinciding with this change in the geographical orientation of Oman, the Hafit culture underwent a transformation into what we now identify as the Umm an-Nar culture. Importantly, the social formation under this cultural horizon was to represent the economic and cultural zenith of third-millennium Oman civilization. The spread of the southeast Iranian black-on-red fine ware tradition into Makkan, which possibly was even accompanied by a minor wave of Marhašian immigrants,[23] is more than anything indicative of the strong cultural ties that were forged across the Strait of Hormuz in the Early Dynastic period.

The Umm an-Nar culture was supported by a diverse economic system that included metal and mineral mining, fishing, herding, and agriculture, and which evolved around oasis centers with fortified stone and mud-brick towers erected over central wells. The towers probably served as markers of water rights, collective storage facilities, and refuges in time of conflict.

Correspondingly, the deceased members of the associated kin group were interred nearby in often elaborate stone-built tower tombs designed for long-term communal use. Possibly beginning around 2400 BC, stone reliefs start to appear above the entrance of the tombs;[24] the reliefs depict symbolic imagery that probably connotes the clan or lineage affiliation of the interred community.[25]

Not long after the dawn of the Umm an-Nar culture, an incipient slowdown in trade with Babylonia can be detected in the interior of Oman. This development is perhaps best attested at the Hili 8 settlement, where the quantity of Babylonian pottery fell from 50% to 25% around ca. 2700–2600 BC (phase IIa–Ic), only to almost completely disappear around ca. 2500–2400 BC (phase IIc2/d–IId/e).[26]

20. Although later activities are attested at the Ayn al-Dila necropolis, the evidence tentatively attributes much of this cemetery's 3000 mounds to the Bronze Age. See Schiettecatte 2014: 25–88.

21. For various tumuli excavated by the Polish Mission at As-Sabbiya in Kuwait, see Rutkowski 2013; Makowski 2013; Reiche 2013.

22. For a similar suggestions, see Potts 1983: 16; Kohl 1986: 367–68.

23. Méry 1996; Potts 2005.

24. Gagnaison et al. 2004.

25. Cleuziou and Tosi 2007.

26. Cleuziou and Méry 2002: 286 and table 3.

Even if the gaze of Makkan was now firmly fixed on the lands to its north and east, the *locus classicus* Umm an-Nar Island represents the major exception in our data, attesting to continued or even intensified trade with Babylonia.

Excavations on this sheltered island located of the coast off Abu Dhabi have uncovered a settlement that, in addition to inconspicuous domestic houses, also features an apparent warehouse facility.[27] The Umm an-Nar warehouse is a stone-built multi-roomed structure with a nearly square 16×16 m ground plan, positioned on the ancient seafront. The building witnessed at least two episodes of fire, the latter of which apparently was the cause of its final abandonment in the late Early Dynastic III or, more likely, the early Sargonic period.[28] Fragments of ingots as well as of casting moulds for ingots and crucibles suggest that copper-processing took place near or inside the warehouse.[29] The interpretation of this facility as a warehouse is based on the fact that nearly all rooms contained, in addition to southeast Iranian and Indus pottery, substantial amounts of Babylonian pottery (43%), large storage vessels in particular. A pottery fragment with an impression of a cylinder seal found in the warehouse has been identified by P. Amiet as being of Syrian provenance, with parallels from Ebla dating to ca. 2500–2400 BC.[30] The impressed vessel evidently represents an import from Syria that, via Babylonian intermediaries, was traded all the way to Umm an-Nar Island.[31]

Fragments in the warehouse and settlement of Indus black-slipped jars, typical beaded-rim jars, and pedestalled bowls of mid-third-millennium BC date and onward[32] document that Meluhhhan traders frequented Umm an-Nar Island or vice versa.

Further evidence of the wide-ranging relations of this trade-orientated Makkan community has been produced through the excavation of seven of the island's numerous circular collective tombs. The grave goods recovered from the tombs date to the Early Dynastic III through early Sargonic period and comprise a broad selection of imported artifacts, of which numerous pottery vessels from Babylonia, Iran, and the Indus are present.[33] Together, the evidence from the settlement and the tombs casts important light on the trade relations of the Umm an-Nar Island community.[34] First and foremost, substantial quantities of high quality painted pottery[35] and incised grey ware,[36] imported from southeastern Iran (Marhaši), attest to the intense relation between Makkan and this region.

Exchange of bulk commodities is demonstrated by different types of standardized Babylonian vessels dating to the Early Dynastic III period. Most illustrative among these is a fairly homogeneous group of round- to pointy-based, pear-shaped jars of a type very common throughout southern Baby-

---

27. Frifelt 1991; 1995.

28. Frifelt 1995: 24.

29. Frifelt 1995: 24.

30. Amiet 1975: 10.

31. Frifelt 1995: 238.

32. Frifelt 1995: 167 fig. 224.

33. Frifelt 1991.

34. Needless to say, perishable goods including cereals and textiles shipped in containers of organic materials such as basketry, leather, woolen cloths, and wooden crates are absent from the record. Consequently, any reconstruction is limited to imported ceramic vessels that were left on the island, either because the goods they contained were consumed there or because they were repacked for further transport inland.

35. E.g. Frifelt 1991: figs. 76–85, 120–21, 138–42, 173–74, 176–78.

36. Frifelt 1991: figs. 122–24 and 199.

lonia (fig. 2 nos. 15–18, p. 13).[37] Vessels of this type frequently occur in the warehouse[38] and were occasionally deposited in the tombs.[39] The pointy base and elongated shape would have made them suitable for stacking in a ship's hull and the long neck, narrow mouth, and banded rim, intended for fastening a cloth or leather cover, may point to a liquid content. Taking into account the relatively small volume of the jars, a likely candidate for the liquid traded would be sesame oil.[40] A host of other variants of Babylonian storage vessels from Umm an-Nar Island among which a couple of the largest are illustrated here (fig. 2 nos. 19–20), possibly also attest to the trade in liquid commodities.

Importantly, metallurgical analysis of Babylonian copper objects dating to the Early Dynastic III and Sargonic periods, respectively, document that it was in these periods that Babylonia acquired the largest portion of its copper from Omani ores.[41]

While Umm an-Nar Island stands out as an exception, having a specialized function as port of maritime trade with Babylonia and Iran (Marhaši), the comparable function of connecting Makkan with the Indus world was primarily maintained from sites in the Ja'alan area, facing the Indian Ocean coast.[42] Among these, Ra's al-Hadd in particular appears to be a primary node in Makkan's eastward trade. This settlement contained a broad selection of Indus pottery, including various painted fine wares, but the import is otherwise dominated by storage vessels of the classic black-slipped type. The Indus presence in the ceramic inventory at Ra's al-Hadd is so pronounced that it has led the excavators to speculate—not without justification—that the site was partly occupied by a small community of native Meluhhans.[43]

From around 2500 BC onward, the seasonally (winter) occupied site of Ra's al-Jinz, which is located 10 km south of Ra's al-Hadd, supplements our picture of Makkan's eastern trade. At this fishing-oriented settlement, Indus pottery, in particular black-slipped jars, makes up one-third of the inventory. Also noteworthy from Ra's al-Jinz are an ivory comb of a common Indus type,[44] and a copper (imitation?) Harappan type seal with the classic "unicorn below text" motif.[45] From Ras al-Jinz, small amounts of Early Dynastic III style pottery possibly evince the easternmost range of Babylonian commodities in the pre-Sargonic period.[46]

Substantial amounts of discarded fragments of bitumen with impressions from sewn-boat planks, found in small caches stored in the houses, probably testify to the ongoing activity of recaulking large plank boats.[47] Importantly, the bitumen found at Ras al Jinz (site RJ-2) by all appearance comes from an Iraqi source, thus raising the possibility that it originally came to Oman attached to Babylonian ships.[48]

---

37. The Babylonian affinity of the vessels has been confidently established by petrographic as well as neutron activation analysis. See Mynors 1983.
  38. Frifelt 1995: 123.
  39. Frifelt 1991: figs. 86–89.
  40. For this suggestion, see already Potts 1993: 425.
  41. Begemann et al. 2010: 157–59.
  42. Cleuziou and Tosi 2007: 216.
  43. Cleuziou and Tosi 2007: 237.
  44. Cleuziou and Tosi 2007: fig. 203.
  45. Cleuziou and Tosi 2007: 237.
  46. Cleuziou and Tosi 1994: 757.
  47. Cleuziou and Tosi 1994: 747–56; 2007: 192–93.
  48. Cleuziou and Tosi 1994: 756.

The above-mentioned Indus black-slipped jars are most instructive when it comes to illustrating the type of standardized import that arrived in Makkan from the Indus world. In analogy to the Mediterranean amphora, it has been suggested that the characteristic pointy base and wide body, which makes these vessels somewhat unwieldy on land, made them ideal for stacking in a ship's hull.[49] The characteristic black slip, which was applied to the exterior as well as interior of the vessels, must have acted as a proofing measure, undoubtedly necessitated because the jars were used to store liquids. The jars, typically ca. 30–70 liters in volume, by all appearance played a significant role in the internal redistribution of foodstuff between the Indus cities and beyond. The products originally shipped in black-slipped vessels is a subject of debate and among the many proposals are wine, liquor, oil,[50] clarified butter, pickled vegetables, fruits, honey, wine, indigo,[51] dried cheese,[52] or ghee.[53]

Importantly, these specialized ceramic vessels are key tracers of bulk export to Makkan in the period from 2500 and 2200 BC. Sherds of black-slipped jars are known in small numbers from sites along the Gulf coast and the inland oases.[54] However, the fact that Indus black-slipped jars reach a much higher frequency in the Ja'alan area demonstrates, perhaps not surprisingly, that the Indus trade was primarily in the hands of the Makkan communities facing the Arabian Sea coast. As an example, the above-mentioned sherds of black-slipped jars from Ra's Al-hadd and at Ras al Jinz RJ-2 make up 30% of the pottery inventory.[55] Considering the shorter distance to the Indus outpost at Sutkagen Dor[56] on the Makran coast or the Indus city of Dholavira in Gujarat,[57] the concentration of black-slipped jars on Oman's east coast is to be expected. Further, if the Indus merchants desired to trade for copper, landing near Ja'alan would also put them in close proximity to the mountainous hinterland that held Makkan's centers of metal production.

In sum, aside from Umm an-Nar Island and a few sporadic occurrences, the record speaks to a decline in Babylonian ceramic import possibly coinciding with the Early Dynastic II–III transition (ca. 2600 BC). In contrast, the gradual decline in Babylonian pottery in interior Oman (Makkan) is met by a massive southeast Iranian (Marhaši) influence on Oman's incipient fineware tradition and by substantial quantities of Indus black-slipped vessels (Meluhhan) along the Arabian Sea coast. These circumstances doubtless portray an authentic development, where Makkan increasingly interacted with communities of southeastern Iran and the Indus world. The strong economic and cultural relations that Makkan society in this way forged with the polities of southeastern Iran and the Indus must have been instrumental in the societal transformations we today observe as the Hafit to Umm an-Nar transition.

While Makkan reinforced her northern and eastern relations, metallurgical analysis at the same time demonstrates that the export of copper to Babylonia intensified in the Early Dynastic III and Sargonic periods.

49. Méry and Blackman 2004: 231.
50. Dales and Kenoyer 1986: 84.
51. Kenoyer 1998: 97.
52. Gouin 1991: 49.
53. Cleuziou and Méry 2002: 295.
54. For references and a distribution map, see Méry 2000: table 59 and fig. 136.
55. Cleuziou and Tosi 2007: figs. 176 and 207.
56. Dales 1962.
57. Bisht 2015.

Endemically, the most important constituents of the social transformation of Oman society were probably advances in metallurgy and pyrotechnics and the intensified use of large fortified settlement towers and circular collective tombs of increasingly more elaborate stone masonry and design.

Texts

The earliest written records of commercial contacts between Babylonia and the Gulf region date to the Early Dynastic III period.[58] It is characteristic that such evidence comes exclusively from the city-state of Lagaš, with the only foreign partner named in this connection being Tilmun. As early as ca. 2500 BC (ED IIIa), the ruler of Lagaš named Ur-Nanše boasts that "he made the ships of Tilmun to submit themselves to him (to deliver goods) from (their) land."[59]

58. A number of data of Uruk III date (ca. 3200 BC) found in the sources suggest the existence of contacts between Babylonia and Tilmun already at that early date. Among them is a mention of ZAG.DILMUN in the archaic version of the so-called "Early Dynastic Lu A," line 83 (ATU 3 82 line 85). Based on the Old Babylonian version of the same list, this entry possibly refers to an official (enkud) responsible for the collection of dues on trade with Tilmun (Green 1984; Carter 2013: 586). However, since the meaning "tax collector" for Sumerian enkud (Akkadian *mākisu*) does not appear before Old Babylonian times (with enkud earlier denoting an official in charge of fisheries), it is more likely that, if this entry refers to trade with Tilmun at all, ZAG in this context instead stands for zag-10, "tithe" (Akkadian *eširtu*). It is interesting to note that this type of duty was levied on Gulf imports in Ur III and Old Babylonian times (Oppenheim 1954: 7). Note especially UET 3 341:1–10 (Šu-Suen 4/vii): 955 ellag$_2$ ^{na4}gug ki-la$_2$-bi 1 ma-na 3 gin$_2$ igi-3-gal$_2$ a-ru-a dil-dil [x]+55 ellag$_2$ ^{na4}gug ki-la$_2$-bi 9 gin$_2$ $^2/_3$ zag-10 nam-gaeš a-ab-ba-ka e$_2$-kišib-ba Ga$_2$-nun-mah-ta za gaba ^{d}Nanna u$_3$ za gaba ^{d}Nin-gal-ke$_4$ ba-ab-dah, "955 beads of carnelian, their weight is 63 and $^1/_3$ shekels, (obtained as) various ex-voto offerings; [x]+55 carnelian beads, their weight is 9 and $^2/_3$ shekels, (obtained) as tithe on the sea-faring trade; (these beads) were added to the gems of the 'breasts' of (the statues of) Nanna and Ningal, from the storeroom of Ganunmah." Apart from the mention of ZAG.DILMUN just discussed, a number of Uruk III economic sources name the sign DILMUN in association with textiles, suggesting a very tentative possiblity of textile exportation to Tilmun. See Englund 1983; Carter 2013: 587. Finally, an Uruk III lexical list of metals and metal objects includes an item called GIN$_2$:DILMUN ("Metal" line 23). See Englund 1983. The same sign-group serves later as a designation of "shekel" in Ebla documentation. However, as we note below (see p. 50 n. 23, below), this term appears to have no connection with Tilmun and/or its weight system.

59. ma$_2$ Dilmun kur-ta gu$_2$ giš mu-gal$_2$ (Frayne RIME 1 83–84 Ur-Nanše 1 c: 4–6, 103–104 Ur-Nanše 17 v 3–5, 106–7 Ur-Nanše 20 iv 1–3, 108–9 Ur-Nanše 22:16–18, 109–10 Ur-Nanše 23:16–18, 111–12 Ur-Nanše 25:1′–3′). Although it is commonly thought that this statement refers to the transportation of timber (see, e.g., Maekawa and Mori 2011: 246; Crawford 2013: 454), it is virtually certain that the word "wood" (giš) appearing here is part of the well-attested idiom gu$_2$-ø giš-a . . . gar/gal$_2$, "to submit oneself," lit., "to place the neck into a wooden neck-stock" (so also Heimpel 1987: 40–41, 70). See gu$_2$-giš-ga$_2$-ga$_2$ = *ku-nu-šu* (Kagal I 376); also gu$_2$-gar = *kanāšu* (CAD K 144); erem$_2$ DU-e gu$_2$ giš ga$_2$-ga$_2$-da, "to submit the evil-doer" (Gudea Cylinder B vi 12); ^{d}A-nun-na-ke$_4$-ne gu$_2$ giš ma-ra-an-gar-re-eš, "the Anunakene have submitted themselves to you" ("Exaltation of Inana" line 113); sag sa$_{10}$-a e$_2$ lugal-[la-ni]-ka gu$_2$ giš ga$_2$-ga$_2$-de$_3$, "to submit a purchased slave to the house of his (new) owner" ("Hendursaga Hymn" Segment C line 62); ^{giš}tukul kalag-ga-nita gu$_2$ giš bi$_2$-in-gar-gar-ra = *in ka-ak-ki-šu da-nim* [ú]-*ka-a*[n]-*ni-š*[u], "he submitted (foreign lands) with his powerful weapon" (Frayne RIME 4 388–391 Samsuiluna 8:29–30). In fact, this idiom also appears, in identical contexts, in Gudea inscriptions (where it likely is a direct borrowing from Ur-Nanše's records): Ma$_2$-gan Me-luh-ha kur-bi-ta gu$_2$ giš mu-na-ab-gal$_2$, "the Makkanites and Meluhhites submitted themselves to him from their lands" (Gudea Cylinder A xv 8); Gu$_3$-e$_2$-a . . .-ra Ma$_2$-gan^{ki} Me-luh-ha^{ki} Gu-bi^{ki} kur Dilmun^{ki} gu$_2$ giš mu-na-gal$_2$-la-am$_3$ ma$_2$ giš du$_3$-a-bi Lagaš^{ki}-še$_3$ mu-na-de$_6$ "Makkan, Meluhha, Kupin and the land of Tilmun indeed submitted themselves to Gudea; they brought to Lagaš for him their ships stacked up with timber" (Statue D iv 4–14). The "timber" mentioned in the last example apparently was "ebony" (^{giš}esi) and "oak wood" (^{giš}ha-lu-ub$_2$), which, elsewhere in Gudea's inscriptions, are said to come from Meluhha and Kupin, respectively: kur Me-luh-ha⟨-ta⟩ ^{giš}esi im-ta-e$_{11}$ (Statue B vi 26–27); kur ^{giš}esi-a-ka $^{⌈giš⌉}$esi ma-

A century and a half later, during the reign of Lugalanda (and thus shortly before the reign of Sargon of Akkade), we read of various merchants being commissioned by the Lagaš royalty to travel to Tilmun with an objective of purchasing copper and tin bronze. The Babylonian merchandise used in exchange consisted of barley, emmer, cedar resin, perfumed oils, lard, textiles, and silver.[60] The same individuals also served as diplomatic envoys, carrying along with their merchandise gifts (nig₂-šu-taka₄-a) intended for the rulers of Tilmun, which consisted of much of the same products (VAS 14 38). As we will see later, this particular assortment of goods was characteristic of Babylonian exports to the Gulf throughout the later history of contacts between these two regions, down to ca. 1600 BC. To reciprocate, the Tilmun royalty sent, via the merchants just mentioned, their own presents to Lagaš. Thus, in one instance, a "queen" of Tilmun gifted her Lagaš counterpart with some choice dates, a number of linen garments, and a quantity of copper (Marchesi 2011).

The marble macehead from Tarut Island we discussed earlier (see above, p. 16), which is an object entirely alien to the material culture of Tilmun, could reflect yet another episode of diplomatic exchanges between Babylonia and Tilmun. Another example of a Babylonian gift could be the copper bull-head also from Tarut, which might originally have been attached to the sound box of a lyre.[61]

Trade and diplomatic contacts were facilitated by a fleet of Lagaš's seaworthy ships, called ma₂-gal-gal, "big ships,"[62] which was based, as later in the Sargonic and Ur III periods, at the seaport of E-Ninmar = Gu'abba.[63] Two sources dating to the reign of Lugalanda (or Urukagina) record the crew of those ships, numbering some forty-three or thirty-three men, who remained under the command of a supervisor named Ur-Ninmar.[64]

Interestingly, the Lagaš sources mention bronze objects called the "bowl (shaped as) a Dilmun ship" (dilim(-da) ma₂ Dilmun), which were presented ex-voto by the Lagaš royalty to various deities of Lagaš.[65] This evidence makes it certain that there existed a distinctive type of Tilmun ship, which apparently differed somewhat in its construction and appearance from the "big ships" of Lagaš and with which the Babylonians were quite familiar. It is likely, therefore, that Tilmun merchants traveled with their cargos to Babylonia as well, but we lack textual confirmation of this (except for the above-cited statement from Ur-Nanše's inscriptions, which talks of Tilmun boats coming to Lagaš).

These textual data strongly suggest that Pre-Sargonic contacts with the Gulf were restricted to Tilmun, with the lands beyond remaining largely unknown to the Babylonians.[66] The absence of any references to either Makkan or Meluhha among this evidence is particularly striking. Although it is possible that the Babylonians had some vague notion of those places, it seems certain that their sea ventures in the Gulf were limited to Tilmun, which, during that time, probably denoted Tarut

---

ra-ni-tum₃ (Cylinder A xii 6–7); Gu-bi-inki kur ˢ¹ˢha-lu-ub₂-ta ˢ¹ˢha-lu-ub₂ im-ta-e₃ (Statue B VI 45–48); sig-ta ˢ¹ˢha-lu-ub₂ giš ne-ha-AN? mu-ra-ta-e₁₁-de₃ (Cylinder A xii 3–4). For Kupin, see below, p. 35 and n. 53.

60. For the attestations, see Maekawa and Mori 2011: 246–47, to which add Foster 1997: 61–62 YBC 12130. The last document is an account of a merchant named Silim-Utu who sold silver and wool in Tilmun, bringing back in exchange copper and tin bronze (nagga zabar).

61. See p. 16 above; Potts 1989: 25–26 and fig. 21.

62. See pp. 104–5 below.

63. For Gu'abba, see in detail chapter 8.

64. See Nikolski 1 12 and 306, discussed on p. 104.

65. VAS 14 13 ii 2; DP 51 ii 4, 69 i 1, ii 6, 70 i 1, 72 iii 1, v 4; BIN 8 390 i 1.

66. Cf. Maekawa and Mori 2011.

Island specifically (see above, pp. 15–16). It was there that that they acquired Omani copper in exchange for cereals, textiles, oils, and silver. It necessarily follows, therefore, that it must have been Tilmunite merchants who serviced the Tilmun–Makkan mercantile connection. While copper undoubtedly was the main commodity Tilmunites purchased in Makkan, it is likely that they obtained a variety of other products as well, such as lapis lazuli, gold, steatite vessels, and carnelian. The latter products arrived in Makkan via the trade routes leading from southeastern Iran (Marhaši) and the Indus Valley (Meluhha). One of the receiving points for those goods evidently was the Umm an-Nar Island, an acknowledged commercial hub in Pre-Sargonic times (see above, p. 18). In particular, Umm an-Nar appears to have been the endpoint of the overland routes over which the Makkanites transported copper from the mines in central Oman to the Gulf. But there may have existed other, still archaeologically unexplored, trading emporia in this general region as well. One thinks here specifically of the coastal area of the Hormozgan province along the Iranian side of the Strait of Hormuz, which would have been a natural receiving place for the products arriving from southeastern Iran. This area could have also serviced some extensions of the Meluhhan trade, especially the routes running along the Makran coast.

Chapter 4

The Sargonic Period
(ca. 2350–2200 BC)

Archaeology

The coarse-grained temporal resolution in the archaeological data poses a number of challenges to any attempt to attribute archaeological evidence from Tilmun and Makkan to the century or so during which the Sargonic dynasty held sway over Babylonia. The confidence with which conclusions can be drawn from correlations between the historical and archaeological data can be said to fall proportionally with the increasingly narrow time-spans under question.

Evidence from Tilmun dating to the time of the Sargonic dynasty comes chiefly from Tarut Island and, as was the case in the Early Dynastic period, the carved chlorite vessels represent by far the most spectacular article of trade. The sheer number in which these Marhašian prestige goods have materialized on Tarut Island is outstanding; originally, the better part of these was doubtlessly destined for re-export to southern Babylonia.[1] Even if it can be questioned whether their presence on Tarut Island reflects the establishment of direct relations between Tilmun and the kingdom of Marhaši, it certainly underlines the unique position that Tarut Island—and by implication Tilmun—now held in the networks of exchange.

Another import, closely related to the chlorite vessels through a shared southeast Iranian origin, are vessels of so-called Bampur black-on-grey ware (fig. 3: nos. 1–3). Significantly, these vessels, which also originate either in Marhaši or the lands immediately to its southeast, have been found in small quantities at several sites on Tarut Island and in mainland Saudi Arabia.[2] In addition to these come a few sherds of the so-called incised grey ware, which are ceramic imitations of the carved chlorite vessels (see below), which also originate in southeastern Iran.[3] The fact that import from Iran is chiefly attested in the form of high-quality prestige goods attests to the strengths of the social and

---

1. Kohl 1986: 368.

2. For sherds that were found at the central tell on Tarut Island, in combination with Mesopotamian pottery, see Masry 1974: 143. Zarins reported both complete vessels and sherds from possible graves at ar-Rafiah. See, e.g., Zarins 1989: fig. 6:16. On the Saudi mainland, black-on-grey wares are known from: the Abqaiq Tumuli (AGM5 and 13), see Piesinger 1983: 257 fig. 50 and 268 fig. 61; "south of Dhahran," see Golding 1974: 29; Dhahran mound cemetery (surface), see Zarins et al. 1984; and finally from Tell Ramad in the Hofuf Oasis, see Piesinger 1983: 336 figs. 106–53.

3. Incised grey ware was found at ar-Rafiah on Tarut Island—see Zarins 1978: nos. 198 and 201; and at Tell Ramad in the Hofuf oasis—see Piesinger 1983: 106–52. Add to this the high probability that some of the Iranian alabaster vessels (see above) that have been found out of context on Tarut Island arrived during the Sargonic period.

Fig. 3. South-East Iranian (Marhaši) Black-on-Grey ware vessels from Saudi Arabia.
a: *Abqaiq Tumuli Field Mound 5 (Piesinger 1983: fig. 50);* **b:** *Abqaiq Tumuli Field Mound 13 (Piesinger 1983: fig. 61);* **c:** *Tarut Island (Zarins 1989: fig. 6/16).*

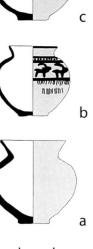

economic bonds that Tilmun had forged with Marhaši or her immediate southern periphery during the period ca. 2400–2250 BC.

Trade relations between Tilmun and Makkan, which first materialize in our data around 2600 BC (see above, p. 16), doubtless continued in the Sargonic period. The evidence, however, only amounts to insubstantial quantities of Makkan pottery (Umm an-Nar black-on-red) and *série récent* steatite vessels from sites in Tilmun that cannot with certainty be assigned to the Sargonic period, because they may well be younger.[4] The same applies to the number of Babylonian artifacts from Tilmun that only with a limited degree of confidence can be attributed to the Sargonic period.[5] Generally, it must be concluded that, until further excavation is conducted on Tarut Island, we will not be able archaeologically to clarify the nature of the social formation that existed in Tilmun at this time nor in greater detail specify what type of commercial relationship it enjoyed with Babylonia.[6] Presently, the Tarut Tell is the best candidate for localizing the type of Sargonic period Babylonian outpost hypothesized elsewhere in this contribution (see p. 31). Awaiting the results of future excavations at the Tarut Tell, we further venture the suggestion that during the Early Dynastic III and Sargonic periods a short-lived Tilmunite "kingdom of Tarut" existed.

Evidence from Makkan is difficult to attribute confidently to the 2350–2250 BC period, and the data only allow us to outline overall trends. Umm an-Nar society appears to have been organized as a tribal system of interdependent specialized economic units that were spatially bound to specific niches of the landscape, where each group engaged in various forms of resource exploitation.[7] Among these, we know the most about domains such as fishing, oasis agriculture, mining/smelting, and trade and pottery production.[8] Comparatively less is known about the practicalities of water-borne transportation, mineral extraction (steatite and diorite), textile and stone vessel industries, and forestry and charcoal burning, although these and related activities doubtlessly constituted equally important components of Makkan's diverse economy. Information on the configuration of the social networks

4. Even if only a few Umm an-Nar (Makkanite) vessels are published from Tarut (Bibby 1973: 37 fig. 33:b; Burkholder 1984: 17b), the statement by Burkholder that "many fine examples of Umm an Nar pottery . . . come from Tarut" (1984: 190) suggests that they were traded in substantial numbers.

5. This is in part so because it remains problematic to confidently assign pottery to the Sargonic dynasty. However, it is likely that some of the Babylonian pottery encountered in the lowest levels in the Tarut Tell soundings by Masry (1974: 143–44) as well as some of the Babylonian pottery found loosely associated with the Bampur grey ware in the Abqaiq tumuli (see p. 18) should be attributed to the Sargonic period.

6. Importantly, there are multiple lines of evidence that suggest that in the Sargonic period Bahrain Island had still neither been intensely populated nor emerged as an important political entity, a point to which we shall return later (see below, p. 44).

7. Cleuziou 1996.

8. *Fishing:* Beech 2004; *oasis agriculture:* Cleuziou 1996; *mining/smelting:* Weisgerber 1981; Hauptmann 1985; *trade and pottery production:* Méry 1996; 2000.

that facilitated the flow of goods and information between these settlement units is as yet lacking but has traditionally been imagined within the broad framework of a tribal organization.[9]

According to the archaeological data from Makkan, the cultural and economic developments that were inaugurated around the Early Dynastic III period with the emergence of the Umm an-Nar culture continued and accelerated during the Sargonic period.

Although the intensity of copper extraction apparently reached a temporary high point in the Sargonic period,[10] the organization of its production and redistribution remained decentralized.[11] In stark contrast to the neighbors of the Oman Peninsula, who (with the possible exception of Tilmun) all were organized in urban and proto-urban systems, Makkan society apparently continued its organization along kinship lines in some stratified tribal or clan-like system. It is significant that, throughout the third millennium BC, Makkan society apparently never aspired to an urban organization nor made extensive practical use of urban technologies such as writing, weights, and seals.[12] Importantly, in the Makkanite burial custom, the telltale signs of a steeply hierarchical structure (as evident in the later Royal Mounds of A'ali on Bahrain) are almost completely absent. Conversely, qualitative and quantitative variation in the collective Umm an-Nar tombs appears to be the result of social competition that aimed to enforce rank hierarchy among groups equivalent to extended households, in contrast to hierarchies between prominent individuals. With the reservations of the above sketch of Makkan's organization in mind, it is, however, not improbable that influential leaders occasionally were able to amass resources and raise the support among the tribes necessary to establish short-lived kingdoms.

From the Sargonic period and onward, sustained or probably even intensified trade with Meluhha is suggested by relatively large quantities of artifacts of Indus origin found in tombs across Makkan, which in particular comprises flasks of Indus painted fine ware.[13] The import associated with black-slipped Indus jars continued in the Sargonic period and was still associated with the settlements facing the Indian Ocean and, only to a much lesser extent, sites in the interior of the Gulf basin, such as Umm an-Nar Island, Tell Abraq, and Ghanadha.[14]

Makkan's intense relationship with Meluhha notwithstanding, stamp seals of the classic square Indus Type apparently hardly ever circulated in Makkan[15] (nor Tilmun for that matter).[16] Conversely, a total of six stamp seals of classic Indus Type and an Indus impressed clay sealing have been

9. Cleuziou and Tosi 2007.

10. See, e.g., Weisgerber 1981; Hauptmann 1985: 34; Weeks 2003.

11. Cleuziou and Tosi 2007: 171.

12. However, as suggested by the three square Indus weights recovered at Tell Abraq by Potts (2000: 128), the Indus weight system possibly found isolated employment in the coastal communities that were particularly active in maritime trade.

13. See Méry 2000: 240–43, figs. 151–52, with references.

14. Respectively: Frifelt 1995; Potts 2000: 130; Al-Tikriti 1985: 13.

15. Among the few exceptions are a classic square Indus Type seal with a short-horned bull and text motif found at the Umm an-Nar settlement tower ST-1 near Salut (Oman). See Avanzini et al. 2012: 16 cat. no. 1; Frenez forthcoming. For an unusual Indus Type seal of copper from a 2500–2300 BC context at Ras Al Jinz RJ-2, see Cleuziou and Tosi 2007: 237. Finally, an Indus seal imitation in chlorite was excavated in an Umm an-Nar Type tomb near Bisyah. See Frenez forthcoming.

16. Although the first Gulf Type seals in Tilmun (ca. 2100–2000 BC) were inspired by the Indus Type seals (cf. Laursen 2010a), not a single classic square Indus Type seal has been found in the thousands of tombs excavated in Bahrain (Tilmun).

reported from contexts in Babylonia, suggesting that the type of interaction between Babylonia and Meluhha was of a different nature.[17] In addition to these come a handful of atypical Indus Type stamp seals and Indus-related cylinder seals.[18] Viewed in light of the dominating position of the kingdom of Lagaš in the third-millennium BC Gulf trade, which is outlined throughout this study (see in particular chap. 8 and Appendix 2), note should be made of the fact that two of the square Indus Type seals known from Babylonia as well as a rectangular Indus Type seal have been found at Lagaš's provincial capital, Girsu.[19] Additionally, two classic Indus Type seals have been found at Kiš,[20] another materialized during the excavations at Nippur,[21] one came from a Sargonic-period grave at Ur,[22] and an unprovenanced specimen is stored in the Baghdad Museum.[23] Finally, to this group one can add a clay sealing bearing an impression of a classic Indus seal with "unicorn below text motif" from the art market.[24]

The contextual information on the classic square Indus Type seals and the clay sealing is inconclusive, but it is certainly possible that every one of them reached Babylonia via the "Meluhhan route" of the Sargonic period. The lack of Indus seals in Makkan (and Tilmun) may cautiously be taken as an indication that the seals represent direct interaction between Meluhhans and Babylonians along trade corridors that bypassed the southern Gulf coast.

Evidence of trade between Makkan and Babylonia is predominantly available in the form of pottery imports at coastal sites such as Umm an-Nar Island, Tell Abraq, and Kalba.[25]

Archaeological confirmation of the military campaigns that Akkade waged against Makkan can be found in the inscribed stone vessels belonging to the so-called "booty of Makkan" taken by Naram-Suen.[26] Among these, the most convincing evidence is the fragments found by Woolley

17. For a presentation of the seals, see During-Caspers 1973: 3–20.

18. For images and descriptions of the four hybrid cylinder seals, see Collon 1987: no. 609 (Tell Suleimeh), no. 610 (Ešnuna = Tell Asmar), and nos. 611–612 (Ur). These hybrid cylinder seals are commonly advanced as an attestation of Babylonian contact with the Indus world, although their relationship arguably is very indirect.

19. One of these classic Indus Type seals bears the rare "tiger below text motif" (Thureau-Dangin 1925) and Parpola states that ". . . according to the dealer from whom it was acquired in 1924, the seal comes from Tello (Girsu)" (1994: 312 no. 24). The other classic Indus Type seal has the "bison below text motif" and was found by de Sarzec at Girsu in an unstratified context termed "époque archäique." See de Sarzec and Heuzey 1884–1912. Last, an unpublished seal of a rectangular type with Indus text only was found at a level belonging to the time of Gudea (or the Larsa period) at Girsu. See Parpola 1994: 312 no. 23.

20. Two classic square Indus Type seals of the common type with "unicorn below text motif" were found at Kiš. The first was found in the foundation of a chamber below a pavement dated to Samsu-iluna. See Mackay 1925: 697–701. The other Kiš seal was found by Watelin in a context about which Langdon states that "according to our stratifications at the site, the object should be Pre-Sargonic, but it was found with a stone pommel bearing an inscription clearly not earlier than Sargon of Akkade. Both objects, therefore, may have fallen from above." See Langdon 1931: 593–96.

21. A classic Indus square seal with the rare "Zebu bull below text motif" was found at Nippur by the Oriental Institute in 1975 but in secondary context of a Kassite date. See Gibson 1976.

22. The square copper stamp seal probably of Indus origin was found together with a Sargonic-period lapis lazuli cylinder seal in PG 489 at the Royal Cemetery of Ur. See Reade 1995: table 44.

23. The seal in question is of the classic Indus Type with "unicorn below text motif," presently in the Iraq Museum collection. See Brunswig, Parpola, and Potts 1983: fig. 1.

24. Scheil (1925) stated that the sealing was allegedly found at Umma but this is most uncertain.

25. For Umm an-Nar Island, see Frifelt 1991; 1995. For Tell Abraq, see Potts 1990: 93–94. The information on Kalba is based on personal communication from C. Philips.

26. Potts 1986b.

at Ur of what is unmistakably an Umm an-Nar styled steatite vessel (*série récente*) (see fig. 4a and below, p. 33).[27]

For evidence along similar lines, we briefly note the stone (esi, *ušû*) that both Maništušu and Naram-Suen claim to have quarried while campaigning in Makkan and the compelling mineralogical matches between known statues of Maništušu and Gudea (olivine-gabbro and diorite)[28] and mineral sources on the Oman peninsula.[29]

Notably, sometime during the late ED III or early in the Sargonic period, the trading post on Umm an-Nar Island was abandoned, possibly after a fire had destroyed the "warehouse" for the second time (see above). Following this event, the port functions of Umm an-Nar Island were apparently taken over by fortified coastal sites such as Tell Abraq.[30] Possibly Sargonic-period Babylonian pottery has appeared on Kalba,[31] and this indicates that during this period the fleet of the so-called "big ships" or Makkan boats (see Appendix 2) may have ranged beyond the Strait of Hormuz and into the Arabian Sea.

The close cultural ties that Makkan had established with southeastern Iran and that first materialized in our data with the emergence of the Umm an-Nar culture (ca. 2700 BC) continued in the Sargonic period. As D. T. Potts has argued, this general southeast Iranian connection is most apparent in the continued strong "Marhaši" influence on Makkan's fine-ware tradition.[32] Additionally, Bampur black-on-grey wares were exceedingly popular on the Oman peninsula during the time of the Sargonic kings and were clearly attributed high status in Makkan, judging from its frequent inclusion in tombs.[33]

Astonishingly, and in stark contrast to the situation in Tilmun (Tarut Island), only very small quantities of sculpted chlorite vessels have ever materialized on the Oman peninsula.[34] In light of Makkan's cultural ties to the greater "Marhaši" region, which are much closer than those with

27. Frayne RIME 2 99–100 Naram-Sin 4, Ex. 4 CBS 14951+14952. It was T. F. Potts who made a connection between this vessel and the "booty of Makkan" by pointing out that "although the geographical name in the final line is entirely broken away, it may confidently be restored as 'Magan,' since that is the only place name which occurs in this context in other vessels inscriptions of Naram-Sin" (1989: 134). D. T. Potts has convincingly argued that, although the other vessels belonging to the so-called "booty of Makkan" are all of Iranian types and made of alabaster (which is practically absent in Bronze Age Oman), this does not necessarily argue against locating Makkan in Oman. Nor does it mean that they must have been taken as booty in Iran, since it is entirely possible that they found their way to Oman through trade or as gifts (D. T. Potts 1986b: 284). This possibility is even more likely in view of the close relationship that appears to have existed between Makkan and Marhaši at that time (see immediately below). Another argument that can be added is the fact that in Tilmun, where alabaster vessels are equally uncommon, types roughly compatible with those belonging to the "booty of Makkan" are known both from Tarut Island (see above) and the Barbar temple (Casanova 2003: 283–88).

28. Heimpel 1987: 65–68; Hauptmann 1985: 15–21.

29. Heimpel 1987: 49 n. 86.

30. For this site, see Potts 1990; 1991; 2000.

31. C. Phillips, personal communication.

32. Potts 2005.

33. Méry 2000: 191–204; Frifelt 1991.

34. Among the few exceptions of sculpted chlorite in Makkan, see the base fragment from Umm an-Nar Island, which Frifelt called a "hut pot"; she has interestingly noted regarding its color that "this pot of greenish steatite unlike the local light grey is probably an import from Iran" (1995: 198, fig. 281 NM). For an example from Mleiha, Sharjah (UAE), see David 1996: 34, fig. 4, and for attestations from Fujairah (UAE), see Ziolkowski 2001: fig. 52 and 80, and David and Phillips 2008.

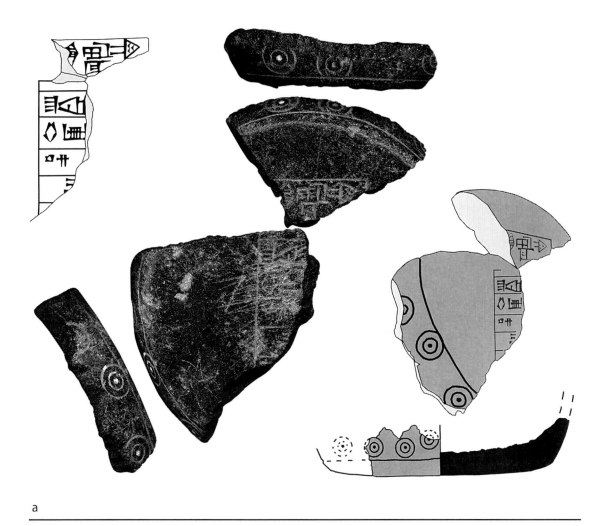

a

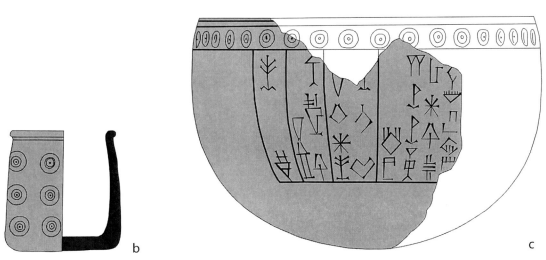

b   c

Fig. 4. ***a:*** *Inscribed fragment of steatite vessels found at Ur which belong to the so-called the "Booty of Magan" (redrawn after T. F. Potts 1989: fig. 10). Photos of the fragments are reproduced courtesy of The Penn Museum.* ***b:*** *a compatible vessels from Maysar 1, Oman (after D. T. Potts 1990: fig. 13 j).* ***c.*** *Inscribed steatite vessels found at Girsu (redrawn after T. F. Potts 1994: 46).*

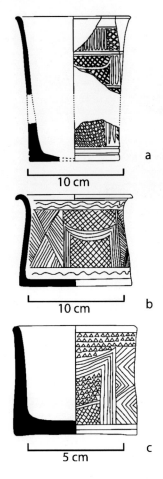

Fig. 5. Examples of Incised Grey Ware with "temple gate with concave lintel" (Hut pot) decoration. **a–b:** *from Hili tomb 1059, Abu Dhabi and Amlah, Oman (after Méry 2000: fig. 126:1 and 7).* **c:** *for comparison, chlorite vessel with the "temple gate with concave lintel" from Tarut island (after Zarins 1978: pl. 66:109).*

Tilmun, the conspicuous dearth of "Marhašian" prestige goods cannot be ignored. The absence is particularly striking in view of the geographical proximity of Makkan to the Hormozgan coast and the Kerman Province, where these vessels are known to have been produced.

Remarkably, in Makkan, the exclusive Marhaši stone vessels generally appear to have been replaced by much simpler ceramic imitations made in so-called "incised grey ware" (cf. fig. 5 a–b). The decoration of incised grey ware draws on models from the Marhaši carved chlorite tradition and frequently employs motifs such as "the temple gate with concave lintel."[35] Importantly, the imitation goes beyond decoration: the clay was intentionally fired in a controlled, reduced atmosphere to achieve a grey-green color superficially reminiscent of chlorite.[36]

In southeastern Iran, where the vast majority of incised grey ware originates, its distribution follows a general pattern: it is rare at sites with an abundance of carved chlorite and infrequent at sites where carved chlorite is absent or rare. This distribution pattern and the low level of craftsmanship involved have given rise to its interpretation as "a cheap substitute" for the more prestigious chlorite vessels.[37]

The characteristic composition of Makkan's import from "Marhaši" and southeastern Iran and the obvious "mimicking" of sculpted chlorite evidenced by the incised grey ware vessels strongly support the hypothesis, previously voiced by P. Steinkeller, that there existed an asymmetrical or at times possibly even client relationship between "urban" Marhaši and "tribal" Makkan.[38]

Texts

The picture of contacts with the Gulf underwent a dramatic change during the Sargonic period. Although foreign trade had figured prominently among the concerns of the pre-Sargonic rulers of Babylonia, who felt the constant need to secure their access to various strategically important prod-

35. The "hut motif" or "hut pot" is a misnomer frequently used to describe the characteristic "gate" iconography.

36. On the basis of petrographic analysis of the incised grey ware found on the Oman Peninsula, S. Méry has identified imported vessels that are compositionally identical to Iranian grey ware (Emir grey) as well as some that are of local Omani manufacture. See Méry 2000: 209–15.

37. See De Cardi 1968: 149. Moreover, when evaluating the interpretive implication of the absence of sculpted chlorite vessels, one must note that alabaster/banded calcite vessels, another luxurious Iranian product, also largely bypassed Makkan. Among the most notable exception to the latter appear to be the alabaster/banded calcite vessels that belong to the so-called "Booty of Magan" dating from the time of Naram-Suen. See below, p. 33, and Potts 1986b.

38. Steinkeller 2006a: 11.

ucts, such as metals, stone, and timber, and sought ways of satisfying their growing taste for a wide range of high-status exotica, none of which were available locally, it was only with the advent of the Sargonic rulers and the creation by them of what may justifiably be identified as the first fully-fledged empire that foreign trade became the main target of Babylonian political strategy.[39] As a result of the Sargonic territorial expansion, which reached its nearly full extent already under Sargon, the founder of the dynasty, the Sargonic rulers succeeded in bringing under their control and turning into a single interconnected system all of the main trade routes of Western Asia, from the Indus Valley in the east to Anatolia in the west, and from Armenia in the north to Lebanon in the south. Most remarkably of all, they created the first international commercial highway, which commenced at the coast of Gujarat and ran, via the Persian Gulf and the Euphrates Valley, all the way to the shores of the Mediterranean. Whenever possible, the Sargonic kings attempted to reach all the way to the sources and ultimate producers of the desired materials (cedar and other conifers in the Amanus, copper and diorite in Oman, chlorite and other semiprecious stones in southeastern Iran, silver in Anatolia, and so on), thereby eliminating most of the middlemen and thus maximizing profits.

As a consequence, the geographic horizon of Babylonia expanded in all directions. Beginning with the reign of Sargon, for the first time we hear of Makkan, Marhaši, and Meluhha. Sargon's abiding interest in the trade is evident from his claim that the god Enlil, the head of the Babylonian pantheon, had himself granted to him the mastery over the "Lower and Upper Seas."[40] A similar claim is made in reference to the middle Euphrates Valley and Syria in Sargon's other inscriptions, where in Tuttul he submits himself to Dagan, and then Dagan presents to him the "Upper Land," including Mari, Yarmuti (probably later Yarimuta, near Byblos), and Ebla, as far as the Cedar Forest and the Silver Mountains (in Anatolia).[41]

There is no evidence that any of the foreign lands conquered by the Sargonic kings were annexed to Babylonia. These territories were neither turned into a system of colonies (settled with Babylonians), nor were they subjected to any systematic economic exploitation (such as taxation), beyond the payment of tribute. All that the Babylonians were interested in was the control of critical nodal points, at which they established military and commercial outposts, staffed with military and administrative personnel. Such outposts existed at Nagar, Mari, Tuttul, and Susa, and closer to home, at Assur and Nineveh. As we suggest below, a similar outpost existed at Tilmun, and there may have been still others in Makkan (at Umm an-Nar?) and on the Iranian side of the Gulf (at Bushire?). Most of the periphery affected by the Sargonic expansion appears to have remained largely independent, with the local rulers simply recognizing Akkade's overlordship and paying occasional tribute. Their relations with Akkade were regulated by dynastic marriages and diplomatic treaties, whose primary objective undoubtedly was to set the terms of trade and to provide protection for the Babylonian traders, who lived in extraterritorial commercial settlements in the periphery or simply conducted regular business there.

In agreement with this picture, the main function of the empire's political and military apparatus was to ensure that the entire commercial network worked smoothly, with the merchandise flowing

---

39. Steinkeller 2013a.
40. Frayne RIME 2 9–12 Sargon 1: 68–73 (Sumerian) = 73–78 (Akkadian); also ibid. Sargon 2 and 13.
41. Frayne RIME 2 27–29 Sargon 11: 14–28 (Sumerian) = 17–35 (Akkadian); also ibid. Sargon 12.

from one end of the system to the other without any disturbances or interruption. When problems arose, punitive military expeditions were sent to restore order. The massive campaign conducted by Rimuš against Elam and Marhaši, which followed an earlier war on Marhaši by Sargon (see the discussion below), undoubtedly was such an operation, whose objective was to restore Babylonia's dominant position in the Gulf region. The same objective may be identified behind the campaigns of Maništušu in southeastern Iran and Makkan. The most drastic example here is the so-called "Great Rebellion" during Naram-Suen's reign, which began in Babylonia itself and spread throughout the periphery, eventually threatening the city of Akkade itself. In the periphery specifically, what this revolt amounted to was a rejection of Akkade's domination of the international trade. After an epic struggle, Naram-Suen managed to restore order in Babylonia and to bring the periphery back under his control. He even extended the geographic compass of the empire still further, introducing a new, more tightly controlled administrative system. Still, in spite of these reforms, the instruments of external control continued to be quite light, with the "empire" amounting to not much more than a commercial enterprise whose existence depended largely on the cooperation and goodwill of allied international powers and the obedience of Akkade's vassals. The absence of a truly imperial infrastructure, in the form of permanent colonies, settled with Babylonians and actively exploiting local agricultural and other resources, explains why the empire collapsed so suddenly and disappeared without leaving hardly any tangible trace (save for its fame preserved in later memory).

The Sargonic expansion in the east apparently commenced with Sargon's capture of E-Ninmar = Gu'abba, Babylonia's main seaport, as well as of its territory and the city of Lagaš, "all the way to the sea." Following this exploit Sargon "washed his weapon in the sea,"[42] a ritual emulated by the later generations of Mesopotamian rulers. Having obtained direct access to the Gulf, Sargon was then in a position to launch a naval expedition against Makkan: "the (land) across the sea revolted (against Sargon); and he heard of this, and crossed (the sea) and smote Makkan, which is in the middle of the sea, (and then) he washed his weapon in the Lower Sea."[43] It appears that, already during Sargon's reign, Babylonia established a modicum of control over the trade routes in the Gulf. This may be gathered from Sargon's boast that "he moored the ships of Meluhha, Makkan, and Tilmun at the quay of Akkade"[44]—meaning that the merchants of Meluhha, Makkan, and Tilmun brought their merchandise all the way to Babylonia. The extraordinary prominence this fact is given in Sargon's inscriptions, which identify it as one of the chief accomplishments of his reign, deserves notice, for it reveals the extent to which Sargonic conquests were motivated by commercial interests.

But the control of Makkan achieved by Sargon must have been only temporary, since his successors needed to campaign there again and again. First came the naval operation against Makkan conducted by Sargon's son Maništušu, which was preceded by an expedition against Anšan and Šerihum. Having transported his army across the Gulf (apparently from Šerihum, which seems to have been situated on the Iranian coast), Maništušu was confronted in Makkan (text says only "across the sea") by a coalition of 32 "towns" (uru/*ālum*).[45] The coalition, led by the "lords" (en/*bēlum*) in charge of

---

42. Frayne RIME 2 9–12 Sargon 1:42–52 (Sumerian) = 44–58 (Akkadian); 13–15 Sargon 2: 47–61.
43. Wilcke 1997: 25 x 15–28, 28.
44. Frayne RIME 2 27–29 Sargon 11:9–13 (Sumerian) = 11–16 (Akkadian); also ibid. Sargon 12.
45. *i-nu An-ša-an*[ki] *ù Šè-rí-ḫu-um*[ki] SAG.GIŠ.RA-*ni ti-a-am-dam sa-bil-dam* MA₂.MA₂ GIŠ.LA-*e u-sa-bì-ir* URU.KI.URU.KI *a-bar-ti ti-a-am-tim* 32 *a-na tamḫārim*(KAS+ŠUDUN) *ip-ḫu-ru-nim-ma iš₁₁-ar*, "when he defeated Anšan and

those "towns," was soundly defeated in an operation that extended as far as the "metal mines" (where copper mines apparently are meant).[46] Maništušu then embarked on a mining operation: "he mined the 'black stone' in the mountains across the Lower Sea, loaded it on ships, and moored (those ships) at the quay of Akkade."[47] Interestingly, the inscription makes no specific mention of mining copper in this connection (as one would expect from the context).

Another Sargonic ruler to campaign in Makkan was Naram-Suen, as part of his efforts to reconstitute the empire after the so-called "Great Rebellion," during which all his territorial possessions had been lost to him, save for his home city and capital Akkade (see above). During this campaign, Naram-Suen defeated Makkan, taking prisoner its "lord" (en/*bēlum*), who was named Mani'um. Like Maništušu before him, Naram-Suen also mined stone (here identified as *ešûm*, "gabbro" or "diorite") in the mountains of Makkan, transporting it eventually to Akkade.[48] Material confirmation of this campaign can be found in the stone vessels that, according to their inscriptions, were brought to Babylonia by Naram-Suen as part of the "booty of Makkan."[49] Among these, by far the most convincing is the unmistakable Umm-an-Nar style vessel made of chlorite (*série récente*), which was found in fragments by Woolley at Ur (see above, p. 28, and fig. 4a).

A digression on Makkan's location is required at this point. The identification of Makkan as the general area of the Oman peninsula (in modern terms, the Sultanate of Oman and the United Arab Emirates) may be considered certain. All the pertinent data were collected and discussed at great length by Heimpel (1987), with a more recent update by Maekawa and Mori (2011). Here we single out the most important facts upon which this identification rests: (1) the royal inscriptions of Sargon and Maništušu locate Makkan "in the middle of" or "across" the Lower Sea (i.e., the Persian Gulf);[50] (2) following his victory over the Makkanite coalition, Maništušu mined "black stone" in the mountains of Makkan, and this stone is likely to be identified as gabbro, a rock well documented in various parts of Oman (cf. Yule and Guba 2001); (3) Naram-Suen mined in the mountains of Makkan a stone called esi/*ešûm*, which is usually identified as "diorite" by Assyriologists, but in this instance almost certainly refers to gabbro as well; (4) Gudea of Lagaš also claims to have obtained esi stone from Makkan; (5) according to the Sargonic and Ur III economic sources, Makkan was a source of copper, a metal known to have been produced in great quantities in Oman during the third and second millennia.

Šerihum, he made the . . . ships cross the Lower Sea; thirty-two 'cities' that are across the sea assembled for battle, and he was victorious (over them)" (Frayne RIME 2 74–77 Maništušu 1:4–19). Misunderstanding the grammar and wording of this passage, Abdi (2000: 279) claimed that Maništušu landed his army on the Iranian coast. But the context makes it certain that the embarkation point of the expedition was *in Iran*, apparently at Šerihum. Moreover, it is completely untrue that *abarti tiāmtim*, "across the sea," always means the Iranian coast (as thought by Abdi).

46. *ù* URU.KI.URU.KI-*su-nu* SAG.GIŠ.RA EN.EN-*su-nu* [*u-s*]*a-am-*[*g*]*i-it ù iš-tu*[*m-ma*] ⌜. . .⌝ *a-ti-*⌜*ma*⌝ *ḫu-rí* KUG *íl-gu-ut*, "and he smote their 'cities' and he killed their 'lords'; and from ⌜. . .⌝ (the coast?) up to the 'metal mines' he plundered (their territory)" (Frayne RIME 2 74–77 Maništušu 1:20–30).

47. SA.TU-*e a-bar-ti ti-a-am-tim sa-bil-tim* NA₄.NA₄-⌜*su-nu*⌝ GI₄ *i-pu-*⌜*lam-ma*⌝ *in* MA₂.MA₂ *i-za-*⌜*na-ma*] *in kar-rí‹-im›* *ši A-ga-dè*^ki *ìr-gu-us* (Frayne RIME 2 74–77 Maništušu 1:31–41).

48. Frayne RIME 2 116–18 Naram-Sin 13 ii 1–14.

49. Frayne RIME 2 99–100 Naram-Sin 4, Ex. 1, 2, 3 and 4.

50. See also a fragmentarily preserved Old Babylonian copy of a Sargonic royal inscription (sometimes incorrectly assigned to Šu-Suen of Ur), which mentions Ma₂-gan^ki *ma-da-*[*ma-da-bi*] *kur x* [. . .] *bala-a-ri a-*[*ab-ba sig-sig*], "Makkan [with its[territories, a [. . .] land, which is beyond the [Lower] Sea" (Frayne RIME 3/2 300–301 Šu-Sin 2:10′–11′).

An important datum bearing on the question of Makkan's geographical extent that has so far escaped proper attention (though it was noted by Heimpel 1987: 37) is a fragmentarily preserved Ur III tablet from Ur (UET 3 1193 = Appendix 1, Text 7), which mentions, following a listing of the typical exports to Makkan, Ma$_2$-gan^{ki} gu-la, "Greater Makkan," as an apparent destination of the goods in question. By analogy with the term Gu$_2$-ab-ba$^{(ki)}$ gu-la, "Greater Gu'abba," which distinguishes in Ur III sources the general area of Gu'abba from the city of Gu'abba proper—the latter written simply Gu$_2$-ab-ba$^{(ki)}$ (see chap. 8), "Greater Makkan" may be taken to have described the entire Oman peninsula. Accordingly, it appears that the Babylonian scribes reserved the designation Ma$_2$-gan^{ki} for the part of Oman usually frequented by the Babylonian merchants, which most probably was the coastal area of Abu Dhabi (today in United Arab Emirates), where the Umm an-Nar island and other sites associated with the Umm an-Nar culture are situated. As for "Greater Makkan," it cannot be ruled out that this geographical designation also included in its compass the littoral region of Iran immediately across from the Strait of Khormuz (modern Hormozgan province), since the two regions have traditionally been very closely linked. The history of the Gulf saw many episodes when these two regions were united under a single rule, with the center of power shifting between coastal Iran and Oman, and with the Iranian and Omani (Arab) populations migrating in both directions.[51] (See Wilkinson 1973; Williamson 1973; Risso 1986.) A good example in point is the medieval Kingdom of Hormuz, whose chief political center originally rested at the city of Hormuz (Old Hormuz) on the Iranian coast (Vasoughi 2009). As a result of conflicts with its rival Kish and Turkic-Mongol enemies, the capital was eventually moved from the mainland to the island of Jurūn, which came to be known as New Hormuz. Apart from the Iranian littoral, the Kingdom of Hormuz ruled over the western and eastern coastal areas of Oman, including even some of Oman's inland territories. In reference to the Sargonic and Ur III periods specifically, the possibility that Makkan embraced the Iranian littoral as well is favored by the fact that Makkan would have been a logical intermediate handler of the merchandise reaching the Iranian coast via the land route leading from Marhaši (modern Kerman, see below), as well as that arriving there from Meluhha. A single center of control (resting either in Oman or in coastal Iran) in charge of both sides of the strait would certainly make sense in this situation—as often was the case in later times. (Cf. Steinkeller 2013a: 416.)

To resume our discussion of the Sargonic conquests in the east: Sargon's operations in that region also included campaigns against Elam (central portions of the Iranian plateau). These operations brought him into direct contact and conflict with the kingdom of Marhaši, whose territory embraced most of the modern Kerman province, probably extending into Baluchistan, and whose political

---

51. "One of the characteristics of the Gulf is that it has always been a creole area, an area of mixed descent, where the line between Arab and Persian was not clearly drawn, with many people bilingual and related to those on the other side. People in the region, as elsewhere, had multiple identities, any of which could be activated depending upon circumstances" (Potter 2014a: 11); "Until modern times . . . tribes traveled freely back and forth across the Gulf. Some have sections on both sides, most famously the Qawasim, based in Sharjah and Ras al-Khaimah, who temporarily governed Bandar Lingeh. Settlements along the Persian coast often had closer relations with those on the Arab side than those in the interior, due to ease of communication . . . There were many Arabs on the Iranian side (especially in the eighteenth and nineteenth centuries) as well as Persians on the Arab side. The second half of the eighteenth cenury was the heyday of the *Hawala*, Sunni Arabs originating on the Arabian coast who moved for a time to Persia and later returned" (Potter 2014b: 132–34).

point of gravity appears to have been situated in the Halil-rud valley (Steinkeller 2014a: 692–93).[52] At that time, Marhaši had become a great power in Iran, which exercised significant political influence in Elam, as well as throughout the entire Gulf region. The conflict with Marhaši continued into the reign of Sargon's son Rimuš, who successfully fought a major Marhašian coalition, one of whose members was, very revealingly, Meluhha. Another ally of Marhaši in this conflict was the land of Kupin, which should possibly be located in the general area of Baluchistan and Makran (Steinkeller 2014a: 693 n. 8).[53] By the reign of Naram-Suen, Marhaši had been neutralized, and apparently even turned into a Babylonian ally, as evidenced in the dynastic marriage arranged between the two royal houses.[54] There is every reason to think that during this time, and continuing into the Ur III period, Marhaši enjoyed a close relationship with Makkan, both economically and politically.

It may be surmised that the Iranian campaigns of Sargon, Rimuš, Maništušu, and Naram-Suen were, like their operations against Makkan, primarily motivated by commercial interests. While the control of the overland routes running through Elam and Marhaši was one obvious goal, the need to eliminate Marhaši's influence and interference in the Gulf region—a condition *sine-qua-non* for the smooth operation of Babylonia's trade connections with Makkan and Meluhha—may have been an even more important consideration.

The question we need to consider next is the status of Makkan as a political entity. From a purely archaeological perspective resting on the existing material data (which, it needs to be emphasized, remain exceedingly incomplete and sketchy), the simplest (and certainly the easiest) answer to this question would be to explain the "political" Makkan as a federation of small and decentralized tribal groups, bound together by inter-tribal alliances, but without a strong permanent leadership. It is conceivable that, like the later coalition of the Germanic tribes lead by Arminius (Herman), such a loose federation might have rallied and become temporarily united in the face of external foes such as the armies of Maništušu and Naram-Suen. Such an explanation was advanced by Cleuziou (1998: 161–62). In a similar vein, D. T. Potts hypothesized that the "lords" of the 32 "towns" captured by Maništušu were "petty lords, each in control of a certain territory centered around a primary settlement . . . dominated by a fortress-tower, bonded together to repulse the Akkadian invasion" (2001: 40).

There are reasons, however, to think that Maništušu's claim of having encountered 32 "towns" (or at least permanent settlements) in Makkan should perhaps be taken seriously and that Makkan

52. Steinkeller (2014a: 693) suggests that the territory of Marhaši extended "all the way to the Persian Gulf and the Straits of Hormuz." However, since the extant documentation never mentions Marhašian ships or any maritime activity conducted by Marhaši, it is possible that the Iranian littoral was politically independent of Marhaši. Be that as it may, it seems certain that this region (possibly a part of "Greater Makkan," as we considered it earlier) was traditionally allied with Marhaši, at times even remaining under Marhaši's hegemony. Cf. the case of the Kingdom of Hormuz, discussed above (p. 34), which, though nominally independent, was a tributary of the ruler of Kerman.

53. Searching for Kupin in the archaeological landscape of southern Baluchistan, the Kuli Culture springs to mind as an excellent candidate conveniently located between the Indus Valley and southeastern Iran. In support of Kupin's identification with the Kuli Culture, it may be emphasized that, as a highland agricultural society, Kuli would have had ample access to the types of trees whose timber is known to have been imported from Kupin to Babylonia during the reign of Gudea of Lagaš (such as the ^{giš}ha-lu-ub$_3$ tree discussed below, p. 84 n. 23). This region further offers a number of navigable waterways by means of which felled trees or logs could have been transported to the coast of the Arabian Sea. See now also R. P. Wright 2016.

54. Steinkeller 2014a: 692.

may have been more than a tribal confederation. Note the suggestion by Reade (2008: 17) that, by the time of Naram-Suen "if not before, the Oman peninsula may have been operating as a unified state and perhaps even attempting to impose some form of control over the Gulf" (criticized by Begemann et al. 2010: 163). That Makkan may indeed have formed a single territorial state is suggested by its *active* involvement in international trade, which presupposes (1) the presence of a settled merchant class, possessing capital and transportation means (ships), and of an agency capable of handling the complicated system of trading arrangements with Makkan's commercial partners (such as Meluhha, Marhaši, and Babylonia); and (2) the existence of an internal organization and control means that would implement the mining of copper and diorite in Makkan's mountains and then the transportation of these materials to the Gulf. The lack of historical parallels for simple tribal groupings successfully engaging in this kind of behavior argues against the likelihood of Makkan being just a tribal federation.

That Makkan indeed possessed a political organization capable of handling the complicated tasks we described above is further suggested by the fact that, in Naram-Suen's account of his campaign against Makkan, only *one* opponent is mentioned, titled "lord," and even identified by name. Was this Maniʾum a royal figure? We submit that one should seriously consider this possibility. Some 150 years later, during the reign of Šulgi, we hear of another ruler of Makkan who sends an object made of gold to king Šulgi as a diplomatic gift (see Appendix 1, Text 1 and discussion below, p. 55). Although unnamed, this Makkanite is afforded the title "king" (lugal), a distinction given only to the most important foreign rulers that the Ur III dynasts interacted with. Yet another ruler of Makkan, named Nadub-ʾel-i and titled ensi₂ Ma₂-gan, is documented during the reign of Amar-Suen, when one reads of his messenger visiting the court of Ur and bringing along with his entourage a gift of exotic animals (see below, p. 55). As a matter of fact, it is known that diplomatic envoys traveled from Makkan to Babylonia already in Sargonic times. A tablet from Umma, dating probably to the reign of Šar-kali-šarri, records an expenditure of travel provisions (bread and beer) to an unnamed ra-gaba Ma₂-ga[n^(ki)], "envoy of Makkan," who possibly was on his way to the royal court in Akkade.[55]

Here it might be instructive to point out that a very similar dilemma faces a student of the political organization in the Zagros region during the Sargonic through the Old Babylonian periods. Although the existing archaeological record shows a very limited number of settlements (of any size) in this entire zone, the written sources bearing on this particular area attest to the presence of a profusion of settlements, not to mention a plethora of highly developed states.[56] This lack of synchroniza-

55. MCS 9 245:25 (= Cripps 2010: 68–69 no. 18). This tablet belongs to the type of document constituting an equivalent of the Ur III "messenger tablets," as known from Umma, Girsu/Lagaš, and Urusagrig. See Foster 1982: 109–14; Steinkeller and Postgate 1992: 51. These documents routinely mention various foreigners (Gutians, Amorites, men from Susa, Pašime, Ḫašuanum, Tilmun, etc.). There is every reason to think, therefore, that the envoy in question was a native Makkanite.

56. A prime example here is the state created around 2100 BC by an Elamite ruler named Puzur-Inšušinak, who united under his rule the Susiana Region, most of the Zagros zone, northern Babylonia, the Diyala Region, and possibly the kingdom of Anšan as well. Because of the vast geographical extent of this creation, it is even justifiable to classify it as an "empire" of sorts. See in detail Steinkeller 2013b: 293–303. In one of his inscriptions (MDP 4 10 and 12), Puzur-Inšušinak claims to have conquered more than 80 individual localities, most of which appear to have been located in the Zagros. If not for the testimony of his inscriptions, one would search in vain for any evidence of this "empire" in the existing archaeological record.

tion between the two types of data means that either many sites are yet to be discovered or that many of the textually-attested settlements in the Zagros zone were single-period sites that have completely disappeared due to the process of erosion. (Cf. the important discussion by Potts 2014: 43.)

We now turn to the specifics of the Gulf trade during the Sargonic period. Though playing a dominant role in the pre-Sargonic period, Tilmun clearly had become marginalized in Sargonic times, serving as but a way-station in the Gulf, a convenient stop for the ships frequenting the routes leading to Makkan and Meluhha and various other points in between. Although occasional mentions of Tilmun ships appear in contemporary economic sources[57] and Tilmunites visiting Babylonia are mentioned as well,[58] it appears that Tilmun no longer was a major independent player in the Gulf trade, that role now having been taken over by the Babylonians, especially once the Sargonic kings had established full mastery over the Gulf, an event that probably took place only in the second half of Naram-Suen's reign. It is possible that earlier, until that dominance materialized and until the Babylonians acquired a merchant fleet and the know-how necessary to navigate in the Gulf, much of the seafaring was done by the merchants from Meluhha and Makkan and possibly by the Tilmunites as well. This may have been especially true of the Meluhhan traders, for there are mentions of Meluhhan boats actually traveling to Babylonia (see below, chap. 9.2), a phenomenon documented textually only in the Sargonic period.

It is also possible that, once the struggle for the control of the Gulf had been won by Babylonia, the Babylonians established permanent merchant outposts or colonies in that region. It appears virtually certain that such an outpost existed in Tilmun. There may have been another one on the coast of Oman, most likely on the Umm an-Nar island. And there may have existed Babylonian outposts on the Iranian side of the Gulf, especially near the Strait of Hormuz and further west along the coast, possibly at modern Bushire.

As for the types of merchandise originating in Makkan, written sources mention only two materials in this connection: copper and gabbro/diorite. The pertinent documentation is scarce in the extreme, since, in the case of copper, only two such attestations survive. Of these, particularly informative is the Lagaš text ITT 1 1422, which is a record of Makkan copper delivered to the "palace" (apparently located in Lagaš). Unfortunately, this text is fragmentarily preserved; even the sequence of the obverse and reverse cannot be determined with confidence. As far as can be ascertained, ITT 1 1422 is an account of transactions conducted between the "palace" and a certain Lumma, who appears to have been a sea-faring merchant involved in the trade with Makkan. It is likely that Lumma had been contracted by the "palace" to purchase copper, and possibly other materials, on its behalf.

---

57. [x (guruš)] ki ma₂ Dilmun, "[x men] assigned to the Tilmun boat(s)" (ITT 1 1418:9′; Lagaš); [DINGIR]-dan šu-gal₅-la₂-um ma₂-Dilmun gaba i₃-ru-a, "(onions for) [Ilum]-dan, a policeman, when he directed the Tilmun boat(s) upstream (apparently from the seacoast to Nippur—and farther north?)" (OSP 2 128 i 13–14 = 132 ii 2′–3′; Nippur). Against Westenholz 1987: 139, who reads the last example du₈-ni ru-a and transliterates it "when he caulked (the Dilmun ship)," we assume that we find here the verb gaba . . . ru/ri, "to confront, to steer the boat upstream" (Akk. *maḫārum*). See, especially, the Akkadian term *ša māḫirtim*, "skipper of the boat traveling upstream," corresponding to the lexical lu₂-ma₂-ru-gu₂ and lu₂-ma₂-gaba-ru-gu₂ in Sumerian (CAM/1 92b). Further, see ᵍⁱˢma₂-gaba-ru-gu₂, ᵍⁱˢma₂-gaba-ri-a-ni = *ma-ḫi-ir-tum* (cited CAD M/1 99a lexical section of *māḫiru*).

58. A Sargonic "messenger" tablet from Umma (for the text type, see above, p. 36 n. 55) lists travel provisions for two Tilmunites (Dilmun 2-bi) named Da-gu-la and Pu-zu-zu (CT 50 55:11–15). Interestingly, both of these names are good Babylonian onomastica.

Lumma has made two (or more) separate deliveries of copper, for which he is now being paid in silver by the "palace." Of special interest are lines 3′–4′ of the reverse(?), which list 50 shekels of silver as a payment for 200 minas of copper, with a resulting rate of 1 shekel of silver per 4 minas of copper. Another interesting point is found in line 2′ of the reverse(?), which implies that, apart from copper, Lumma was also commissioned to buy šuba gems. The identication of this semi-precious stone (called *šubûm* in Akkadian) is uncertain, though it has been speculated that it may be a type of agate. Whatever the exact meaning of šuba was, and even if in fact it could be purchased in Makkan, it is unlikely that šuba was native to Makkan itself. Rather, the Makkanites obtained it through intermediary trade, either from Iran or Meluhha. Because of its importance, we offer a full edition of ITT 1 1422 below:

Obverse?	(beginning broken off)	
1′)	[x] gin$_2$ ⌜12 še (kug-babbar)⌝	[x] shekels and 12 grains (of silver)
2′)	la$_2$-NI-am$_3$	is the outstanding balance;
3′)	Lum-ma i$_3$-da-gal$_2$	it is owed to Lumma;
4′)	uruda a-ra$_2$ 2-[kam]	the second (installment of) copper;
5′)	e$_2$-gal-še$_3$ mu-de$_6$	he (Lumma) delivered it to the palace;
6′)	nam-ga-eš$_8$-ak	the sea-faring trade with
7′)	Ma$_2$-gan$^{k[i]}$	Makkan;
8′)	⌜nam-ga-eš$_8$-ak⌝ b[a?-x]	the sea-faring trade ⌜. . .⌝;
	(rest broken off)	
Reverse?	(beginning broken off)	
1′)	[x] GAR [x]	⌜. . .⌝ (that was expended?)
2′)	šuba(MUŠ$_3$.ZA) uruda ba-sa$_{10}$-a	to buy the šuba gems and copper.
3′)	1 ma-na la$_2$ 10 gin$_2$ (kub-babbar)	50 shekels (of silver),
4′)	sag uruda 3 gu$_2$ 20 ma-na-še$_3$	in exchange for 200 minas of copper,
5′)	e$_2$-gal-še$_3$ mu-de$_6$-a	which he had delivered to the palace,
6′)	ib$_2$-ta-zi	were expended (to him).
	(space)	
	(rest broken off)	

The other Sargonic source mentioning Makkan copper is STTI 68. This text simply lists five bushels of barley and ten minas of Makkan copper, the written receipts for which were placed in a leather bag.[59] It is unclear if the barley represented the payment for the copper. If it did, the price of copper was half that paid in the earlier text (assuming that 1 bushel of barley cost 1 shekel of silver).

These meager data contrast sharply with the archaeological record bearing on Makkan, which shows, during the second half of the third millennium BC, evidence of a massive copper industry that involved both ore extraction and copper production.[60] The huge size of this industry, whose *floruit* belonged to the Sargonic and Ur III periods (Begemann et al. 2010: 137–40), permits one to conjecture that, the paucity of relevant textual data notwithstanding (for the Ur III references to copper trade with Makkan, see below, Appendix 1, Texts 5 and 6, pp. 94–96), the volume of copper that was exported from Makkan to Babylonia during these periods must have been enormous.

59. 5.0.0 še gur / 10 uruda ma-na Ma$_2$-gan / ^{kuš}⟨a-⟩ga$_2$-la$_2$ ke[š$_2$-ra$_2$] (lines 1–3).
60. See Weisgerber 1987, 1988, 1991; Heimpel 1987; Begemann et al. 2010.

Another consideration supporting this conclusion is the fact that the Sargonic and Ur III kings obtained copper *directly* from its producers in Makkan, without the use of middlemen in the Gulf (such as Tilmun), which enabled them to import it at a lower cost and therefore also in larger quantities, especially since they had large navies at their disposal. This opens a possibility that, contrary to what the written record appears to indicate (see below, p. 68), the copper trade in the Gulf as it existed in the Isin-Larsa and Old Babylonian periods, when it was controlled by Tilmun, probably was considerably smaller than during the third millennium. [61]

As for gabbro/diorite, the other material associated with Makkan, there is even less information about its import to Babylonia, since it is named only in the inscriptions of Maništušu and Naram-Suen cited earlier. In the later periods, this Makkanite stone is explicitly mentioned only in the inscriptions of Gudea (for which, see below, p. 54; for the sources of gabbro in various parts of Oman, see Yule and Guba 2001).

As noted earlier, it is likely that Makkan was also involved in the transshipment of the materials originating in (or percolating through) the lands of Marhaši and Meluhha. In the case of merchandise that Makkan obtained from Marhaši, one thinks of chlorite and finished chlorite vessels, which are known to have been produced in Marhaši locally. Marhaši must have also served as a middleman in the trade in lapis lazuli, gold, and tin, all of which were imported from Afghanistan and, in the case of tin, also from Central Asia. As for the goods brought to Makkan from Meluhha (and from the various localities situated between the Indus Valley and the Strait of Hormuz), one may list carnelian, ebony, and possibly gold. For other materials associated with Meluhha, see chap. 9. The šuba stones we discussed earlier—if indeed one could purchase them in Makkan—would have been obtained by Makkan via these mechanisms as well.

Although we have no records of the merchandise that the Sargonic traders brought to Makkan, it seems fair to assume that it involved the same assortment of goods that were sent to Makkan in Ur III times, as well as to Tilmun in the Pre-Sargonic period: textiles, wool, barley, perfumed oil, and silver. [62]

---

61. Because of the mentions of large volumes of Tilmun copper in a group of Old Babylonian sources from Ur, Weeks (2007: 89) thinks that it was only in the Isin-Larsa and Old Babylonian periods that the copper trade in the Gulf "reached its peak." However, as we emphasized earlier (see above, p. 5), foreign trade finds exceedingly little reflection in the cuneiform record. When such information is given, it is usually accidental.

62. H.-P. Uerpmann and M. Uerpmann (2008) have argued that the large domestic sheep kept at Saar and Qala'at al-Bahrain (and perhaps even those found in the Indus Valley) originated in Babylonia. This is a very likely proposition, though written sources offer no support of it. On the other hand, there is evidence of the transfer of animals from the Gulf region to Babylonia. The documented cases here are the "goat of Makkan" (see below, p. 55) and the water buffalo, which is depicted in Sargonic art and which possibly appears in texts as ab_2-za-za, Akk. *apsasûm* (see p. 88).

Chapter 5

Makkan and Tilmun
between ca. 2200 and ca. 2100 BC

The chronological resolution in the archaeological data from the Oman Peninsula is not sufficiently fine-grained to confidently identify developments temporally confined to the short "post-Sargonic period." Nonetheless, it is important to note that, all together, the last quarter of the third millennium BC stands out as the cultural and economic zenith of Makkanite society (the Umm an-Nar culture). In general, there appears to have been a culmination of settlements in the last quarter of the millennium,[1] and the collective tomb-building tradition peaked as the stone masonry reached a technological and artistic climax.[2] Judging from settlements such as Maysar 1, the extraction of copper flourished beginning ca. 2200 BC.[3] Even if the abandonment of the warehouse and trading station on Umm an-Nar Island occurred well before the Sargonic collapse, trade-oriented coastal sites at locations such as Tell Abraq and Ras al Jinz thrived in the post-Sargonic period onward. It is quite conceivable that Makkan, which in comparison with Tilmun was probably much less economically dependent on Babylonia, was relatively unaffected by the post-Sargonic breakdown and perhaps simply intensified her commercial activities with Meluhha and Marhaši.

That major changes unfolded in Tilmun in the wake of the collapse of the Sargonic dynasty and/or the breakdown of the Gulf trade is suggested by the entirely peripheral position Tilmun came to occupy in the mercantile order that emerged with the advent of the Ur III state. Hitherto, the important question regarding what conditioned the decline of Tilmun after the Sargonic collapse has largely been ignored.

As noted below (see chap. 8 and Appendix 2), in the Ur III period the operational range of the long-distance trade fleet of "big ships" at Gu'abba must have been unprecedented and certainly must have contributed to the decline of Tilmun as an intermediary. However, archaeological and, to a lesser extent, textual data suggest that other elements of the explanation for Tilmun's decline should be sought in developments within Tilmun—a subject on which we shall now digress.

After 2250 BC, everything in the archaeological record suggests that a significant reorganization of the Tilmun polity had occurred. Following a drought of evidence of occupation on the island,

1. Weisgerber 1981.
2. Gagnaison et al. 2004.
3. Weisgerber 1981; Hauptmann 1985.

Bahrain suddenly emerges from the archaeological record as the dominant component in Tilmun's settlement hierarchy.

On the northern tip of the island, a coastal settlement was founded at Qala'at al-Bahrain,[4] a site that around 2050 BC was to emerge as the fortified city and economic center of Tilmun (see below).[5]

Concurrently, flat-topped so-called "Early Type" burial mounds appeared in scattered areas on the island in numbers that ultimately reached 28,000 before that tomb style fell out of fashion around 2050 BC.[6] Based on the number of recorded burials, the average size of the living community populating Bahrain Island during this period has been estimated at about 10,000 individuals.[7] Since Cornwall has reported similar but now vanished burial mounds in roughly compatible quantities from the Dammam Dome, one is probably faced with a living regional population that on average ranged well above the 20,000 mark.[8] That a substantial pastoral population lived in the borderlands of Tilmun is suggested by mound cemeteries such as al-Rufaya 1–3 and Ayn al-Dila in the Al-Kharj region, KSA[9] and As-Sabbiya south of Kuwait City,[10] of Bronze Age and later dates.

Judging from the corresponding lack of finds from the Qatif, Hofuf, and Yabrin Oases dating to this period,[11] one must envision that these mainland oases either fell into decline or that the proposed population contraction simply left the oases communities almost entirely deserted.[12]

The new burial mounds of so-called Early Type generally display modest proportional variation and in doing so exhibit architectural continuity with older models on the mainland, such as the Abqaiq tumuli (see above). However, even if the burial mounds typically are small, they do exhibit

4. Højlund and Andersen 1994; 1997.

5. Højlund 1989a.

6. The accurate count of the original population of burial mounds has been obtained through an extensive and systematic program of mapping conducted on the basis of preindustrial 1959 aerial photography. See Laursen and Johansen 2007; Laursen 2010b; 2010c.

7. This figure is based on a statistical model that draws on the highly accurate counts of the burial mounds obtained from aerial photography recorded in 1959 before any mounds had been removed. The model that estimates the size of the average living population operates with a life expectancy rate of 35 to 40 years, but it obviously does not take into account individuals or population groups that potentially were not afforded a mound burial. See Laursen in press.

8. Cornwall published a sketch map that indicates the distribution of what he describes as "many thousands of burial mounds" around most of the Dammam Dome as it appeared in 1941 (Cornwall 1946: 36 fig. 2). The geography of the area that is occupied by Early Type mounds on Cornwall's map is strikingly similar to that occupied by this mound type on Bahrain. In this respect, it is particularly important to make note of the fact that around 2250 BC the Dammam Dome was a sheltered peninsula enclosed on three sides by *sahbka* and by the sea to the east.

9. Although later activities are attested at the Ayn al-Dila necropolis, the excavator tentatively attributes much of the cemeteries' 3,000 mounds to the Bronze Age. See Schiettecatte 2014: 25–88.

10. See above, p. 17 n. 21.

11. Zarins 1989.

12. J.-J. Glassner (1998: 156) has expressed disagreement with the hypothesis that Al-Hufuf oasis—which he prefers to connect with the Ekarra/Hakara of cuneiform sources—was surpassed by Bahrain in the late third millennium BC. However, even if there are limited data for earlier periods with which to compare, the beginning ca. 2250 BC of this massive accumulation of burial mounds on Bahrain Island and the Dammam Dome undoubtedly reflects a substantial increase in the size of the regional population. Based on the archaeological evidence alone, one cannot draw a qualified inference as to whether this population increase was the result of an endemic contraction of a previously more widespread regional population or the infiltration of external ethnic groups or, perhaps more likely, a combination of these two phenomena.

Figure	References	Artifact No.	Volume
6.1	Laursen 2011: fig. 1/6	A19075	0.23L
6.2	Laursen 2011: fig. 1/5	A6144	0.24L
6.3	Laursen 2011: fig. 1/3	A4599	0.21L
6.4	Laursen 2011: fig. 1/4	A17368	0.26L
6.5	Laursen 2011: fig. 1/2	A19072	0.32L
6.6	Laursen 2011: fig.1/1	472-2-88	0.35l
6.7	Laursen 2011: fig. 1/8	A19068	1.2L
6.8	Højlund 2007: fig. 145	213.h	0.83L
6.9	Højlund 2007: fig. 138	211.m	1.20L
6.10	Laursen 2011: fig. 3/8	A4740	1.06L
6.11	Laursen 2011: fig. 3/7	A461	1.51L
6.12	Højlund 2007: fig. 137	211.L	1.50L
6.13	Højlund 2007: fig. 151	214.h	2.00L
6.14	Aali Unpublished BNM	N/A	10.80L
6.15	Aali Unpublished BNM	N/A	7.21L

an incipient social hierarchy[13] that apparently had not yet developed in the early- to mid-third-millennium BC tumuli record at Abqaiq. Unambiguously, the emergence in Tilmun of a socially pre-eminent class is paralleled by a population influx to Bahrain, as reflected in the mound-type encircled by an outer ring wall that amounts to less than one-per-thousand of the entombed cemetery population. The "ring mounds" are only found centrally on Bahrain Island and were apparently reserved for the entombment of the highest-ranking individuals in Tilmun's tribal hierarchy.[14]

Significantly, imported vessels of both incised grey, Bampur black-on-grey, and sculpted chlorite are completely absent in the almost 1,000 Early Type burial mounds excavated to date. These southeastern Iranian imports are also nearly nonexistent in the substantial soundings at Qala'at al-Bahrain.[15] Accordingly, we can confidently assume that, by the time of the major population transfer to Bahrain Island, direct trade between Tilmun and southeastern Iran (Marhaši and its environs) had been brought to a halt. By contrast, evidence of the trade in which Tilmun was still involved is now chiefly confined to pottery and steatite vessels from Makkan (Umm an-Nar types)[16] and pottery from Babylonia.[17] Imported artifacts in the burial mound are henceforth restricted to a selection of Makkan fine ware[18] and the repeated occurrence of a specific, small Babylonian vessel type (see fig. 6: nos. 1–7 and Appendix 3). At Qala'at al-Bahrain, storage vessels from Babylonia of late Sargonic types make up approximately 10% of the ceramic inventory, while fine ware from Makkan

13. Laursen in preparation (a).
14. Højlund et al. 2008; Laursen 2008.
15. Højlund and Andersen 1994.
16. Højlund 1994: 111–17.
17. Højlund 1994: 102–10.
18. Laursen 2009.

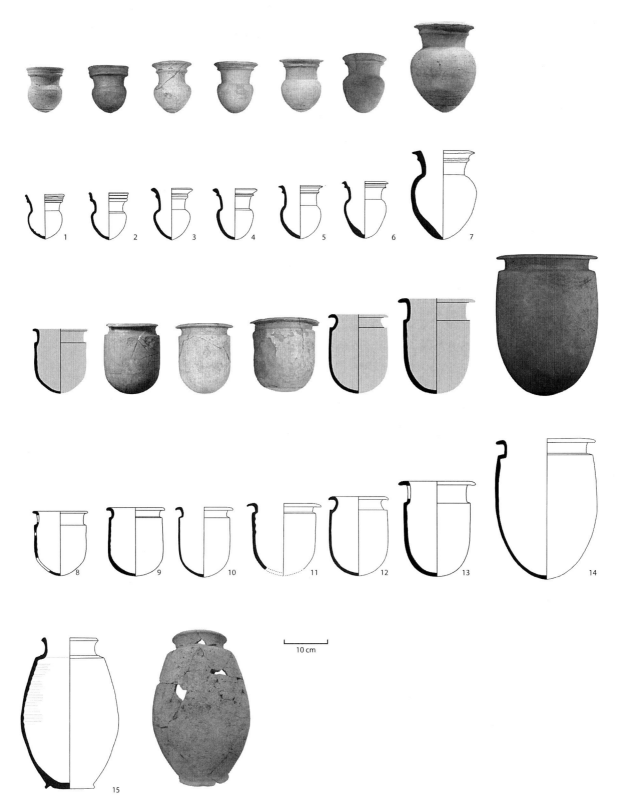

Fig. 6. Late Sargonic and Ur III period (nos. 1–7) and Isin-Larsa period (nos. 8–15) Babylonian vessels from the burial mounds of Bahrain. Details, vessel volume and references are listed in the table opposite.

only amounts to 2%.[19] This pattern reflects a situation in which Tilmun, after ca. 2250 BC, generally speaking had been reduced to a minor way station for the Makkan trade, which was bypassing it.

Taken in the aggregate, the evidence suggests that the population of Tilmun around 2200 BC had contracted to Bahrain Island and a similarly protected environment on the adjoining mainland near the Dammam Dome (see fig. 7). From this time onward, the elite fraction of Tilmun tribal society was entombed centrally on Bahrain Island in burial mounds encircled by a special outer ring-wall. At its stage of recent translocation, the polity of Tilmun was apparently only able to attract exotic articles from the trade connecting Babylonia with Makkan, which otherwise passed by Tilmun.

Importantly, the disappearance of southeast Iranian imports from the inventory in Tilmun allows us to conclude that, when this major translocation unfolded, the once significant trade to Tarut Island in carved chlorite vessels from Marhaši had ended.[20]

Given the character of the situation in Tilmun at this time, it is evident that in order for us to provide a nuanced answer to the question as to what conditioned the decline of Tilmun, one needs first to identify the causes behind of the major translocation to Bahrain Island.

There are multiple lines of evidence that suggest that around 2200 BC sudden environmental deterioration affected the Eastern Province at a scale that had considerable consequences for human security and that made Bahrain Island and Damman Dome, with their abundant fresh-water springs and defensive coastline, emerge as optimal safe havens (see fig. 7).[21]

The subsistence economy in the interior of Saudi Arabia outside the oases would to a large degree have depended on herding and would, as such, have been highly sensitive to grassland fluctuations. Of particular interest in this connection is the massive global aridification event (the 4.2 kiloyear event),[22] which began about 2200 BC and lasted into the nineteenth century BC and has been suggested as a possible contributing factor behind major reorganizations in the Indus Civilization[23] and the collapse of both the Sargonic empire[24] and the Old Kingdom in Egypt.[25]

Locally, in the Al Hasa Province, the onset of extreme prolonged aridification ca. 2200 BC must have presented multiple challenges to both the pastoral and the oasis economies, and seen in isolation, a cluster of extreme droughts alone could account for the population's translocation to Bahrain Island and Damman Dome.

However, from the perspective of human security, the 2200 BC aridification probably posed an even greater threat to the Tilmun polity, since the resultant droughts must have disrupted the seasonal patterns of movement of the mobile pastoralists all across the Levant and central Arabia.[26] The amplified mobility of pastoralist groups is most clearly attested by the historically documented migrations of the Hurrians, the Gutians, and the Amorites toward the well-watered alluvium in

19. The percentages derive from Højlund's counts of rims, respectively, from period Ia levels (1994: fig. 390).

20. Two carved chlorite vessels from Marhaši have materialized in early-second-millennium BC burials in Bahrain. One of them comes from the burial complex at the Saar Mound Cemetery (see Crawford and Al Sindi 1996), while the other from a burial mound in the Janabiyah Mound Cemetery (see Lombard 2014: 37).

21. Zarins 1986; Højlund 1989a: 52.

22. Weiss 1993; 2012: 1; Cullen et al. 2000.

23. Dixit et al. 2014.

24. Weiss et al. 1993: 1002; Weiss 2012.

25. Bernhardt et al. 2012.

26. For the concept of "mobile pastoralism," see Frachetti 2008, with further literature.

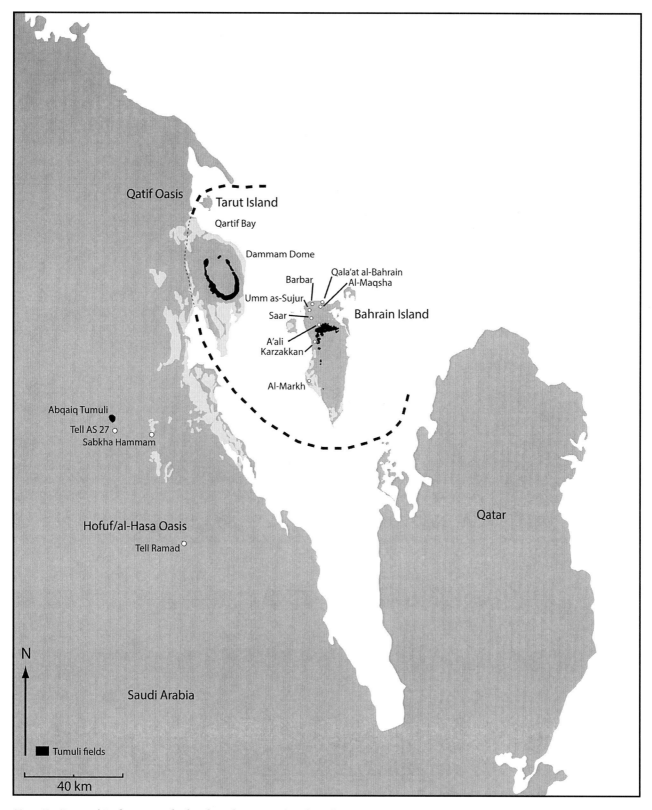

Fig. 7. Bay of Bahrain with the distribution of 3rd-millennium BC burial mounds shown in black. The distribution of sabkha (possible mangrove or swamp land in prehistory) is shown in light grey. Note how a belt of sabkha virtually cuts the Dammam Dome from the adjacent Saudi mainland. The dotted line indicates the ca. 2200 BC populous contraction or refugee zone and the subsequent core of the early 2nd-millennium BC Tilmun state.

Babylonia.[27] The much closer interval at which droughts occurred must thus have sent branches of many other pastoralists on the move at an unprecedented scale, with a resulting negative push and domino effect on most sedentary societies in the region. That pastoralist groups (the Ahlamu) in the Kassite period were causing problems in Tilmun by stealing the date production is evidenced by texts found at Nippur.[28]

Projecting this line of reasoning onto our present case, the threat from mobile pastoralists emerges as the most likely cause of the major translocation to Bahrain Island.[29] Similar ideas have been voiced in the past in connection with the rise of the Tilmun State around 2050 BC,[30] and the question of the Amorites' involvement does carry with it important ramifications for how we should evaluate Babylonia's relationship to Tilmun from ca. 2200 BC onward. Accordingly, the textual evidence that may point to an infiltration of Amorites as the catalyst for the massive translocation of Tilmunites to Bahrain Island is discussed later in this monograph (see p. 60 below).

27. Weiss et al. 1993: 1002.
28. Cornwall 1952; Potts 1986c.
29. Against Cleuziou 1998: 163.
30. Zarins 1986; Højlund 1989a: 52–53.

Chapter 6

The Ur III Period
(ca. 2100–2000 BC)

Archaeology

The archaeological data from Tilmun suggest that in the middle of the century marking the rule of the Ur III dynasty over Babylonia, major changes transpired in Tilmun and ultimately led to the formation of a state on Bahrain Island from around 2050–2000 BC.[1]

This notwithstanding, the archaeological record dating to the first half of the 21st century BC only displays limited signs of economic and social change. By all appearances, at this stage, Tilmunite society was organized around a number of kinship groups, each of which evidently enjoyed a status of relative autonomy. Exclusive mound burials encircled by outer ring-walls[2] and the obvious status-related architectural variation in the chamber layouts demonstrate that within these kin groups a social hierarchy with some form of preeminent social elite had been firmly established.[3]

At Qalaʾat al-Bahrain, the frequency of pottery imports from Babylonia reaches an all-time peak of 19% of the total ceramic inventory.[4] Essentially, these Babylonian ceramics attest to the fact that, even if Tilmun in the Ur III period was cut off from most of the organized trade (e.g., in textiles, oils, and cereals) that would have been passed down to us in economic texts, Babylonian products continued to reach Tilmun. Conceivably, much of this pottery arrived on the Babylonian "big ships" or Makkan ships (see Appendix 2) that were passing by, anchoring to stock provisions or make ship repairs, en route to or from the Oman Peninsula. However, the quantity of larger Ur III period storage vessels at Qalaʾat al-Bahrain[5] demonstrates that the Babylonian merchants probably also engaged in bulk and more organized trade with Tilmun. Among the most noteworthy evidence here stands out

1. Højlund 1989a.
2. Laursen 2008; Højlund et al. 2008.
3. Laursen in preparation (a).
4. Højlund 1994: 140 fig. 390. The fact that the relative percentage of imported Babylonian pottery in Qalaʾat al-Bahrain culminated at the very time when Babylonia's trade with Makkan completely dominates in the texts has multiple explanations. It should primarily be attributed to the simple fact that at this time the domestic production of pottery in Tilmun was very limited and simple and that the Tilmunite households at Qalaʾat al-Bahrain as a consequence held wheel-thrown Babylonian pottery in high regard.
5. For example, Højlund 1994: figs. 249 and 271.

Fig. 8. Rim sherd of Ur III period Babylonian storage vessel with cuneiform inscription from Qala'at al-Bahrain. Photo: Moesgaard Museum. Inscription after Læssøe (1958: fig. 2).

a rim fragment of an Ur III vessel of this category (see fig. 8). An inscription on the inside of the rim records a volume of 167 sila$_3$ or "liters."[6] The very large volume of this vessel suggests that the object in question originated in some official Ur III institution, such as a palace or temple household.[7]

The sole evidence for the use of the Babylonian system of measure in Tilmun at this time is a two-shekel (16.4 g) hematite weight from Qala'at al-Bahrain.[8]

The earliest observed settlement on Failaka Island comes from Tell F6 and centers around a dry stone wall corner of either a house or a courtyard that is associated with late-3rd-millennium BC deposits. The pottery found in and outside the corner structure is completely dominated by Babylonian forms of known Ur III period types. The assemblage also contains Umm an-Nar (Makkan) and Barbar ware (Tilmun) and a few probable Indus valley sherds (Højlund 2016: 93–95). Of note is a fragment of an Indus valley ladle made of shell (*Chicoreus ramosus*) that probably derived from the Gulf of Kutch (Højlund 2016: 223 fig. 1122). A number of Ur III period cylinder seals found in secondary contexts at Tell F6 (Pittman 2016: 157) should also doubtlessly be attributed to this Babylonian phase in Failaka's occupational sequence. The Ur III period settlement that was probably a way-station for Babylonia's east–west trade seems to have been deserted by the end of the Ur III period and was overlain one or two centuries later by the Early Dilmun period temple (Højlund and Laban 2016).

The small and standardized Babylonian vessel type that was included in Tilmun burials from the Late Sargonic period (see above, p. 42, and Appendix 3) continues to appear in the burial mounds

6. 2(pi) 4(ban$_2$) 7 sila$_3$. Cf. Eidem 1994: 301–2.

7. A parallel for this sherd is provided by a nearly identical vessel on which a volume of 175$^5/_6$ sila$_3$ or "liters" is inscribed. See D. T. Potts 1990: 159. The latter vessel comes from a secure Ur III context at Nippur (McCown and Haines 1967: pl. 87:14). During the 2013 excavation season at the A'ali Royal Tombs, an imported Babylonian vessel fragment with a similar but fragmentary cuneiform inscription on the shoulder/neck transition was found in "Mound P," which dates to the Old Babylonian period. See Laursen in preparation (a).

8. Højlund 1994: 396, fig. 1989.

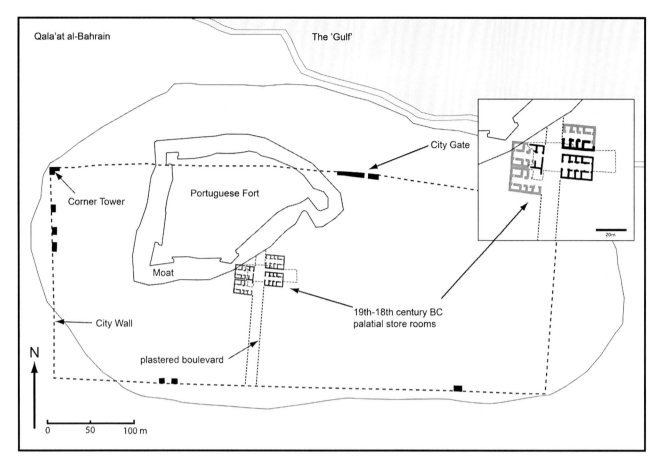

Fig. 9. The Bronze Age tell and Portuguese fortress Qala'at al Bahrain. The most important structures from the late 3rd and early 2nd millennium BC "Tilmun City" are emphasized. Inserts show 2nd-millennium palatial warehouses (after Højlund 1997: 11, fig.4; Højlund 1999: 74).

of the Ur III period (fig. 6: nos. 1–7, p. 43).[9] The only other foreign ceramic that appears in the burial mounds dating to the Late Sargonic and Ur III period also illustrates Tilmun's situation at this stage: they are Makkan fine ware types (Umm an-Nar Black-on-Red), which occur eight times more frequently than the Babylonian vessel type.[10] Pottery from Makkan (domestic as well as fine wares) is also present at Qala'at al-Bahrain, but here the ratio to Babylonian pottery is almost exactly the opposite of that observed in burials.[11] The number of carnelian beads found in the almost 1,000 mounds excavated from this period (Early Type) is very small,[12] and this suggests little or no direct contact with the Meluhhans. That Tilmun on the whole was detached from the Meluhha trade, which at this

9. Laursen 2011: 33–35 Type 1. In Appendix 3, we note the conspicuous similarity between the practice of including these small Babylonian vessels in burials of the Ur III period and the habitual inclusion, during the early third millennium BC, of small Jamdat Nasr style vessels in contemporaneous burials (Hafit tombs).

10. Laursen 2010c; 2011: n. 8.

11. Højlund 1994: fig. 390.

12. In his extensive database of ancient beads from Bahrain, Waleed Al-Sadeqi has recorded only 21 carnelian beads as coming from third millennium (period Ib) burial contexts (2013). We owe this observation to Al-Sadeqi.

time must have been facilitated through Makkan, is also demonstrated by the fact that two sherds of Indus black-slipped jars[13] represent everything of certain Indus affinity that has been recovered from Qala'at al-Bahrain dating to this time.[14]

Approximately halfway through the 21st century BC, Tilmun society suddenly underwent a series of major reorganizations that are concordantly suggestive of an explosion in both social complexity and economic prosperity. In every respect, this period marks an era of major transition that witnesses, among other things, the launch of a tradition of large public buildings that becomes characteristic of the Tilmun state proper during the early second millennium BC. One of the hallmarks of this transitional phase is the construction at Qala'at al-Bahrain, around 2050 BC, of a defensive stone wall that encircled 15 ha of the site (fig. 9); by implication, this is commonly believed to have assumed the position of paramount center of Tilmun.[15]

The temporary segregation from the Meluhha trade, which Tilmun hitherto had been subjected to, comes to a conspicuous end. Most important in this respect is the introduction in Tilmun of major urban innovations associated with the administration and organization of trade, each of which clearly are inspired by the mercantile protocol of the Indus Valley civilization.[16]

The first Indus-inspired circular stamp seals of "Gulf Type" appear in the layers at Qala'at al-Bahrain concurrent with the construction of the city wall ca. 2050 BC.[17] The synchronous introduction of Indus "writing" is suggested by the occasional presence on the Gulf Type seals of short inscriptions written in the characters of the Indus script.[18] The distribution of this class of inscribed "Gulf Type" seals ranges as far as Babylonia in the west to Sindh[19] and Gujarat (Dholavira) in the east.[20] By all appearances, this first series of stamp seals native to the Gulf is connected with a league of Tilmun-associated merchants that was now actively involved in the Meluhha trade.[21]

The introduction of sealing technology was accompanied by the introduction of a formal weight system, as evidenced in the cubical and spherical stone weights that correspond perfectly to the standard weight unit of the Harappans.[22] In Babylonia, Tilmun's newly adopted Meluhhan weight system became known as the *Tilmun norm* (na_4 Tilmun[ki]) (UET 5 796).[23]

Significantly, toward the end of the 21st century BC, the iconic Makkanite (Umm an-Nar Black-on-Red type) pottery completely disappears from the settlements[24] and burial mounds in Tilmun.[25]

13. Dales and Kenoyer 1986: fig. 6.
14. Højlund 1994: 118.
15. Højlund 1989a, against Glassner 1998: 156.
16. Laursen 2010a.
17. Bibby 1986: fig. 26; Kjaerum 1994: 319–20.
18. Parpola 1994; Laursen 2010a.
19. Laursen 2010a.
20. Bisht 2014.
21. Laursen 2010a.
22. For the examples found in Bahrain, see Bibby 1971: 345–53; Højlund 1994: 395–96; Moon and Killick 2001: figs. 5.30b and 5.36g.
23. See Bibby 1971: 345–53; Roaf 1982. It is important to note that the item GIN$_2$:TILMUN of pre-Sargonic Ebla sources, which some scholars interpreted as "Tilmun shekel" (e.g., Pettinato 1981: 182; De Maigret 1980; Pomponio 1980: 173; Carter 2013: 591), is almost certainly unrelated to the toponym Tilmun. There is likewise no archaeological evidence that, before the late Ur III period, Tilmun possessed any formal weight-system of its own.
24. Højlund 1994: fig. 390.
25. Lowe 1986; Højlund 2007; Laursen 2009.

This radical development positively reflects the demise of the Umm an-Nar culture in Makkan and probably coincides with the fall the Ur III dynasty[26] and the ensuing breakdown of Babylonia's long-distance trade fleets stationed at Gu'abba (see chap. 8 and Appendix 2).

The secondary effects of the reorganization of Tilmun society also echo in the burial custom: the previously scattered mounds are replaced by the emergence of vast, compact mound cemeteries. Ten such compact mound cemeteries are "founded" on Bahrain and over time accumulate a collective total of ca. 47,000 burial mounds.[27] Synchronous with this development on Bahrain, three equivalent cemeteries emerge on the mainland on the southern slopes of the Dammam limestone formation near Dhahran (cf. fig. 7, p. 45).[28]

A new conical burial mound of the so-called "Late Type" is introduced in tandem with the spatial allocation of new burial mounds to cemeteries proper. These new burial mounds display more variation than previous ones in terms of diameter, height, chamber layout, and grave goods. These developments unquestionably mirror the formation of a much more ranked society, with considerable social inequality. Importantly, the Gulf Type seal is introduced as a personal grave good parallel to the establishment of the compact mound cemeteries.[29] This suggests that the merchant class became an increasingly important aspect of social identity marking (real or imagined) in Tilmun society.

Detailed analysis targeting the transition to mound cemeteries by focusing on the "commoners" in Tilmun's social hierarchy has documented a distinct but short-lived type of burial mound that was in use only during the first 50 years or so of the emerging cemeteries.[30] These so-called "Radial Wall Type" mounds are characterized by a number of stone walls radiating from the central chamber to the edge of the mound, forming a star-like pattern.[31] Significantly, a burial mound strongly resembling the Radial Wall Type mound has recently been reported from the outskirts of the major Meluhha city of Dholavira in Gujarat,[32] which further underscores the importance of Tilmun's relationships with the Indus world at this stage.

The by now time-honored custom of erecting an outer ring wall around the burial mound of pre-eminent individuals continues with the emergence of the compact mound cemeteries. However, regardless of this continuity, the rise of a new ruling political body is possibly, more than anywhere else, expressed in Tilmun's second-generation "ring mound" burials. From ca. 2050 BC on, this symbol of rank becomes exclusively reserved for a small number of individuals entombed in sizable burial mounds in the largest cemetery at A'ali (fig. 10, p. 52). These "ring mounds" are significantly larger than any previous examples and were never constructed in any of the other cemeteries, so each of the latter, by implication, must have been associated with communities of inferior rank.

In effect, the outer ring wall that centuries earlier had appeared in Tilmun together with the earliest burial mounds as a symbol of preeminent rank was now completely monopolized by a privileged group of a select few—the first "Royal" Dynasty of Tilmun.[33]

---

26. Laursen 2009; 2010c.
27. Laursen 2008.
28. Cornwall 1946.
29. Lowe 1986; Højlund 2007; Laursen 2008; 2010c.
30. Laursen 2010c.
31. Laursen 2010c: fig. 6.
32. Bisht 2014.
33. Højlund 2007; Laursen 2008. The precise chronology of the Royal Cemetery of Tilmun is currently subject to

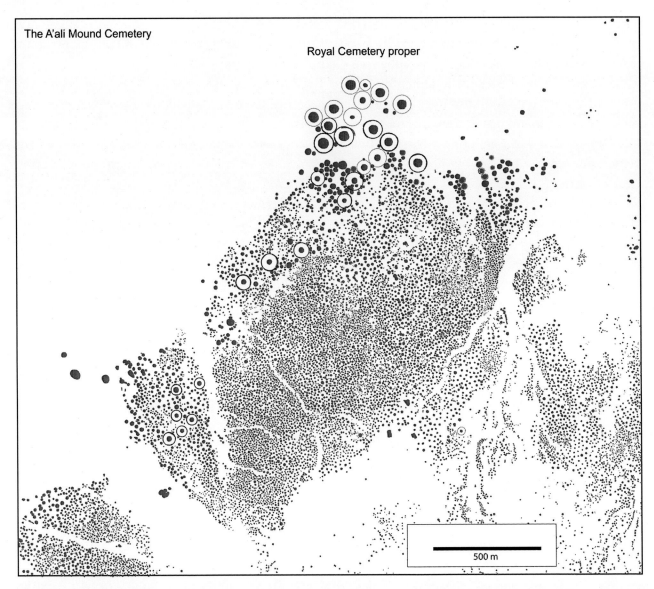

Fig. 10. The A'ali Mound Cemetery with elite ring mounds marked in black. The Royal Cemetery proper is located in the northern corner.

In Makkan, the 21st century generally marks the apogee of Umm an-Nar society and culture. However, data from Makkan enable us to make detailed statements about the cultural and societal developments only to a limited extent.

The distinct dot-in-circle decorated steatite vessels (*série récente*), which must have been strongly associated with the visual identity of the Makkan tribes, having materialized during or a little earlier than the Sargonic period, continued to be produced throughout the 21st century.

---

a detailed program of C14 dating and architectural analysis. The preliminary results suggest that the first "Royal" Tombs proper were constructed around 2000 BC. For further details, see Laursen in preparation (a).

That Makkan had established more intense contacts with the Ur III state can be gleaned, among others things, from the fact that the majority of the *série récente* steatite vessels found in Babylonia date to the Ur III and subsequent periods.[34]

The most notable example among these steatite exports is an open bowl (height 9 cm, diameter 16.2 cm), recovered during the excavations at Tello (Girsu).[35] The bowl is of the classic Umm an-Nar Type in the *série récente* style, with an incised decoration consisting of a single row of dot-in-circles (fig. 4c, p. 29). Exceptionally, a 21st-century BC dedicatory inscription has been added to it by the son of a Lagaš merchant, who almost certainly originally obtained this vessel on an expedition to Makkan.[36]

During that time, Ur III-period Babylonian pottery also reached costal sites in Makkan as far as Kalba,[37] indicating that the "big ships" or Makkan boats (see Appendix 2) ultimately ranged as far as the Indian Ocean/Arabian Sea.

Around the third- to second-millennium BC transition, marked changes in the patterns of interaction in the Gulf occurred, and Tilmun pottery started to appear on Makkan sites along the coast.

The pottery sequence from the fortified tower settlement Tell Abraq is particularly instructive when it comes to monitoring the changing relationships among Babylonia, Makkan, and Tilmun toward the end of the 21st century BC.[38] The stratigraphic sequence from Tell Abraq dating to the late third and, in particular, the earliest second-millennium levels[39] contained large quantities of red-ridge pottery imported from Tilmun.[40] This pottery probably shows that Tilmun merchants at this time began to venture east on trade expeditions. The levels containing the largest quantities of Tilmun imports belong to the early second-millennium layers associated with local pottery made in the Wadi Suq tradition, which emerged after the disintegration of Umm an-Nar society (see below, pp. 66–67)). Because these strata are the most important and were found directly superimposed over an abandoned late Umm an-Nar tomb type, it follows that Tilmun's eastbound trade must have picked up immediately after the collapse of Umm an-Nar society.

Texts

Following the disintegration of the Sargonic empire ca. 2200 BC—which probably was primarily caused by the inherent weaknesses of the Sargonic political structures, although the intrusions of new ethnic groups (Gutians, Amorites, and Hurrians) into the area must have played an important part in this development as well—Babylonia reverted to the traditional mode of decentralized political and economic organization that characterized its history before the advent of Sargon. During this transitional phase, which lasted roughly one century, northern Babylonia fell under the domination

34. For this conclusion, see already T. F. Potts 1994: 262.

35. Gros 1910: 250–51.

36. For a drawing, see p. 29, fig. 4c; for a photograph, see Amiet 1986: 278 fig. 88. Amiet dates this vessel to the time of Amar-Suen (1986: 278), but this attribution is unfounded.

37. C. Phillips personal communication.

38. Laursen 2010c: 133.

39. Potts 1990.

40. Grave et al. 1996.

of the Gutians.[41] The Gutian presence was particularly strong along the Tigris valley. The Gutians eventually took hold of Adab, where they established an independent dynasty. They also turned Umma into their vassal. Other southern city-states, such as Uruk and Lagaš, remained independent and even enjoyed relative economic prosperity. On the whole, however, this period—often called "Gutian"—saw a general decline in international trade. This decline is epitomized by the famous historical line: "In the north he (i.e., the Gutian) closed off trade routes, he made grass grow high in the highways of the Land."[42] Chances are, therefore, that the commercial exchanges between Babylonia and the Gulf region ceased as well. Still, in view of Lagaš's independence in this period, it cannot be excluded that some contacts of that nature continued to persist. But the absence of written data makes it impossible to reach any firm conclusions regarding this matter.

Sometime toward the end of this period, an Elamite ruler by the name Puzur-Inšušinak, the last member of the so-called "Awan dynasty," conquered and annexed to his "mini-empire" the Diyala Region and much of northern Babylonia.[43] This event put an end to Gutian rule over that region. Shortly thereafter, a king of Uruk named Utu-hegal launched a military campaign against Tirigan, the last king of the Gutian dynasty based at Adab. By defeating Tirigan, Utu-hegal eliminated Gutian presence from the south as well, thereby laying foundations for the reunifaction of Babylonia.

Utu-hegal's unification efforts were continued by Ur-Namma, the founder of the 3rd dynasty of Ur (ca. 2100 BC). Ur-Namma's main achievement was his successful war on Puzur-Inšušinak, which put him in control of all of Babylonia and probably of the Diyala Region as well. Ur-Namma also succeeded in conquering Susiana, thus beginning a new phase of Babylonia's territorial expansion in the east. Although the chronology of the events remains uncertain, there are strong reasons to believe that, in his war efforts against Puzur-Inšušinak, Ur-Namma was actively assisted by Gudea of Lagaš.[44] It was apparently as part of this military cooperation that Gudea campaigned in southwestern Iran, conquering the city of AdamDUN.

It was these developments combined, no doubt, that led to the reestablishment of Babylonia's commercial contacts with the Gulf. We learn this from the inscriptions of Ur-Namma, who claims to "have returned ships of Makkan to Nanna" (meaning to Ur, Nanna being the divine proprietor of Ur) and to "have made sea-faring trade flourish on the coast of the sea."[45] Gudea's sources corroborate this picture. Thus, the inscriptions on his statues talk of the importation of diorite from Makkan (one proof of which are the statues themselves),[46] while three economic tablets attributable to his reign (Appendix 1, Texts 2–4) record shipments of textiles to Makkan.

Although it is possible that the plans for further territorial expansion and for the reconstruction—though on a considerably more modest scale—of the Sargonic empire were formulated already under Ur-Namma, it was only during the reign of Šulgi, Ur-Namma's son and successor, that these designs were put to action. During the second and third decades of his reign, Šulgi launched a concentrated diplomatic effort to create a coherent international order in which the entire terri-

---

41. For this period, see the recent discussion by Steinkeller 2015.
42. Frayne RIME 2 283–93 Utu-hegal 4: 43–45.
43. Steinkeller 2013b: 294–303.
44. Steinkeller 2013b: 298–302.
45. Steinkeller 2013b: 302 and n. 58.
46. Gudea Statues A, B, C, D, E, G, H, K, and Z; Wilcke 2011.

tory between eastern Iran and northern Syria was divided into clearly defined spheres of influence. The foundation on which this order rested was political and economic alliances with the powers of particular strategic importance to Ur. In the east, the main partners of Ur were Marhaši and Anšan, both relationships being cemented by dynastic marriages, which took place in the years Šulgi 18 and Šulgi 30, respectively.

There is every reason to think that another important ally of Ur in the east was Makkan. The earliest evidence of diplomatic contacts between Babylonia and Makkan dates to Šulgi's twenty-eighth regnal year, when an unnamed ruler of Makkan sent a gift of gold to Ur (Appendix 1, Text 1, p. 92).[47] These exchanges continued to flourish in Šulgi's later years and during the reigns of his successors. Thus, Makkan served as a base for the Babylonian troops in the conflict with Anšan (which, having reneged on its earlier commitments, needed to be punished), which occurred in years Šulgi 33 and 34.[48] Eighteen years later, in year Amar-Suen 4, we read of a diplomatic visit paid to Babylonia by a certain Wedum, an emissary of the ruler of Makkan named Nadub-ʾel-i.[49] There are strong reasons to believe that, on that occasion, Wedum brought along with his entourage a group of exotic animals called maš₂ Ma₂-gan$^{(ki)}$, "Makkanite 'goats.'"[50] These animals, which in all likelihood are to be identified as "oryxes,"[51] must have represented a gift of Nadub-ʾel-i to the king of Ur. Another proof of good relations between Ur and Makkan are the records of economic exchanges between these two lands during the reigns of Šu-Suen and Ibbi-Suen (see Appendix 1, Texts 5–9).

The existence of these contacts confirms that Makkan enjoyed a friendly relationship with Babylonia, which likely was formalized through commercial and military agreements. It is highly probable that, as appears to have been the case during the Sargonic period (see above, p. 35), Makkan was also allied with the kingdom of Marhaši. At the very least, Makkan and Marhaši must have been

47. See also above, p. 36.
48. See below, p. 105.
49. 1 gud niga 3 udu 2 maš₂ gal We-du-um lu₂-kin-gi₄-a Na-du-be-li₂ ensi₂ Ma₂-gan^{ki}, "1 grain-fed ox, 3 sheep, and 2 mature goats (for) Wedum, the envoy of Nadub-ʾel-i, the ruler of Makkan" (CTMMA 1 17 iii 20–22; year Amar-Suen 4/ vii; Puzriš-Dagan). Cf. Steinkeller 1995: 62 n. 13.
50. This animal is documented exclusively in the Ur III period. There survive only 15 attestations of maš₂ Ma₂-gan$^{(ki)}$, all of them found in the sources from Puzriš-Dagan. Of special interest are two texts, TCL 2 5632 and TAD 13, that date respectively to the 27th day and the 30th day of the sixth month of year Amar-Suen 4 and thus only briefly before the visit of Wedum (which is said to have taken place in the seventh month of year Amar-Suen 4, but whose arrival in Puzriš-Dagan/Nippur may have taken place sometime earlier). These texts record the disbursements made by the chief receiving official of Puzriš-Dagan of six male breeders and five females of this species (TAD 13:1–2), as well as of one unspecified maš₂ Ma₂-gan (TCL 2 5632:5). We can be confident that all of these animals formed part of the same delivery, which, as indicated by the virtually same date of these documents and the one mentioning Wedum, had been made by Wedum. It appears that the same herd is also referred to in several texts dating to Amar-Suen's later years: PDT 1 130:1 (Amar-Suen 5/ii/7), SACT 1 91:1 (Amar-Suen 5/viii/8), SACT 1 94:2 (Amar-Suen 6/viii/25), OIP 121 512:1 (Amar-Suen 6/xi/9), Torino 1 361:1 (Amar-Suen 7/viii/23), and AUCT 1 786:3–4 (Amar-Suen 8/xii/28). The remaining attestations of maš₂ Ma₂-gan$^{(ki)}$ belong to the late reign of Šulgi and year Amar-Suen 1: Hirose 28:1 (Šulgi 44/iv/28), SANTAG 7 17:6 (Šulgi 45/xi/2), BPOA 7 2732:2 (Šulgi 45/xii/-), TRU 210:4 (Šulgi 47/iv/25), Hirose 75:2 (Šulgi 47/vii/28), JCS 40 112 1:4 (Šulgi 47/ix/11), and SET 29:5 (Amar-Suen 1/i/30). It is possible that these animals also had been brought to Babylonia from Makkan as a diplomatic gift.
51. For this identification, see Steinkeller 1995: 50 and nn. 12–15. Another possible candidate is the Arabian Tahr (*Arabitragus jayakari*), as suggested by Heimpel (1987: 64). But the Tahr is an ordinary, plain-looking wild goat, and thus it is unlikely that it would have been deemed sufficiently attractive to be imported or presented as prestige gifts. See Steinkeller 1995: 50 and nn. 16–17.

linked by common economic interests, since Makkan was a natural market for the merchandise arriving from Marhaši and areas farther north (such as Afghanistan). It is also significant that, as noted earlier, Marhaši was one of Babylonia's closest partners.

A very important historical development that took place sometime during the last few centuries of the third millennium BC was the migration of Amorite tribes into Oman and the teritorries along the Arabian side of the Gulf. This migration appears to have formed part of the same phenomenon that had brought other Amorite tribes to northern Syria and the middle Euhprates Valley. These Amorite newcomers must have settled down and become acculturated very quickly, since, already in Ur III times (and probably even earlier), they assumed positions of power. Our evidence is the fact that the earlier-discussed Nadub-ʾel-i and Wedum of Makkan bore names that are unquestionably Amorite.[52] A good Amorite etymology may likewise be posited for Maniʾum, the name of the ruler of Makkan during the reign of Naram-Suen (see above, pp. 33, 35–36).[53] Other indications of the strong Amorite presence in this general geographical area is a passage from one of Gudea's inscriptions, where Tilmun is described as the land of the Amorites and the place where Amorite "towns" are situated,[54] and an Ur III tablet from Puzriš-Dagan, which records an expenditure of animals for the "Amorites (and?) the exorcist(s) coming from Tilmun."[55] This picture is further corroborated by the fact that Amorite (or at least West Semitic) names are documented in the general area of Tilmun also during the Old Babylonian and Kassite periods.[56]

Although the pattern of the Gulf trade in the Ur III period was quite similar to that which existed under the Sargonic dynasty (see above, pp. 37–39), it also differed in some respects. The main difference was that, in Ur III times, the Gulf trade was dominated by Babylonia to a much greater degree than in the Sargonic period. Particularly telling here is the nearly total disappearance of Meluhha's name from the Ur III documentation. This evidence strongly implies that Meluhha had ceased to be directly involved in exchanges with Babylonia and the Gulf area more generally, a conclusion that is also supported by the archaeological record, which shows no intrusive Meluhhan presence of any kind throughout the whole region. Although various kinds of merchandise of Meluhhan origin is mentioned occasionally in Ur III sources, one no longer hears of the Meluhhan ships arriving in Babylonia, nor is there any evidence that the Meluhhan traders continued to be actively involved in the Gulf trade. Their participation in the maritime exchanges probably terminated in Makkan, from whence the Meluhhan goods were shipped farther west by the Babylonians, perhaps with the active assistance of the Makkanites.

Equally conspicuous is the virtual absence of mention of Tilmun in Ur III sources.[57] While in the Sargonic period Tilmunite ships were able to reach the shores of Babylonia, indicating at least a

---

52. See Steinkeller 1995: 62 n. 13.

53. See Steinkeller 1995: 62 n. 13.

54. kur Dilmun^ki-na uru^ki Mar!-tu!^du-t[a] . . . i⟨-na⟩ *ša-du-ú* Dilmun[^k]^i *ma-at A-mu-ri-im!* (Wilcke 2011: 40 no. 22 iv 3–4).

55. See below, n. 57.

56. For a complete list of the personal names attested in the sources from Failaka and Bahrain, see Glassner 1996: 240; 2002: 346–47.

57. Only three such attestations survive. Of these, only one concerns commercial contacts with Tilmun (Appendix 1, Text 10). This tablet, which comes from Ur and dates to year Ibbi-Suen 1, records a shipment of wool from Ur to Tilmun. The other two texts refer to individuals traveling from Tilmun: an undated tablet from Girsu/Lagaš lists food provisions for a runner (lu$_2$-kas$_4$) named Ur-Dumuzi and an unspecified number of sick/wounded royal soldiers (aga$_3$-us$_2$

degree of Tilmunite participation in the Gulf trade, this situation apparently no longer existed under Šulgi and his successors. As was the case already under the Sargonic rulers, Tilmun served as but a way station for the Babylonian fleet, with Tilmunite merchants playing no independent role in the maritime trade.

Recent excavations at Tell F6, the later Tilmun colony on Failaka Island, Kuwait, have demonstrated the existence there of a Babylonian settlement dating to the Ur III period (Højlund and Abu-Laban 2016: 15–30, 251–52). This so-called Phase 1 occupation is the earliest yet encountered on the island and is firmly dated to the Ur III period on the basis of dominant pottery types (Højlund 2016: 93–95), radiocarbon dates (Heinemeier and Højlund 2016), as well as by the discovery of a number of inscribed cylinder seals (Eidem 2016; Pittman 2016). The abandonment of this outpost probably coincides with the collapse of the Ur III empire. The limited architectural remains that were exposed at Tell F6 are insufficient to draw any firm conclusions regarding the nature and function of this settlement. However, the finds of such exotic materials as the pottery from Tilmun, Makkan, and Meluhha (Højlund 2016: 95), the beads made of agate, carnelian, chalcedony, and lapis lazuli (Andersson 2016: 185–87), and the fragments of steatite and calcite vessels (Hilton 2016: 165–66), strongly suggest that its role was that of a way-station for Ur III merchants—and probably also for Ur III military personnel, who are known to have been stationed throughout the Gulf region. As shown by the discovery in the Ur III layers at Tell F6 of numerous fragments of bitumen (Højlund and Abu Laban 2016: 210–13, 251; Van de Velde 2016), this foreign enclave was probably involved in the servicing of Babylonian ships. (Cf. above, n. 57.)

The void left by the elimination of Meluhha and Tilmun from active participation in the Gulf trade was filled by Makkan. As is indicated primarily by the archaeological record, in the Ur III period, Makkan became a major player in the Gulf trade, with a role second only to that of Babylonia. It is fair to say that these two polities together practically monopolized commercial exchanges in the Gulf. However, while Makkanite ships are reported to have visited Babylonian ports during the reign of Ur-Namma, there is no textual evidence that they did so later. Therefore, it appears that the balance of power in the Gulf was skewed in Babylonia's favor.

In view of Makkan's political importance in this period (as shown by its high international status vis-à-vis Babylonia), it is possible that it held an upper hand in the commercial contacts with Meluhha, with the Makkanite traders perhaps even taking their ships all the way to Meluhha's coast.

Although the specifics of Makkan's participation in the Gulf trade are difficult to ascertain (at least from the textual perspective), the nature of the Babylonian involvement is known in considerable detail. During the period in question, Babylonian commercial ventures in the Gulf were strictly controlled by the state through the medium of an organization comparable to a modern foreign-trade ministry. This organization was headed by a merchant named Puʾudu, who had under his command an extensive naval organization that included eight captains of "big ships" (nu-banda$_3$ ma$_2$-gal-gal-me) and six "officers in charge of sixty men (each) (ugula-geš$_2$-da)."[58] From these data, it

tu-ra), who were coming from Tilmun (Dilmun^{ki}-ta du-ne-ne) (RA 5 93 AO 3474 [AS 2/vi/4]); a tablet from Puzriš-Dagan, dating to year Amar-Suen 2, records an expenditure of three sheep for the Amorites (and?) the exorcist(s) coming from Tilmun (Mar-tu maš-maš Dilmun-ta e-ra-ne) (CST 254:1–2 [AS 2/vi/3]; TRU 305:1–3 [AS 2/vi/4]; Ebla 1975–1985 287 A:1–3 [AS 2/vi/-]).

58. Steinkeller 2004:104; 2013a: 417.

may be extrapolated that Pu'udu commanded more than 360 men. Pu'udu's organization was based in the town of Gu'abba, which belonged to the Girsu/Lagaš province and functioned as Babylonia's main seaport. For a detailed discussion of Gu'abba and its role in maritime operations, see chap. 8.

Pu'udu was a person of exceedingly high social rank, as underscored by the fact that his son Kug-Nanna married into the royal family. Another son of Pu'udu, named Lu-Enlila, was likewise involved in the Gulf trade. He eventually succeeded Pu'udu in his office. Lu-Enlila held the title of the "seafaring merchant" (ga-eš$_8$ a-ab-ba-ka), which he apparently inherited from his father. He also officiated as a royal judge at Ur. Lu-Enlila's seal was of the extremely rare in-na-ba type, which represented a personal gift from the king.[59]

According to one Ur III tablet,[60] the state had at its disposal in the Girsu/Lagaš province a flotilla of 223 ships, most of which were of 60-bushel (Sumerian gur) cargo capacity (1 bushel = 300 liters). Included among them were also 11 ships of 180 bushel capacity. It is likely that it was these 11 ships that were specifically used by Pu'udu's organization in their voyages in the Gulf.

As the written evidence makes clear, the main destination of Ur III maritime expeditions was Makkan. Commencing in Gu'abba, trips to Makkan followed the Gulf's southern rim, making re-provisioning stops in Tilmun and probably in a number of other places situated farther east. Another important sea route, which also began in Gu'abba, ran along the Gulf's northern coast to the mouth of the Karun river. From there, ships sailed up the Karun deep into the Susiana region, to the cities of Susa and AdamDUN, to name only the most important localities situated there.

The merchandise traded from Babylonia to Makkan and southern Iran consisted essentiallly of the following four articles: barley, finished textiles, wool, and perfumed oil.[61] What the Babylonians brought back from Makkan was copper and diorite,[62] plus an assortment of luxury materials of Meluhhan and Iranian origin, such as carnelian, lapis lazuli, chlorite (vessels),[63] various other stones, gold, tin, ivory, mangrove wood, sissoo wood, ebony, and possibly bamboo.[64] From the Susiana re-

---

59. Steinkeller 2004: 104; Maekawa and Mori 2011: 255–57.

60. BPOA 6 37 (undated).

61. See the sources edited and discussed in Appendix 1.

62. Mentions of the importation of diorite from Makkan come exclusively from the display inscriptions of Gudea.

63. In all probability, chlorite is identical with a stone called duḫ-ši-a, which is said to come from Marhaši. See Steinkeller 2012: 263–66. It is important that the aforementioned Pu'udu, head of the Ur III "foreign-trade ministry," is known to have delivered the duḫ-ši-a stones to the court of Ur (Steinkeller 2004: 104). It is highly likely that Pu'udu obtained these stones from Marhaši in the course of his trips to Makkan. Another foreign material Pu'udu is known to have procured (probably from Marhaši as well) is tin. See AUCT 2 289 (date not preserved), discussed by Maekawa and Mori 2011: 257.

64. An important source likely bearing on imports from Makkan is the Ur tablet UET 3 751, dating to year Ibbi-Suen 2, which enumerates the following items: 308+[x] minas of copper, 38 minas of ivory (na4zu$_2$-am-si), 180 minas of lump *algamešum* stone (lagab na4bur-šu-sal), large volumes of two other stones (identity unclear), 20 liters of unidentifiable plant (u$_2$-MIN?), and 10 liters of the "garlic of Makkan" (sum^{sar} Ma$_2$-gan^{ki}). All these items are identified as zag-x ^{d}Nanna-kam. The uncertain sign x begins with a numeral 10, suggesting that we find here the term zag-10, "tithe," for which compare UET 3 341, mentioning zag-10 nam-gaeš a-ab-ba-kam, "the tithe on the sea-faring trade" (discussed above, p. 21 n. 58). If so, the objects listed in UET 3 751 would constitute the tithe collected by the household of the god Nanna. For the unique "garlic of Makkan," compare the very rare "onions of Marhaši" (sum-sikil Mar-ha-ši^{ki}) (ITT 2 3802:9′; CUSAS 3 1113:1, 1168:1). The ultimate source of the ivory here listed must have been Meluhha. For a detailed discussion of Meluhhan imports, see chap. 9.2, pp. 82ff.

gion, Babylonian traders brought back various types of timber, as well as sesame, large plantations of which existed in Susa and AdamDUN.[65]

The volumes of barley that the Ur III state traded to Makkan and various other localities in the Gulf region must have been enormous.[66] A good idea of the scale of these shipments is given by two sources from Girsu/Lagaš, which involve the aforementioned Pu'udu and his son Ur-Enlila. In the first of them (Appendix 1, Text 8), Pu'udu is commissioned to ship to Makkan 600 bushels of barley. An even larger volume is recorded in the other source (Appendix 1, Text 9). There, Lu-Enlila sends to Makkan a whopping 1,800 bushels of barley, an amount that would call for 10 ships of 180-bushels capacity (the largest ships at his disposal; see above) to carry out this assignment. In both instances, the person authorizing the shipment was the chancellor Aradmu, the most important official of the realm after the king.[67]

It is evident that the exports of Babylonian textiles to Makkan and other places in the Gulf region equaled (if not exceeded) those of barley, both in terms of their bulk and monetary value. Although only a few records of these shipments survive (see Appendix 1, Texts 2–7), some of them involving Lu-Enlila (Appendix 1, Texts 5 and 6), it may be estimated that, in the course of the 40 years of the effective existence of the Ur III empire, Babylonia exported to the Gulf region substantially more than 100,000 individual textiles. This estimate rests on the fact that the town of Gu'abba and its neighbors housed an enormous weaving operation (probably the largest such operation in the entire Ur III empire), employing some 10,000 weavers and related personnel. As we argue in detail in chap. 8, the only explanation for this great concentration of weaving activity at Gu'abba, Babylonia's chief seaport and its window into the Gulf, is that most of the textiles produced there were intended as exports for Makkan and the neighboring areas.

It appears that the importation of Gulf merchandise to Babylonia (either by the state or private merchants) called for the payment of local "taxes." One such payment was the "tithe of sea-faring trade" (zag-10 nam-gaeš a-ab-ba-ka) that was due to Nanna and Ningal, the patron deities of Ur and of the Ur III state as well. This tithe is uniquely mentioned in the text UET 3 341 (cited and discussed above, p. 21 n. 58) in connection with the importation of carnelian beads (whose ultimate place of origin must have been Meluhha).

---

65. Maekawa 2016.

66. D. T. Potts (1993: 425) opined that the "putative mass export of Mesopotamian cereals to Magan is illusory," by reasoning that "the arguments raised [by himself and E. Carter] against P. L. Kohl's suggestion that surplus grain was being exported *en masse* from Mesopotamia to the Iranian plateau in the third millennium . . . are just as appropriate in the case of alleged cereal exports from Mesopotamia to Magan." However, the two situations are completely different because of the drastically different transporation costs involved in each case. It has been estimated that water transport is four to five times cheaper and more efficient than overland transport (Algaze 2008: 53). Thus, while the proposition that the Babylonians exported large volumes of cereals to their eastern periphery by using overland transport (which, during the third millennium BC, would be restricted to donkeys and human carriers) certainly lies beyond the realm of possibility, there is no objection to assuming that, as is corroborated by at least some textual data, Babylonian cereals were transported into the Gulf area on ships as a matter of course. In fact, given the relatively low cost of water transport, it is inconceivable that the Babylonians would not have taken advantage of such an obvious—and undoubtedly highly profitable—commercial opportunity.

67. In these two transactions, Aradmu acted in the capacity of governor of Girsu/Lagaš, one of the many offices he had amassed. It appears that during the reigns of Šu-Suen and Ibbi-Suen (to which these two tablets belong), Aradmu usurped most of the royal powers for himself, becoming the de facto ruler of the empire.

All these data show that the Ur III period witnessed an unsually high level of commercial exchange between Babylonia and the Gulf region. This picture is corroborated by Sumerian literary sources. Particularly instructive is the mythological poem "Enki and the World Order," which offers a systematic description of how the creator-god Enki organizes the world, assigning to everybody, gods and humans alike, their specific domains and functions. This composition, which probably originated in the Ur III period,[68] is likely to be read as an idealized apotheosis of the well-ordered Ur III empire: a place untouched by wars, where everybody lives in peace and harmony with his neighbors, playing his own particular role, and enjoying the benefits of international trade. In lines 191–249 of this poem, Enki determines the destiny of Sumer and its neighbors and commercial partners, with the latter being identified as Meluhha, Tilmun, Elam, Marhaši, and the Amorites, "the ones without cities and houses." This stress on the Gulf area, to the total exclusion of Babylonia's other neighboring lands, is a telling indication of the paramount importance this region played in the international commerce of the Ur III empire.[69]

To sum up, the Ur III kings successfully recreated the system that had been installed in the Gulf by the Sargonic rulers, but, in the typical Ur III fashion, they put it under a much more direct, firm control. As was the case throughout the empire, Ur III commercial operations in the Gulf involved considerably more state participation. It appears that this trade network had a strong military underpinning (which probably was more pronounced than in Sargonic times). On the whole, however, Ur III trade in the Gulf relied primarily on diplomatic contacts. Quite remarkably, with the exception of the conflict with Anšan in years 33–34, there is no evidence of any Babylonian military or policing actions in the greater Gulf region throughout the entire period in question.

The Role of Amorites in Tilmun and Makkan

We have hypothesized above that an accumulation of Amorites in the Gulf was one of the main causes for the massive population transfer to Bahrain Island around 2250 BC. There is, however, evidence to suggest that mobile pastoralists may have occupied the desert fringes of Tilmun (and Makkan) long before they become visible in the historic sources. It is of interest that Juris Zarins, on the basis of his evaluation of archaeological data, has argued that, during the period from 4000 to 2000 BC, a distinctive "pastoral technocomplex" expanded over much of the Levant, Yemen, and central Arabia.[70] As defined by Zarins, this "technocomplex" is characterized by, among other things, the presence of large stone rings, tumuli, rock art, a distinctive lithic inventory, and extensive evidence of animal husbandry.[71] Through recourse to various historical data, Zarins sought to connect this hypothetical cultural phenomenon with the Amorite people. Of relevance to our present

---

68. Possibly during the reign of Šulgi, since lines 242–47 appear to allude to a conflict with Elam and Marhaši, which may have been be connected with Šulgi's operations against Anšan in years Šulgi 33–34. Note that the epithet lugal ᵈEn-lil₂-le a₂ sum-[ma], "king [given] power by Enlil," found in line 244, finds an echo in the formula of year Šulgi 23: mu ᵈŠul-gi lugal-e ⌈a₂⌉ mah ᵈEn-li[l₂ su]m-ma-ni (variant: mu lugal-ra a₂ m[aḫ] sum-ma).
69. A closely similar geographical and commercial horizon is described in the composition "Enki and Ninhursag" (see below, p. 69). However, this composition seems to reflect the realities of the early Old Babylonian period.
70. Zarins 1986: fig. 68.
71. Zarins 1986: 241–43.

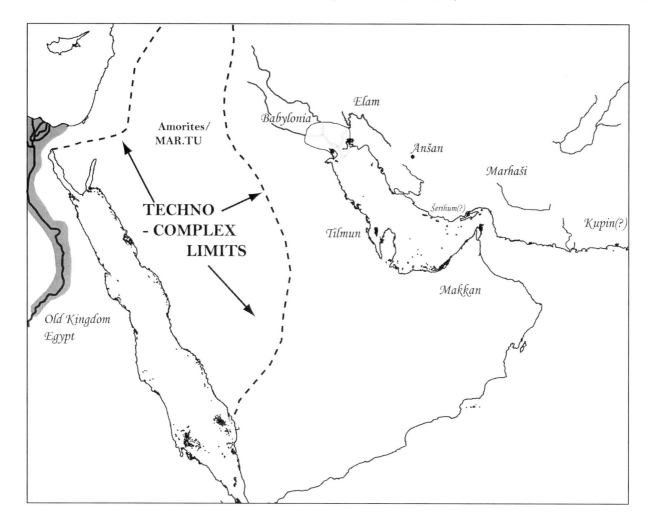

Fig. 11. The geographical extent of the proposed Amorite (MAR.TU) techno-complex after Zarins 1986: fig. 68 and the approximate location of major political entities around 2200 BC loosely after Steinkeller 1982 fig. 2.

case is the fact that the eastern limits of this "pastoral complex" roughly coincide with the western margins of Tilmun (cf. fig. 11). Consequently, if this (Amorite?) population, in a drought-induced mass migration, set out for the water sources in Tilmun, it would in all probability have lead to exactly the type of domino effect we suggest led to the population transfer to Bahrain Island. (See above, pp. 42, 44–46.)

Independently of the theory of an Amorite "technocomplex," a number of Assyriologists have speculated in the past that an Amorite group expanded into the Gulf region during the Bronze Age.[72] This hypothesis is corroborated by various new textual data that demonstrate that just such a migration began as early as the Sargonic period (if not earlier) and that already during Ur III times this

72. For example, Landsberger 1954: 56 n. 103; Buccellati 1966: 249.

region showed the presence of Amorite communities and even political organisms. (See, in detail, above, pp. 54–56.)

Evidence for an Amorite involvement in the translocation to Bahrain Island and the Damman Dome goes beyond texts. The appearance of burial mounds at Abqaiq (ca. 3200–2800 BC) provides a distant link between the Tilmun culture proper, as it appeared on Bahrain Island, and a nomadic past of doubtless much greater antiquity. Along these same lines is the possible relation between the use of stone circles in association with burial cairns in the "Amorite technocomplex" and the stone rings that came to encircle the earliest elite burial mounds on Bahrain Island around 2250 BC.

Taking into account the environmental, textual, and archaeological data, the following scenario can be outlined: the serial droughts induced by the 2200 BC aridification, which sent mobile pastoralists such as the Hurrians and Gutians into Babylonia, also initiated the southeastward habitat-tracking of Amorites, as previously hypothesized.[73] In response to the pressure from Amorites and their livestock, the oasis settlements on the Saudi mainland, which had hitherto been the constituents of the Tilmun polity, were deserted. This branch of the Amorites may thus have been responsible for the breakdown of the elusive social formation that, up until now, had orchestrated the success of Tarut Island in the third-millennium BC Gulf trade. In search of safe havens and ample fresh water supplies, the population of Tilmun contracted to Bahrain Island and the Damman Dome and regrouped (cf. fig. 7, p. 45). Notably, trade in carved chlorite vessels and other products from Marhaši ceased simultaneously. Judging from the evidence of texts (see above, pp. 55–56) and the use of stone rings around the earliest elite burial mounds on Bahrain, the indigenous Tilmunite elite was, in spite of its probable efforts toward the contrary, soon infiltrated by Amorites.[74]

Why did Tilmun decline after the Sargonic collapse? It appears that there is ample evidence to conclude that Amorites most probably were instrumental in both the translocation to Bahrain Island around 2250–2200 BC and that they contributed to the ensuing economic decline of Tilmun at the same time. Needless to say, this explanation for the temporary setback of Tilmun in the struggle for a share of the Gulf trade should also be accompanied by consideration of the influence of the other regional actors involved.

73. Zarins 1986.

74. Among the evidence demonstrating the Amorite presence in Bahrain, of special interest are the votive inscriptions recently excavated in an A'ali Royal Tomb (Laursen in preparation): they were dedicated to the god Inzak by a ruler bearing an Amorite name, Yaglī-'el (Marchesi forthcoming). Based on their paleography, Marchesi dates these inscriptions to the time of Hammurabi or slightly earlier.

Chapter 7

The Post-Ur III Period
(2000–1800 BC)

Archaeology

From the beginning of the second millennium BC, the archaeological record from Tilmun ubiquitously speaks of a prosperous era, characterized by cultural and economic florescence, unequivocally marking the zenith of the Tilmun Culture. Tilmun society is evidently profoundly affected by the thriving trade economy, and it is possible to observe a significant increase in public building activities that approximately half a century earlier had been launched by the construction of the city wall around the settlement at Qala'at al-Bahrain (see above, pp. 49–50). Around 2000 BC, modest domestic quarters at Qala'at al-Bahrain give way to monumental stone buildings with walls up to 1.75 m in width. Little is known about these large buildings, as they already, around 1900 BC, made way for new monumental architecture (fig. 9 with insert; see p. 49). This time, at least four apparently identical storage facilities built with well-dressed ashlars are laid out on both sides of a 12-m-wide, plastered "boulevard," which ended at a monolithic threshold measuring ca. 3.6 × 1.3 m.[1] This colossal threshold evidently marks the entrance to the metropolis's central palace, any remains of which must have been completely eradicated in the fifteenth and sixteenth century AD by the construction of a Portuguese fort.[2]

The city wall and its northern gate were rebuilt several times during the first centuries of the second millennium, after which they apparently fell into ruin, some time after ca. 1800 BC.[3]

The palatial "warehouses" flanking the central boulevard should obviously be understood within the context of the site's function as a center of trade, but quite possibly the primary function of the city wall was also connected to trade. Although the wall certainly offered the town dwellers considerable protection against raids, its circumference of 1.8 km must have rendered it an ineffective defense against any regular siege. Accordingly, the city wall should primarily be seen as the instrument by

---

1. Højlund 1999: 75; Lombard 1999. For a photograph of the stone threshold, see Lombard 1999: 123, upper left corner.
2. For this conclusion, see already Lombard 1999: 123; Højlund and Andersen 1997: 40–41; Højlund in press.
3. Højlund and Andersen 1994: 32–44.

which any incumbent monarch of Tilmun was able effectively to impose taxation on incoming goods and as a guarantee for the safeguard of the Tilmun market.

Around the onset of the second millennium BC, a "Royal Cemetery" proper was founded 8 km south of Qalaʾat al-Bahrain in the northern corner of the Aʾali Mound Cemetery.[4] Over the next two centuries, 14 colossal "Royal" tombs that by far exceed any previous efforts in terms of monumentality and investment of resources were erected in this "Royal Cemetery" (fig. 10, p. 52).[5] Recent excavations have shown that some of the Royal Mounds originally were in excess of 15 m in height and had ring walls of up to 37 m in diameter. A small number of the Royal Mounds display elaborate stone architecture in a manner that evidently mimics the style of contemporary palatial buildings.[6]

It is more than likely that, among the rulers entombed in the "Royal Cemetery" of Aʾali, were the anonymous recipients of the "royal gifts for Tilmun," which were sent to Tilmun from Isin around 1990 BC (see Appendix 1, Texts 12, 13, and 14). The Tilmunite king whom king Shamshi-Addu of Assyria gifted with perfumed oil more than a century later[7] probably is buried here as well.

To the immediate south of the "Royal Cemetery," an east–west band of 150 large mounds evidently marks the burial ground of senior courtiers and members of the royal family (cf. fig. 10, p. 52). These are followed still farther south by the smaller burial mounds of more than 11,000 lower-ranking Tilmunites, who also were buried in the Aʾali Cemetery.[8]

Parallel to the developments in Aʾali and at the fortified settlement at Qalaʾat al-Bahrain, the formerly modest temple at Barbar is replaced by a succession of monumental "water temples" constructed of well-dressed stone ashlar masonry.[9] The succession of temples at Barbar exhibits an exponential increase in dimensions, which around 1800 BC culminates with the final and grandest temple (III) complex.[10] A similar but possibly even larger temple is constructed over Bahrain's allegedly once largest artesian spring, "Umm as-Sujur," but stone robbing has almost completely deprived the building of its well-dressed ashlar building blocks leaving little but two subterranean wells.[11] What perhaps says most about the organizational power behind temple building after 2000 BC is the fact that each of the thousands of ashlars of the characteristic oolitic limestone used for these temples was quarried and transported from the small Jiddah island located ca. 4 km west of Bahrain Island.[12]

The abrupt replacement of the "Gulf Type" seal by the "Dilmun Type" seal ca. 2000 BC represents another important development at this juncture. The new series of stamp seals is evidently publicly sanctioned and more centrally regulated than the former Gulf Type. This change is most clearly expressed in the collective "trademark" that now invariably appears on the reverse of Dilmun Type seals in the form of "three grooves and four dots-in-circles."[13]

    4. Højlund 2007; Laursen 2008: fig. 6.
    5. Højlund 2007: 25–32; Laursen 2008; for a detailed absolute chronology based on C14 dating, see Laursen in preparation (a).
    6. Laursen in preparation (a).
    7. Eidem and Højlund 1993; 1997; Ziegler 2008.
    8. Laursen 2008.
    9. Andersen and Højlund 2003.
    10. Højlund 2013a: fig. 3.
    11. Bibby 1954; Konishi 1996; Andersen and Højlund 2003.
    12. Højlund 2013b.
    13. Kjærum 1994.

Stylistically, the former Harappan influence on Gulf Type seals yields to a series of new motifs that now suddenly borrow profoundly from scenes in contemporary Babylonian and Syrian glyptic art.[14] The vast network of the new class of Tilmun traders possibly finds reflection in the geographic distribution of the Dilmun Type seals, which range from the Indus site of Lothal[15] in the east to Ešnuna (Tell Asmar) in the northwest. The Dilmun Type is confidently fixed to the Middle chronology by an impression in its earliest style (Kjærum's IA) on a tablet dated to the tenth year of Gungunum of Larsa (1923 BC).[16]

Simultaneous with, or shortly after the introduction of the Dilmun Type seals and the founding of the Royal Cemetery at A'ali, a trading colony with a substantial community is established on Failaka Island ca. 400 km northwest of Bahrain. This small but distinctly Tilmunite town is directly superimposed over the Ur III period Sumerian trading station mentioned above (see p. 57).[17]

More than 500 seals of Dilmun Type, found at this (Tell F6-F3)[18] and smaller settlements (al-Khidr)[19] around Failaka Island, hint at a thriving merchant community. At a slightly later, not well-defined point in time, the colonists construct a monumental 400 m^2 industrial "palace" facility next to a temple at a short distance from the domestic quarters of the settlement. The data from Failaka Island generally bear witness to a substantial Tilmunite community from ca. 1900 BC onward.[20]

At the same time, on the Iranian side of the Gulf, a node of contact between southwestern Iranian communities (Anshan and Elam?) and the kingdom of Tilmun has been documented at a site at Bushire.[21] The imports of Tilmunite affinity include numerous sherds of pottery[22] and a several-hundred-liter complete storage vessel.[23] The storage vessel is of a distinct Tilmunite type and has a Tilmun "potter's mark" incised on the rim.[24] Other evidence attesting to Gulf trade comprises fragments of Makkanite steatite vessels of late third- and early second-millennium types,[25] as well as a typically bun-shaped copper ingot from Makkan[26] and at least one Indus sherd.[27]

Beginning ca. 1700 BC, the quantity of archaeological evidence becomes exceedingly limited and consequently the developments in Tilmun after this time are poorly understood. What seems certain is that the near silence in our record from Bahrain Island and the Saudi mainland reflects a substantial economic and cultural decline. The evidence from Failaka Island indicates that the

14. Kjærum 1980; Peyronel 2008; Laursen in preparation (b).
15. Rao 1963.
16. Hallo and Buchanan 1965.
17. Højlund 2012; 2013a; Højlund and Abu-Laban 2016.
18. Kjærum 1983.
19. David-Cuny and Azpeitia 2012.
20. Calvet and Pic 2008; Højlund 1987; 2012; 2013a; Kjærum and Højlund 2013.
21. See Pézard 1914 for the tell at Bushire. For the connection between the Bushire assemblage and Tilmun, see Højlund 1994: 98 n. 9.
22. See Højlund 1994: 98 and n. 9. Among these is a red-ridged sherd (Pézard 1914: pl. V no. 9) with a pseudo-sealing clay appliqué typical of the Tilmun pottery tradition, for which see Højlund 1994: 98 and Laursen in preparation (b).
23. For photos of this 1.15 × 2.2 m "pithos" vessel, see Pézard 1914: pl. III nos. 3–4 and pl. VI no. 5.
24. According to Højlund (personal communication), the "potter's mark" found on the pithos rim (BB 136 in the Louvre collection) can be compared to Højlund 1987: fig. 114.
25. See Pézard 1914: pl. VIII nos. 2 and 5 (Wadi Suq style) and 4 (Umm an-Nar style).
26. See Pézard 1914: pl. VIII no. 16.
27. For the identification of the Indus sherd (BB97 in the Louvre collection), see Højlund 1994: n. 9.

period of prosperity lasted longer at this location,[28] and Højlund has suggested that this northern colony was eventually absorbed by the enigmatic Sealand Dynasty before the lands of Tilmun finally fell under Kassite rule.[29]

In Makkan, society also experiences a string of rapid developments, and the artistic sophistication and strong cultural cohesion that had characterized the communities of the Umm an-Nar culture start to disintegrate after 2000 BC.[30]

A widespread desertion of the fortified settlement towers and the communal circular tombs—the very constituents of third-millennium BC Makkan society—suggests some sort of breakdown of the social order. A recent study by L. Gregoricka (2014) makes it virtually certain that the Makkanite population was faced with much dryer climatic conditions at the time of the Umm an-Nar to Wadi Suq transition, ca. 2000 BC.[31] With the exception of a few sites, such as Tell Abraq[32] and Hili 8,[33] discontinuity is prevalent in the settlements, and large portions of Makkan's population are by all appearance forced to abandon their former territories, possibly due to climatic deterioration and/or incoming pastoral nomadic groups.[34] From the vestiges of Umm an-Nar society, the so-called Wadi Suq Culture emerges as a new culturally less homogeneous social formation.[35] The now conspicuously unsubstantial occupation record points to some degree of transhumance combined with a sedentary adaptation to new economic and climatic conditions. In addition, the smelting of copper ore may have witnessed a drastic drop in intensity at this time.[36]

The Marhaši-inspired Umm an-Nar fine-ware tradition, by then ca. 600 years old, comes to a sudden end and is replaced by the technologically and stylistically different pottery of the Wadi Suq tradition.[37] However, elements of continuity from the former Umm an-Nar pottery document that the new Wadi Suq tradition was born out of Umm an-Nar related groups.[38] The stone-vessel tradition also undergoes some significant modifications as the style of steatite vessels changes,[39] but here there are also clear elements of continuity from the former tradition.

As noted above, there is some continuity in the burial rituals: the ancestral custom of inhumation in stone-built communal tombs continues, albeit in a modified form. The classic circular Umm

---

28. Højlund 1994: fig. 395; 2013a.

29. Højlund 1989b: 12. This point is now confirmed by a tablet excavated at Qal'at al-Bahrain, dated to Ea-gamil, the last ruler of the Sealand Dynasty (text QA 94.46 in Cavigneaux and André-Salvini forthcoming).

30. Cleuziou 1996: 162.

31. Gregoricka's study of human remains from Umm an-Nar and Wadi Suq tombs in Shimal (2014) demonstrates a marked change in oxygen isotope composition between the late Umm an-Nar and Early Wadi Suq populations that is highly indicative of increased aridity.

32. Potts 1990b.

33. Cleuziou 1989: 71–78.

34. Parker et al. 2006.

35. This new heterogeneity can, among other things, be seen in the rough divide that emerges between new types of single inhumation burials in Oman and the continuity in collective tombs (although of very varied architecture) in the north of the peninsula. See Vogt 1998: 275.

36. Begemann et al. 2010: 140.

37. Méry 1996: 171–72; 2000: 249–71.

38. Vogt 1998: 278–79.

39. The style of steatite vessels changes from the so-called *série récente* (Umm an-Nar) to the *série tardive* (Wadi Suq).

an-Nar Type tomb is replaced by a rectangular collective tomb that is architecturally and technologically less sophisticated than the former. This development probably in part reflects a loss in ritual *savoir-faire* during what must have been dramatic societal transformations.

Several extensive "graveyards" of Wadi Suq Type collective tombs begin to accumulate along the western foothills of the Hajjar Mountains. Judging from the burial record at Simal in the modern emirate of Ras al-Khaimah, this area emerges as a major early-second-millennium BC population center.[40] Because water generally is more available here at the piedmont, the apparent accumulation of the Wadi Suq population at this and similar locations also points to more arid conditions elsewhere on the Oman Peninsula after 2000 BC. By inference, this identifies climate change as a contributing factor behind the decline of Makkan. It is possible that the Simal region, in particular, should be regarded as a Wadi Suq period *refugium*, where the population was able to cope—more successfully than elsewhere—with the increased aridity.[41]

It is almost certain that, after the disintegration of Umm an-Nar society, the "big ships" of Babylonia ceased to land in Makkan. Yet, it is less clear if this collapse of the Makkan trade alone was the result of domestic institutional changes in Babylonia that followed in the wake of the fall of Ur or if the major (climate-induced) societal changes in Makkan momentarily made it impossible to obtain copper. Be that as it may, the complex chain of copper production and redistribution that must have played a key role in the integration of Umm an-Nar society eventually disintegrated (for external or endemic reasons) and so did the Makkan trade and the more than half-a-millennium-old Umm an-Nar way of life.

Texts

The heyday of the Ur III empire belonged to the reigns of Amar-Suen and Šu-Suen. Its collapse came suddenly at the beginning of the reign of Ibbi-Suen, the last ruler of the dynasty. It was marked by the successful revolt of the Zagros land Šimurrum (in year Ibbi-Suen 3) and the concommitant takeover of the Susiana region by the Šimaskian ruler Yabrat. With these events, the entire northeastern periphery gained independence, and so the empire effectively ceased to exist. Subsequent years saw the gradual loss of much of northern and southern Babylonia, with some of those territories becoming completely independent of Ur (like the state of Isin under Išbi-Erra and various entities in northern Babylonia) or falling under the control of the Šimaškians (the former provinces of Girsu/Lagaš and Umma). In this way, the possessions of Ibbi-Suen were reduced to the city of Ur and its immediate surroundings. This truncated state lingered for another 15 years or so, during which, it appears, a degree of contact with the Gulf region continued to be maintained.

The end of the dynasty came in year Ibbi-Suen 25, when the Šimaškians sacked Ur, capturing Ibbi-Suen and carrying him off as a prisoner to Anšan. The Šimaškians occupied Ur for roughly 10 years, to be eventually chased out by Išbi-Erra of Isin. The capture of Ur and the neighboring regions established Išbi-Erra firmly in control of southern Babylonia, thereby opening another active

40. Vogt 1998: 273.
41. For this reason, the continuity of the community at Simal observed by Gregoricka (2014) does not necessarily apply to other regions of the Oman peninsula.

phase of commercial contacts between Babylonia and the Gulf region. These contacts continued under Išbi-Erra's successors, as well as during the period of the dynasty of Larsa, which, ca. 1920 BC, wrested the city of Ur away from Isin.[42] Babylonia continued to interact with the Gulf during the subsequent Old Babylonian and Kassite periods, but these events fall outside the time-frame of the present investigation.

Four tablets dating to the reigns of Išbi-Erra and his successor Šu-ilišu (Appendix 1, nos. 11–14) attest to the existence of vigorous contacts between the kingdom of Isin and Tilmun.[43] Of particular importance here are texts nos. 12, 13, and 14, which refer to the shipment of "gifts" (nig$_2$-šu-taka$_4$-a) from Isin to Tilmun. The "gifts" in question, which consisted of garments, fine oil, apples, another type of fruit, and the *kukru* aromatic, probably were diplomatic presents that the rulers of Isin sent to the Tilmun royalty. Among the conveyors of these presents, one finds a merchant named Lugal-itida and the man of "big ships" named Ešhegal. Another man of "big ships," by the name of Lu-balašaga, is documented as a recipient of bitumen, which was to be used to caulk a boat traveling to Tilmun (text no. 11). The likely explanation of these data is that the royal presents were sent along with the shipments of merchandise that the private merchants and sailors regularly transported from Babylonia to Tilmun.

As already noted, commercial exchanges between Babylonia and Tilmun continued to thrive during the period of Larsa domination. At the peak of its political importance, the kingdom of Larsa counted among its possessions the cities of Larsa, Ur, Eridu, Lagaš, Umma, and Adab. In addition, it controlled various northern Babylonian localities along the Tigris, reaching all the way to Maškan-šapir and the land of Emutbal. Some 50 texts from Ur, dating to the reigns of Gungunum through Rim-Sin,[44] bear evidence of a brisk trade between Ur[45] and Tilmun, which was conducted by a group of private seafaring merchants, designated by the term *alik Tilmun*, "the one going to Tilmun."[46] The merchandise brought by these individuals from Tilmun consisted primarily of copper (which the Tilmunites undoubtedly imported from the Oman peninsula = Makkan), though it also included an assortment of luxury goods, among them pearls, raw ivory and objects made of ivory, gold, lapis lazuli, carnelian, chlorite, various other semiprecious stones, exotic woods, and kohl (UET 5 279–96, 526, 546, 549, 678). Although the pearls were available locally in Tilmun, most of other luxury items must have been imported by the Tilmunites from Meluhha and southeastern Iran.[47] The goods exported to Tilmun from Ur were silver, garments, and sesame oil (UET 5 367, 428, 848).

42. This happened during the reign of Gungunum (1932–1906 BC), the fifth ruler of the dynasty.

43. It needs to be noted that texts 11 and 12 date to Išbi-Erra's "19th" regnal year—i.e., to the time when Ur still remained under the Šimaškian occupation (which apparently came to an end only in Išbi-Erra's "27th" year). This means that lines of communication with Tilmun remained open (or at least accessible to the more northernly parts of Babylonia) even during the time when the Šimaškians were in control of Ur.

44. A number of these documents actually belong to the reign of Išme-Dagan of Isin (UET 5 278–81), thus preceding the period of domination by Larsa.

45. It is striking that these documents never mention Gu'abba, which, as we have seen earlier (see above, p. 58, chap. 8 below), was the main (if not the only) seaport in Ur III times, with no evidence of such activity being documented at Ur. It appears, therefore, that although the region of Gu'abba was controlled by the Larsa kings, it no longer frunctioned as a seaport, that function now being performed by the (newly constructed?) facility at Ur.

46. See, in detail, Oppenheim 1954.

47. In one instance, a šuba gem is specifically associated with Me-luh-ha, meaning that it either came from Meluhha or was of Meluhhan type: 1 na4šuba Me-luh-ha . . . šag$_4$ kaskal Tilmun^{ki}-na (UET 5 549:1–3).

The fact that only Tilmun is mentioned in the Isin and Larsa sources just discussed, with the names of Makkan, Meluhha, and Marhaši being conspicuously absent, makes it quite certain that the horizon of Babylonian ventures in the Gulf during the Isin and Larsa periods was strictly limited to Tilmun. There is also no evidence of any extensive state involvement in these operations (such as existed earlier in Ur III times). This is especially true of the Larsa period, when the trade was clearly in the hands of private entrepreneurs. Given the limited nature of the Babylonian involvement, we need to assume that the Gulf trade was now dominated by Tilmun, probably also to the exclusion of merchants from Makkan and Meluhha. This would mean that, in the period in question, all the maritime contacts with the Oman peninsula (Makkan) and southeastern Iran (Marhaši)—and perhaps those with the Indus Valley (Meluhha) as well—were conducted by Tilmun's commercial fleet. This picture is corroborated by the independent historical data, which convincingly support the argument that, precisely around this time (1900–1800 BC), the kingdom of Marhaši had been eclipsed (and probably also partly absorbed) by the kingdom of Šimaški, which had now become the paramount political, economic, and commercial power on the Persian plateau. The rise of Šimaški also marked the growing importance of the overland trade-routes in Iran (especially, the Great Khurasan Road), a shift that would be fully completed by ca. 1500 BC, when the age of long-distance sea ventures in the Gulf and the Indian Ocean would reach its effective end. It would not be until the days of the Persian empire that the maritime exploration in the East could claim a comparably vast geographic horizon and that the whole region would develop a similar level of cultural connectivity.[48]

It appears that a similar decline was experienced by Marhaši's ally, Makkan, whose name also disappears from the historical record. Clearly, the evaporation of Marhaši and Makkan from the political map, combined with the diminished role of the Babylonians, offers a perfect scenario for the ascent of Tilmun to the status of the sole maritime power in the Gulf. In many ways, this ascent represented a return to the conditions that existed in this region prior to the Sargonic involvement.

That, subsequent to the Ur III period, Tilmun assumed a dominant positon in the Gulf is even more emphatically demonstrated by the archaeological record, especially by the appearance, precisely at that time, of monumental architecture at Qala'at al-Bahrain and of collosal tombs at the A'ali Mound Cemetery, both of which should be interpreted as the expressions of a highly prosperous, full-fledged monarchy. This record further documents the spread of Tilmunite influence over the entire Gulf region. Other archaeological data demonstrate the concomitant decline of the Umm an-Nar culture (the assumed cultural marker of the Makkan state), thus agreeing with the absence of textual mentions of Makkan in post-Ur III times.

Lines 49a–o of the composition "Enki and Ninhursag" paint a picture of Tilmun as a commercial emporium. Therein, Tilmun is said to be a receipient of goods incoming from Tukriš and its gold bearing mountain Harali, as well as from Meluhha, Marhaši, Makkan, the "Sea Land" (probably a general designation of the coastal regions of the Gulf), the "Tent Land" (the inland Gulf areas inhabited by the Amorites), Elam, and Ur. It is interesting to note that, according to this source, the merchandise supplied by Ur to Tilmun (also on "big ships"!) consisted of barley, textiles, and sesame oil—that is,

---

48. The unique character of the third-millennium contacts between Mesopotamia and the East—in particular, their vast geographical scale—was first noted by Oppenheim (1954: 14–15). Building on Oppenheim's observations, one might today justifiably talk of the existence, during the third millennium, of one enormous, mutually interconnected cultural and commercial *koiné* that extended from the Mediterranean to the Indus Valley.

materials similar to those that are mentioned in the economic sources from Isin and Ur discussed earlier and those exported to Tilmun and Makkan from Babylonia in Ur III times: eš$_2$ Urim$_2^{ki}$ barag nam-lugal-la uru$^{k[i]}$ [. . .] še i$_3$-giš tug$_2$ mah tug$_2$ sig$_5$ ma$_2$-gal-[gal] hu-mu-ra-ab-[sa$_2$], "may the shrine of Ur, the dais of kingship, direct to you (i.e., Tilmun) 'big ships' with barley, sesame oil, great/sumptuous textiles, fine quality textiles" (lines 49n–o).[49] Because of the prominence it ascribes to Tilmun, this passage (which is found only in the version from Ur), probably represents an early Old Babylonian addition, which was appended to an earlier (Ur III?) version of this composition in reflection of the dominant position of Tilmun in the Gulf during the Isin and Larsa periods and of the close commercial contacts that existed between Ur and Tilmun at that time.

Elsewhere in the same composition, Tilmun is called a "town" or "city" (Sumerian uru) and identified as "the chief(?) quay of the Land (i.e., of Sumer)" (e$_2$-gu$_2$-kar-ra kalam-ma, lines 49, 60, and 61).[50] There can be no doubt that the place meant by these descriptions is the early second-millennium settlement of Qalaʾat al-Bahrain.

49. The "big ships" (ma$_2$-gal-gal) are also mentioned in lines 49c–e of the same composition, in connection with Meluhha.

50. The term e$_2$-gu$_2$-kar-ra, attested only here, is difficult. Cf. Marchesi 2014, who speculates that it may mean "house of the harbor taxes."

Chapter 8

The Role of Gu'abba as Babylonia's Main Seaport and a Major Textile Production Center

1. *Gu'abba, the Seaport*

During the second half of the third millennium BC, Babylonia's main seaport was situated at the town of Gu'abba, which formed part of the city-state of Lagaš. The original designation of Gu'abba, which is used in pre-Sargonic and Sargonic sources—occasionally appearing as an alternative name of Gu'abba also in Ur III documentation—is E_2-^{d}Nin-mar^{ki}, "household of the goddess Ninmar."[1] Ninmar was thought to be a daughter of the goddess Nanše, the chief deity of the southern section of the city-state of Lagaš, whose own urban centers were at Nimin/Nina and Sirara, both to the north of Gu'abba. Another town situated in that region was Kinunir, a domain of the goddess Dumuzi-abzu, who likewise belonged to the circle of Nanše and Ninmar.

The term Gu$_2$-ab-ba, which means "Coast/bank of the Sea,"[2] is found for the first time in the pre-Sargonic sources from Lagaš,[3] where it functions as a general description of the coastal region of the city-state of Lagaš where the seaport and the temple-household of Ninmar were situated. This original meaning of Gu'abba is preserved in the toponym Gu$_2$-ab-ba$^{(ki)}$ gu-la "Greater Gu'abba," which is occasionally mentioned in Ur III sources (sometimes together with Gu$_2$-ab-ba)[4] and which appears to describe Gu'abba's more general area.[5] The connection of Ninmar with the sea is further

---

1. See RGTC 1 48; Selz 1995: 256–61. Among the Ur III attestations of E_2-^{d}Nin-mar^{ki}, see, e.g., BPOA 1 440, from Umma, which records a boat trip from E-Ninmar to Ur and Umma, a trip that took 21 days, as well as a walking expedition from Kamari (in the Umma province) to E-Ninmar, lasting 3 days.

2. This etymology is confirmed by the spelling Gu$_2$-a-ab-ba^{ki}-še$_3$ (Messenger Texts, Diss. No. 537:5), which explicitly names a-ab-ba, "sea." Cf. gu$_2$ a-ab-ba-ta gin-na (Nisaba 3/2 13:16; CUSAS 16 216:4) and gu$_2$ a-ab-ba-a-ta gin-na (MTBT 192:4), "who came from the seacoast."

3. Nikolski 1 19, which records a transfer of several families from Girsu to Gu'abba (Gu$_2$-ab-ba-še$_3$), among them two sailors and a fisherman. Note the absence of the semantic indicator KI following Gu'abba's name, which corroborates the conclusion that this toponym originally designated a geographical area rather than a specific settlement.

4. For Gu$_2$-ab-ba$^{(ki)}$ gu-la, see TCTI 2 695:11; MTBM 260:12; OBTR 96:6; AUTBM 1 621:9; etc. The two toponyms are named together in TCTI 2 695 and OBTR 96, demonstrating that the distinction is intentional.

5. For this conclusion, see already Selz 1995: 257 n. 1228.

demonstrated by the fact that one of her chief cultic officials was called šita-ab-ba, "šita-priest of the Sea" (Edzard 1997: 8–9 Ur-Ningirsu I 2 ii′ 7′).

That E-Ninmar = Gu'abba functioned as a seaport already in pre-Sargonic times is demonstrated by the fact that it was at Gu'abba that Lagaš's fleet of "big ships" (and, along with it, its personnel) was stationed (see Appendix 2). This conclusion is corroborated by other textual data from Lagaš. In Nikolski 1 313, a merchant traveling from Elam is charged a duty of some sort in E-Ninmar. It appears that this individual followed the classic sea route between southern Babylonia and the Susiana region, which, as later in Ur III times, ran from Gu'abba along the Iranian coast to the mouth of the Karun, continuing then over the Karun into the Susiana (see below, p. 75).

A similar itinerary is suggested by Sollberger Corpus 46 (= FAOS 19, pp. 25–29), a letter written by a certain Lu-ena, the head of the temple-household of Ninmar, in which he informs his counterpart in Girsu (En-entarzi, the head of the temple-household of Ningirsu) about a raid on Lagaš (modern Al-Hiba south of Girsu = modern Telloh) carried out by a band of 600 Elamites. Following the raid, the attackers tried to retreat to Elam with their loot. They were subsequently intercepted at E-Ninmar = Gu'abba by the said Lu-ena, who defeated them in battle, managing to recover some of the looted goods (among which were silver mirrors, high quality textiles [^{tug_2}nam-lugal "royal garments"], and wool). Like the merchant discussed earlier, these Elamite invaders probably followed a sea route: from the Susiana over the Karun to the Persian Gulf, then along the coast to Gu'abba, and then they continued (probably also on ships) to Lagaš.

It may be assumed that the same route is also alluded to in a pre-Sargonic tablet from Lagaš, which refers to the "long-distance trade of Elamite ships" (nam-ga-eš$_8$-ak ma$_2$ Elam-ma-ka-kam). This document lists various merchandise that was purchased in Elam by a long-distance trader (gaeš) named Girni-badab.[6]

Gu'abba's importance as a seaport continued in the Sargonic period. This is shown by the prominence it is given in one of Sargon's inscriptions, which highlights the conquest of Gu'abba and its territory, clearly in reflection of its strategic position on the coast, with the capture of Lagaš being mentioned there almost as an afterthought: "he conquered E-Ninmar and destroyed its walls; and he captured its region and Lagaš as far as the sea; he washed weapons in the sea."[7] Another interesting contemporary reference to Gu'abba is found in Banca d'Italia 1 63 iii 1–6, an Adab tablet dating to Sargon's reign, which is a record of the trips undertaken by a certain Ur-e: iti [x] E$_2$-^{d}Nin-Ma[r^{ki}] iti 4 A-ga-de$_3$^{ki} gir$_3$-gin Ur-e$_2$-kam, "[x] months in E-Ninmar; 4 months in Akkade; these were the trips of Ur-e." Finally, a Sargonic tablet from Lagaš talks of the goods (identity uncertain) that were brought to Gu'abba as part of the "long-distance trade with Elam."[8]

As the following discussion will show, Gu'abba continued to be Babylonia's principal seaport at least down to the end of the Ur III period. It is possible that there was also a seaport in the vicinity

---

6. RTC 21. A closely related text is RTC 20, where Girni-badab delivers to the palace of Lagaš similar merchandise, here designated as the "long-distant trade of the Elamites" (nam-ga-eš$_8$-ak Elam-me-ne-kam). For a recent edition of these two documents, see Maekawa and Mori 2011: 247. The merchandise listed in these tablets included large volumes of the alkali salt (naga) and the substance called arkab (possibly bat droppings), as well as various spices and objects.

7. Frayne RIME 2 9–12 Sargon 1:42–52 (Sumerian) = 44–58 (Akkadian).

8. [1] gu$_2$ 30 ma-˹na˺ ˹x˺-[(. . .)] / nam-ga-˹eš$_8$˺-[(ak)] / Elam-[ma] / 1 gu$_2$ [. . .] / (broken) Šu-[. . .] / dub-sar / Gu$_2$-ab-ba / mu-de$_6$ / [a-r]a$_2$ 2-kam (STTI 63). Although it would be tempting to think that the merchandise in question was wool, the traces of ˹x˺ as copied do not support the reading ˹siki˺.

of Ur, conceivably at Eridu. While not confirmed textually any time during the third millennium, the existence of a seaport such as this appears particularly likely in pre-Sargonic times. This is indicated by the political prominence of the city-state of Ur during that period and the fact that Ur was involved in commercial exchanges with the Gulf (as shown from the presence of a rich assortment of eastern goods in the so-called Royal Tombs), which probably were of a direct nature. Given the political climate of pre-Sargonic times, which was characterized by a high level of competition for elite and strategic materials among the leading city-states, it is doubtful that Lagaš would have allowed its rival Ur to have a free use of Gu'abba, thus forcing Ur to seek an alternative access to the seacoast. Be that as it may, Ur III sources contain no references to any form of maritime activity in the area of Ur (or Eridu).[9] Therefore, it appears certain that, even if such a port existed, it was not used extensively in Ur III times.[10] Since the early Old Babylonian sources from Ur bearing on the trade with Tilmun place this operation at Ur (though not identifying Ur specifically as an embarkation point),[11] it appears that, at that time, a port existed at Ur, which was directly linked by a waterway with the Gulf. It is also important that the same sources mention a "harbor" of Ur, where various types of boats could be hired.[12] On the other hand, the name of Gu'abba is not attested in Old Babylonian times. These facts should perhaps be interpreted as implying that, following the disintegration of the Ur III empire, Gu'abba ceased to be a seaport, that role having been taken over by Ur or Eridu.

2. Gu'abba, the Town

The town of Gu'abba was the site of a temple-household of Ninmar, which constituted the largest religious and economic institution in the area. In addition, a number of other, smaller temple-households were located there, among them those of [(d)]Na-du$_3$-a, [d]Igi-ama/ma-še$_3$, Enki, and Dumuzi.[13]

---

9. It is characteristic that Eridu is mentioned exceedingly rarely in Ur III economic documentation. The general impression is that, during this time, Eridu played an only marginal economic role. A notable exception is a tablet from Umma (BPOA 2 2095) that mentions a worker who spent one month "towing a boat with wool from Eridu." The unusual length of this operation suggests that the tablet describes a round trip, which involved transportation of wool from Umma to Eridu, possibly with an intention of exporting it farther, to the Gulf. In fact, the existence of a waterway between the region of Ur and the seacoast is indicated by an inscription of Ur-Namma, which describes how Ur-Namma excavated a border canal named Nanna-gugal, extending its outlet all the way to the sea (id$_2$-da [d]Nanna-gu$_2$-gal mu-bi kun-bi a-ab-ba-ka i$_3$-la$_2$) (Frayne RIME 3/2 63–65 Ur-Namma 28:10–14). This canal is perhaps identical with the waterway running through Eridu at the beginning of the second millenum (H. T. Wright 1981: 330 and 331 fig. 21).

10. In all probability, this situation arose from the fact that, by the end of the third millennium, the main channel of the Euphrates (the so-called Kiš branch) carried much less water than before, due mainly to the diversion of its water into a new, western branch (Arahatum), along which the cities of Babylon, Borsippa, and Dilbat were situated. Already in Ur III times, the Euphrates levels were too low to allow large-boat navigation, with the river traffic south of Nippur being conducted predominantly over the Tigris (Steinkeller 2010: 375–76 and n. 37). This picture is corroborated by the archaeological survey data from the region of Ur and Eridu, which show that, during the period in question, the main branch of the Euphrates virtually ceased to exist to the east of Ur (H. T. Wright 1981: 328–34), having been replaced by a body of marshes and estuaries (J. Pournelle, personal communication). There is every reason to think, therefore, that in Ur III times the city of Ur did not have a viable waterway connecting it to the Gulf. A detailed discussion of this issue will be offered by Steinkeller elsewhere.

11. Oppenheim 1954.

12. UET 5 196:9, 229 rev. 9', 230: 23, 371:7, 420:11.

13. See Selz 1995: 257–59; Priests and Officials 101 App. 4a-b; PPAC 4 267 iv 2–4; MTBM 260:12; TCTI 2 3482:8; CT 7 26 BM 18371:32.

Ninmar's temple household owned extensive tracts of arable land, orchards, tree plantations, and flocks of sheep.

Apart from these temple households, Gu'abba housed at least three establishments of a purely economic character: (a) a shipyard; (b) a caravanserai for the state personnel who were traveling and various foreign visitors who either traveled to Babylonia or were returning to their native countries; and (3) a weaving facility.

2.1. The Shipyard

The shipyard, which is identified in the Ur III sources as $(e_2\text{-})$mar-sa Gu$_2$-ab-ba^{ki}, undoubtedly was a component of Gu'abba's port.[14] This facility had extensive personnel, numbering between 30 and 60 individuals,[15] among whom were two scribes (dub-sar mar-sa), caulkers, reed-workers, leather-workers, and various support staff. Attached to the shipyard was a warehouse where timber, reeds, bitumen, and other materials used in the construction and maintenance of ships were stored. This warehouse was manned by a separate group of workers called the "personnel of wood and reeds."[16]

Much of the timber used in ship-building at Gu'abba came from tree plantations, which were located at Gu'abba as well as in the neighboring towns.[17] There is no doubt that these plantations had been established with the specific objective of supplying timber for Babylonia's fleet. Particularly instructive here is TLB 144, which is a record of an inspection conducted at one of those plantations.[18] The plantation grew pine trees exclusively, which from the inception were designated for specific ship parts (here note that the object of the inspection were *live* trees, not harvested timber!). There is no doubt that this is an instance of the arboricultural practice (which is known in the Gulf area in modern times as well[19]) in which young trees are trained into specific shapes to suit the timber's later applications. The text records 9,833 individual pines, which were to be used as steering oars (^{giš}gi-muš), punting poles (^{giš}mi-ri$_2$-za), and the keel's ribs or frames (^{giš}girah(ŠU.DIM$_2$)),[20] the last coming in four different sizes, to fit ships of the capacity of 20, 30, 40, and 60 bushels (Sumerian gur).

14. Other shipyards are known to have operated in Girsu and Nimin. The one at Nimin, for which see ASJ 20 110 8 ii 19–iii 6; MTBM 233, 324; TUT 130:25; etc., was the smallest of the three.

15. See SAT 1 422, which records barley and garments allotments for 59 employees of the shipyard (lu$_2$ mar-sa Gu$_2$-ab-ba^{ki}-ke$_4$-ne). ASJ 20 110 8 iii 1–v 2 names 29 shipyard workers and specifies their professions. A similar text is Priests and Officials 101 App. 4a-b rev. vi 15–23, which lists 40 members of this group. In Zinbun 34 no. 129 vii 19–20 they are assigned 27,480 liters of barley as their yearly allotment.

16. See gir$_3$-se$_3$-ga giš-gi šag$_4$ Gu$_2$-ab-ba^{ki} (PPAC 5 314 vi 9–10); gir$_3$-se$_3$-ga giš-gi-me . . . šag$_3$ Gu$_2$-ab-ba^{ki} (TUT 146 rev. iii 16), gir$_3$-se$_3$-ga šag$_3$ giš-ka . . . šag$_4$ Gu$_2$-ab-ba^{ki} (BPOA 2 1942:7); UN-il$_2$ giš-gi-me . . . šag$_4$ Gu$_2$-ab-ba^{ki} (CT 7 26 BM 18371:23, 36). The grain allotments of these workers are recorded in Zinbun 34 no. 129 viii 4–5: 168.0.0 gur še-ba gir$_3$-se$_3$-ga giš-gi.

17. Such tree farms, which are documented only in the Ur III province of Girsu/Lagaš, are called ^{giš}kiri$_6$ giš gal-gal, "orchards of big trees." See, especially, JEOL 33 127 13, which documents them at Nimin, Kinunir, and Gu'abba. The grain allotments of the personnel (nu-^{giš}kiri$_6$ giš-gal-gal-me) attached to the plantations in Girsu, Nimin, Ki'eša, and Gu'abba are specified in Zinbun 34 no. 129.

18. ^{giš}u$_3$-suh$_5$ šid-da ^{giš}kiri$_6$ [giš gal-gal] šag$_4$ Gu$_2$-ab-ba^{ki}, "the counted pine trees in the orchard of [big trees] in Gu'abba" (vi 2–3). The work-force attached to these plantations (nu-^{giš}kiri$_6$ giš gal-gal-me) must have been substantial, since in CT 7 BM 18371:12–13, a list of wool allotments distributed among the various types of personnel at Gu'abba, these individuals receive one of the largest volumes of wool recorded there (252.5 minas). In Zinbun 34 no. 129 vii 17–18 the same group of workers is assigned 66,660 liters of barley as their yearly allotment.

19. As observed by Laursen on Bahrain.

20. For this ship part, see Appendix 2, p. 107.

2.2. The Caravanserai

There is every reason to think that Gu'abba's caravanserai or rest house (e$_2$-kas$_2$), which is known to have been a large and important operation,[21] formed an integral part of the seaport. Its presence there is explained by Gu'abba's role as Babylonia's main seaport and one of the most important communication hubs. In addition to providing access to the Gulf region, Gu'abba's seaport also facilitated overland traffic leading onto the Iranian plateau and points farther east, especially the lands of Anšan and Marhaši and other places situated in the southern reaches of Fars and Kerman.

At least two main sea routes commenced at Gu'abba. The first of them led to Tilmun (Failaka, Tarut, and Bahrain) and then, skirting the Iranian coast, to Makkan.[22] The second route, which was equally important, ran eastward along the coast to the mouth of the Karun river. From there it followed the Karun deep into Khuzestan, where the cities of Susa and AdamDUN were situated and the overland routes leading into southeastern Iran could be accessed.[23] The latter route remained in constant use, with ships being sent regularly from Babylonia to provision the Babylonian military stationed in Khuzestan and to bring back timber and other materials that the agents of the empire acquired in that region and in the neighboring Zagros zone.[24] The same ships also transported Babylonian troops back and forth, as well as messengers, merchants, and various other state employees traveling on official business and, at times, foreign soldiers, large numbers of whom were supplied by the various Iranian polities situated in southeastern and central Iran, among them the lands of Šimaški, Anšan, and Marhaši. All of these individuals routinely passed through Gu'abba, often making a stop at its caravanserai, where they could rest and obtain food supplies for their further travel. Thus, for example, in year Šu-Suen 8, visitors to the caravanserai included a group of elite royal soldiers, various runners (kas$_4$), soldiers transporting a boat with birds, the governor of Susa named Beli-arik, the Elamite mercenaries from Anšan, Huhnuri, Barbarahuba, and Sabum, and a similar detachment of soldiers sent by the Šimaškian ruler Yabrat (TÉL 46).

2.3. The Weaving Establishment

Gu'abba's weaving facility (e$_2$-uš-bar) was the main center of textile production in the province of Girsu/Lagaš, likely constituting the largest such operation in the entire Ur III state (Waetzoldt 1972: 94–95; Steinkeller 2013a: 420–22). In the sources from the reign of Šu-Suen, this establishment is

---

21. See Veldhuis 2001: 85–109. The importance of this institution is underscored by the mentions of an associated "palace" (e$_2$-gal), which may have served as living quarters for the more privileged travelers. See gir$_3$-se$_3$-ga e$_2$-gal e$_2$-kas$_4$ (CT 7 26 BM 18371:6–7; RTC 399 vi 6, 8–9), gir$_3$-se$_3$-ga e$_2$-gal gibil$_4$ u$_3$ e$_2$-kas$_4$ (HLC 1 29 iv 20–22). For the "personnel" (gir$_3$-se$_3$-ga) working there, see also Priests and Officials 101 App. 4a–b iv 12–v 1. In Zinbun 34 no. 129 vii 13–14, these workers are assigned 22,500 liters of barley as their yearly allotment.

22. Gu'abba is explicitly identified as the embarkation point for Makkan in a tablet from years Šulgi 34–35 (TLB 3 145 ii 12–15, iii 10–12). This document records deliveries of various materials to E-Ninmar = Gu'abba, which were intended for the soldiers about to be transported to Makkan (eren$_2$ Ma$_2$-gan^{ki}-še$_3$ bala-a). Without doubt, the amphibious operation in question was connected with the campaign(s) against Anšan that took place in years Šulgi 33 and 34 and involved the movements of troops between Makkan and Anšan. See Steinkeller 2007: 226 and n. 45, with reference to the related tablets MVN 10 149 and TLB 3 146.

23. See Steinkeller 2013b: 297 and nn. 30–33; 2013a: 419–20.

24. For the deliveries of timber, see, e.g., the sources cited in Steinkeller 2013b: 297 and n. 31, which date to the time of Gudea of Lagaš. In addition, see 12.0.0. (še) gur šag$_4$-gal šu-ku$_6$ giš A-dam-DUN^{ki}-ta ma$_2$-a gar-ra kišib Ze$_2$-lu-u-bi-i$_3$-li$_2$ sukkal lugal . . . šag$_4$ Gu$_2$-ab-ba^{ki} (Zinbun 34 no. 129 ix 4–6, × 1; Šulgi 47; courtesy of K. Maekawa).

referred to as é-uš-bar ^{d}Šu-^{d}Suen-ka, "weaving house of Šu-Sin" (BPOA 1 61:24; ITT 2 651:6–7; PPAC 5 783:10–11; TCTI 1 844:6; TCTI 2 4104:4–6; MVN 22 229:2). This renaming may have resulted from the state having assumed more direct control of its operation. It is also possible that Šu-Suen had been responsible for a major physical expansion of this facility.

That Gu'abba was Babylonia's main center of textile industry in Ur III times is strongly indicated by the information on the numbers of weavers employed there. According to the sources dating to years Šulgi 48 and Amar-Suen 1, there were ca. 4,300 female weavers residing in Gu'abba at that time, which is four times more than the number of weavers documented for the city of Girsu, the province's capital (Steinkeller 2013a: 420–21). In addition, a very substantial population of female weavers—likewise exceeding in number those attested at Girsu—is known to have resided in Gu'abba's satellites, Kinunir and Nimin. All in all, when the children of the weavers and the various other personnel are included in the tally, one may estimate that the total number of people involved in textile manufacture in the Gu'abba region must have been in the range of 10,000 individuals.

This estimate finds confirmation in the text Zinbun 34 no. 129, an account of the barley expenditures of the province of Girsu/Lagaš (the localities of Girsu, Lagaš, Nimin, Ki'eša, Kinunir, and Gu'abba) in year Šulgi 47. The section listing the expenditures of Gu'abba names a truly astronomical figure of 2,290,050 liters of barley that was distributed during that year among the weavers, the fullers, and the personnel of Gu'abba's weaving establishment: 2 kuru$_7$ (= 7,200 gur) 433.2.3 gur še-ba geme$_2$-uš-bar azlag$_7$ u$_3$ gir$_3$-se$_3$-ga e$_2$-uš-bar . . . šag$_4$ Gu$_2$-ab-ba^{ki} (viii 8–9, x 1). The corresponding expenditures in Kinunir amounted to 233,835 liters of barley (vi 21–22, vii 7), while the total in Ki'eša (which appears to have been situated near Nimin and Kinunir) was 20,810 liters (v 21–vi 1, 6). Unfortunately, the figure for Nimin is not preserved. In contrast, the expenditures for the weavers, the fullers, and the personnel of the weaving establishments operating in Girsu and Lagaš were 744,360 liters and 66,215 liters of barley, respectively (ii 17–18, iv 5–6), which is less than one-third of the costs incurred at Gu'abba, Kinunir, and Ki'eša combined (and not including Nimin).[25]

An important additional insight into the scale of this operation is provided by the text PPAC 5 301 (undated), which is a detailed listing of the managers and the supporting staff employed at Gu'abba's weaving establishment. More than 600 individuals are itemized, among them 21 administrators (pisan-dub-ba, dub-sar, and um-mi-a), 29 weavers' foremen, 446 fullers (azlag$_7$) and their menial assistants, plus various specialized workers such as carpenters, felters, reed-workers, handlers of mordants and dyes (naga and im-babbar), thread-makers (lu$_2$-gu), reed-counters (lu$_2$-gi-šid), as well as guards, door-keepers and chair-carriers.

Although direct information on the output of this operation is scarce, it is clear that Gu'abba and its satellites produced huge quantities of textiles, whose numbers likely were in the tens of thousands per year. Just in one instance (TCTI 2 3506; ŠS 1) we read of 33,360 $^{5}/_{6}$ pounds of wool that was assigned to Gu'abba's weavers (a$_2$-giš-gar-ra geme$_2$-uš-bar Gu$_2$-ab-ba^{ki}-še$_3$) to produce four types of

---

25. See also MVN 2 75 and BPOA 1 308, both from year Šu-Suen 9, recording expenditures of 204,000 and 159,510 liters of barley for the weavers, respectively. These two sources record only what had been issued for the weavers from two separate grain-storing facilities, and thus the total volume of barley expended to the weavers of Gu'abba during that year undoubtedly was much higher. For related records, see Nisaba 17 26 (AS 4/viii); MVN 22 17 (Š 47/i); TUT 162 (AS 1/i); RTC 404 (IS 5/i); HLC 3 238 (date not preserved); BPOA 1 279 (date not preserved); etc.

garments. At an estimated rate of six pounds of wool per garment,[26] this amount is the equivalent of 5,560 individual garments. Occasional records of textiles produced corroborate this picture. A text dating to Šulgi 48 (AUTBM 1 327) lists 1,167+[x] individual garments, many which were of the highest ("royal") quality, produced in Gu'abba during that year.

The fact that Gu'abba and its region housed what (as far as we can tell with the data presently available) was the largest textile production center in the Ur III Babylonia[27] raises the question as to why this operation was situated on Babylonia's coast, not in a more central location that would fit the logistics of wool procurement and finished-product distribution better. As recently argued by Steinkeller (2013a: 421–22), the obvious answer to this question is that Gu'abba's textile production was geared primarily toward trade with the Gulf and other areas in the east that could be reached by water (such as the Susiana Region and the lands beyond, which could be accessed from Gu'abba via the Karun river).

Only a few records of garments being shipped to the Gulf area survive, all of them involving Makkan.[28] But the paucity of this information is not surprising, since, as we noted earlier (pp. 5–6), foreign trade as a rule has practically no reflection in administrative records. Therefore, the single fact that in Ur III times Gu'abba was the main center of the weaving industry and Babylonia's window on the Gulf and southeastern Iran is sufficient to support the conjecture that most of the textiles produced there ended up as exports. There are also strong reasons to think that this textile operation was closely tied to the activities of the Ur III "foreign trade ministry" (see above, p. 57), which, like its fleet of "big ships," probably was based in Gu'abba as well.

It is difficult to estimate how large these textile exports may have been, but if one considers the production capacity of Gu'abba and its neighbors (as we discussed it above), it is conceivable that, during the 40 or so years of the effective existence of the Ur III empire (from ca. year Šulgi 30 through year Ibbi-Suen 3), Babylonia exported into the Gulf and neighboring areas well over 100,000 individual textiles (if not twice that number).

Excursus: The Textile Industry at Ur

Ever since the appearance of T. Jacobsen's article "On the Textile Industry at Ur under Ibbī-Sîn" (1953), a view (especially common in secondary literature) has persisted that the city of Ur was a major (if not the main) center of textile production in the Ur III state. In fact, in that article, Jacobsen never offers any opinion as to the relative importance of weaving at Ur. However, by tacitly assuming that all the references to wool production and weaving activity appearing in the economic sources from Ur describe a local Ur-based industry, he created an impression that this operation had

---

26. This is the ancient estimate of wool needed to produce the garment called "ordinary [= fifth class] guz-za" (Waetzoldt 1972: 116–18), which is one of the items listed in TCTI 2 3506.

27. The possibility cannot be excluded that there existed (as yet undocumented textually) similar concentrations of textile manufacturing in other border zones of Babylonia, geared toward the supply of other foreign markets. The existence of such centers could find support in the fact that, in the immediately following period, the Assyrians obtained huge volumes of textiles from Babylonia, possibly from a weaving operation located on the fringes of northern Babylonia (Ešnuna in the Diyala Region?).

28. See above, p. 59, and Appendix 1, Texts 2–7.

a considerable size. To be sure, there were some weavers at Ur and its vicinity. But, when examined in detail, the relevant sources show that most of the weaving activity referred to therein actually took place in the Girsu/Lagaš province, primarily at Gu'abba = E-Ninmar. E-Ninmar is identified specifically in six sources by the use of the label šag$_4$ E$_2$-^{d}Nin-mar^{ki}-ka (UET 3 1518:6, 1519:3, 1546:13, 1672:18; UET 9 204 ii 5, 910 rev. iii 19'–20').[29] Another possible reference to it is found in UET 3 1636:2–3, which talks of the "weavers of the household of Šu-Suen" (uš-bar ⌈e$_2$⌉ ^{2}Šu-^{d}Suen-ka-še$_3$). In this example, the facility in question likely is the "weaving house of Šu-Suen," which, during the reign of Šu-Suen, was the name of Gu'abba's weaving house (see above, pp. 75–76).

Other producers of textiles named in Ur documentation are Lagaš (UET 3 98:24, 1649:6, 1658:16) and Girsu (UET 3 1651:5). Outside of Girsu/Lagaš, textiles were supplied by the city of Umma (here appearing under its alternative designation E$_2$-^{d}Šara$_2$$^{(ki)}$) (UET 3 1545:7–9, 1599:9, 1686:9) and a provincial Umma town named Šu-na-mu-gi$_4$ (UET 3 978:4, 1721:30, 1779:4).

At Ur itself, weaving activity is documented only at its neighboring settlements of Ga'eš/Karzida (UET 3 1584:2, 1664:23; UET 9 910 rev. iv), ^{d}Nanna-gú!-gal (UET 3 978:5, 1668:16), Ambar-mah (UET 3 1518:5, 1519:6, 1665:13), and uru-bar-ra, the last representing, apparently, one of Ur's suburbs (UET 3 55:5).

---

29. All of these attestations (save one) concern a weaver-foreman (ugula-uš-bar) named Ur-Igalim. It is possible that he is identical with the weaver-foreman of that name appearing in Girsu/Lagaš documentation (CT 10 20 BM 14308 ii 35, iii 13, 23; DAS 332bis:7; MVN 20 19 iii' 10'; ZA 12 261 5:4).

Chapter 9

Contacts between Babylonia and Meluhha in the Late Third Millennium

1. A Meluhhan Settlement in Southern Babylonia?

In an article published in 1977, S. Parpola, A. Parpola, and R. H. Brunswig (S. Parpola et al. 1977) brought attention to a rural settlement named E_2-duru$_5$-Me-luh-ha$^{(ki)}$, which existed in the Girsu/Lagaš province in Ur III times. They also noted the personal name Me-luh-ha, which occasionally appears in the Girsu/Lagaš economic sources of the very same date. On the basis of these data, Parpola et al. suggested that the village in question "may originally have been founded as a [Meluhhan] commercial settlement or a mercantile enclave," implying (though not stating it explicitly) that the founding of that settlement belonged to Sargonic times. At the same time, these authors acknowledged that, by the time when this settlement is attested textually, it was a typical Babylonian village, whose dwellers were fully assimilated into the local society.

While generally dismissed by Assyriologists,[1] the idea that there existed a distinctive Meluhhan settlement in southern Babylonia, which had been founded by merchants from Meluhha, was enthusiastically (and quite uncritically) embraced by archaeologists. Even today, the Parpola hypothesis is presented as a fact in archaeological literature, often in an absurdly exaggerated form.[2]

However, this theory finds no support in the written sources in hand. As far as we can ascertain, E_2-duru$_5$-Me-luh-ha$^{(ki)}$, "Village/hamlet of Mr. Meluhha," was a small agricultural settlement situated somewhere in the province of Girsu/Lagaš, which, apparently, was named after an individual who conceivably (but not necessarily) had some connection with Meluhha. As of this writing, 14

---

1. See, e.g., the perceptive criticism by D. O. Edzard in S. Parpola et al. 1977: 145–46, 164–65.
2. It will suffice to cite the following five examples: "the textual evidence dealing with individuals qualified as 'men' or 'sons' of Meluhha or called with the ethnonym Meluhha, living in Mesopotamia and of a 'Meluhha village' established at Lagash (and presumably at other major cities as well) unexcapably [sic] points to the existence of enclaves settled by Indian immigrants" (Vidale 2004: 261); "the trading settlements that, we know, were active at least since the middle of the 3rd millennium BC (referring to Eduru-Meluhha)" (Salvatori 2008: 116); "Mesopotamian documents indicate the presence of Meluhhan . . . interpreters and even larger acculturated communities in some Mesopotamian cities" (Kenoyer 2008: 24); "Mesopotamian texts refer to merchants from Meluhha living in Mesopotamia" (Wright 2010: 224); ". . . there is again presence for a Meluhhan village" (Crawford 2013: 457).

references to this village survive, most of which concern the grain-storing facility (i$_3$-dub) located there.[3] Granaries of this sort were typical of small rural settlements in Ur III Babylonia.[4] In the immediate vicinity of Eduru-Meluhha, there was also an orchard.[5] In agreement with its rural character, Eduru-Meluhha was involved in agriculture and grain storage. Nearly all of the sources mentioning it are records of barley expended from its granary. There is no indication whatsoever that this village was the focus of any other type of activity nor that merchants, native or foreign, resided there.

The question of Eduru-Meluhha—and with it, the Parpola hypothesis—has recently been revisited by P. S. Vermaak (2008), who claims that this village was identical with the *town* of Gu'abba, the principal seaport of the Ur III state and an important center of textile industry (for which see, in detail, chap. 8). However, this suggestion is baseless. Vermak's sole "evidence" is the Girsu/Lagaš tablet MVN 7 420 (Š 34/ix), which he transliterates (but does not translate), alleging that "the importance of this text is that the *Meluḫḫan* village often referred to is now connected to the well-known place/village of Gu$_2$-ab-ba^{ki} which is also mentioned twice in this text" (ibid., 561). In reality, however, the tablet in question does not "connect" Eduru-Meluhha with Gu'abba in any way. Instead, it makes it absolutely clear that these were two completely different settlements:

1) 490.0.0 še gur lugal 1 sila$_3$-ta
2) še-ba gab$_2$-us$_2$ udu gukkal
3) Gu$_2$-ab-ba^{ki}-ka E$_2$-duru$_5$-Me-luh-ha-ta
4) ki Ur-^{giš}gigir ka-guru$_7$-ta
5) mu Ur-^{d}Lamma dumu Ka$_5$^{a} ka-guru$_7$ Gu$_2$-ab-ba^{ki}-ka-še$_3$
6) Ur-^{d}Ig-alim dumu Ur-^{d}Ba-u$_2$ šu ba-ti
7) gir$_3$ Ur-DUN šeš-na
8) iti-mu-šu-du$_7$
9) mu An-ša-an^{ki} ba-hul

1) 490 bushels of barley, (distributed at the rate of) 1 liter (per 1 man per day) each,
2) (are) the allotments of the herders of long-tailed sheep
3) (stationed) in Gu'abba. From Eduru-Meluhha,
4) from Ur-gigir, the granary superintendent (of Eduru-Meluhha),
5) on behalf of Ur-Lama, son of Ka, the granary superintendent of Gu'abba,
6) Ur-Igalim, son of Ur-Bau, received (this barley).
7) The conveyor was Ur-DUN, his brother.
8–9) Date.

The tablet records a transfer of barley from the village of Eduru-Meluhha to the town of Gu'abba. The transaction was conducted between the granary superintendents of Eduru-Meluhha and Gu'abba, who were Ur-gigir and Ur-Lama, respectively. For Ur-Lama, see Appendix 2, p. 105, n. 7. The actual recipient of the barley was Ur-Lama's representative, Ur-Igalim, whereas the person who oversaw its transport from Eduru-Meluhha to Gu'abba was Ur-Igalim's brother, Ur-DUN. The purpose of this transfer was to provide grain allotments for the sheep-herders resident in Gu'abba.

3. Called i$_3$-dub E$_2$-duru$_5$-Me-luh-ha$^{(ki)}$ or, more commonly, i$_3$-dub Me-luh-ha. For the attestations, see BDTNS online.
4. See Steinkeller 2006b.
5. ^{giš}kiri$_6$ Me-luh-ha (SAT 19 ii 15).

That Eduru-Meluhha and Gu'abba were two different settlements is further shown by BPOA 2 1881, a list of barley expended from various granaries (i₃-dub) of the province of Girsu/Lagaš, where the i₃-dub Me-luh-ha (i 4) is listed *separately* from the i₃-dub Gu₂-ab-ba^{ki} (iii 1).

As for the individual after whom Eduru-Meluhha was named, the Ur III sources from Girsu/Lagaš do in fact mention a couple of men bearing this name. One of them was the son of a certain Ur-Nadua,[6] who bore a good Sumerian name. Furthermore, we find references to Ur-Lama and Ur-Igalim (probably brothers), likewise bearing Sumerian names, who are identified as the sons of Me-luh-ha,[7] the latter probably being the same person as the Meluhha mentioned earlier. There are also references to a supervisor of that name,[8] who could be the same person as well.

It is possible that the eponymous founder of Eduru-Meluhha did in fact have some connection with Meluhha. We may speculate that he had traveled to Meluhha at some point in time or, alternatively, he had been involved in contacts with the Meluhan traders. Compare the Arabic name Hajji, which is a common designation of someone who has completed the Hajj. Alternatively, he may have possessed some physical characteristics that were associated with the Meluhhan people (dark complexion, for example). Cf. German *Mohr*, Italian *Moro*.

The same personal name also appears in a post-Sargonic tablet (CT 50 76),[9] which, like the earlier-discussed sources, comes from Girsu/Lagaš:

1)   10 gin₂ kug
2)   kug eme gul-la-kam
3)   Ur-ur ni-is-ku
4)   dumu Amar lu₂-tukul
5)   Lu₂-Sumun₂-zi-da
6)   lu₂ Me-luh-ha-ke₄
7)   i₃-na-ab-su-su

1)   10 shekels of silver,
2)   the silver (restitution) for a damaged "blade,"
3)   (to) Ur-ur, an elite soldier,
4)   son of Amar, a military man,
5)   Lu-Sumunzida,
6)   a subordinate of / belonging to Mr. Meluhha,
7)   will restore/return to him.

Although the exact sense of the "blade" (lit., "tongue") in question is unclear, the fact that it belonged to a soldier makes it likely that a spearhead or dagger blade is meant here.[10] In line 6, lu₂ Me-luh-ha-ke₄ evidently means "man/subordinate of Mr. Meluhha." A possibility that Meluhha here could be an ethnic designation is most improbable. Since Lu₂-sumun₂-zi-da is a genuine Sumerian

---

6. ¹Me-luh-ha dumu Ur-^{d}Na-du₃-a (ITT 1 1426:7–8).

7. Ur-^{d}Lama dumu Me-luh-ha (OBTR 242:22–23; UDT 64:13; ASJ 13 230 74 ii 3; CT 3 17 BM 14594:4, 7; MVN 22 181:8; PPAC 5 323 rev. ii 2, 612 ii 8–9, iii 8–9); Ur-^{d}Ig-alim dumu Me-luh-ha (Orient 16 88 131 ii′ 7′).

8. ⌜ugula⌝ Me-luh-ha (MVN 7 411:10).

9. This text was also edited by Parpola et al. 1977: 160, though with different readings and interpretation. Note, in particular, that in line 2 Parpola et al. incorrectly read eme (KA×ME), "tongue," as zu₂(KA), "tooth." The sign EME is clear in Sollberger's copy.

10. For this sense of eme, see below, p. 86 n. 28.

name,[11] this individual could not have come from Meluhha. Moreover, in this example, Me-luh-ha lacks a semantic indicator KI, which would be expected in such a case.

In consideration of all these facts, it is not unreasonable to suggest that the village in question had been founded, shortly before the Ur III period, by the Mr. Meluhha referred to in CT 50 76 (or one of his possible namesakes).[12] Although we lack any information about his identity, it is possible that the few persons bearing that name mentioned in Ur III texts were his descendants. As already emphasized, neither they nor the hamlet in question was in any way connected with Meluhha or Meluhhan traders.[13]

2. *Contacts between Babylonia and Meluhha*

We may use this occasion to offer a discussion of the data bearing on contacts between Babylonia and Meluhha, the gist of which was presented in the main part of this book. Direct contacts between these two lands are documented only during Sargonic times. Most important, it is only then that we read of Meluhhan ships. Apart from their mention in an inscription of Sargon (Frayne RIME 2 27–29 Sargon 11:9), such vessels are referred to in four Sargonic tablets:

(1) 10 i$_3$-šah$_2$ ⌜giš⌝ sum-ma sila$_3$ e$_2$-⌜nig$_2$⌝-gur$_{11}$-ta Mu-ni-ra an-na-sum gir$_3$-gin-na ma$_2$ Me-luh-ha-še$_3$, "10 liters of aromatic lard was given to Muni from the warehouse for the expedition of the ships of Me-luhha" (Banca d'Italia 1 102:1–6; Adab).[14] The tablet probably dates to the reign of Sargon, based on the text Banca d'Italia 1 63, from Adab, which deals with the gir$_3$-gin of Sargon, and trips to A'azbum, E-Ninmar (= Gu'abba), and Akkade.[15]

11. "The One of the Faithful Wild Cow (i.e., of the goddess Nin-sumun)." Against Parpola et al. 1977: 160 and 164 n. 57 (who think that this name is a hapax and explain it as a Proto-Dravidian word!), Lu$_2$-Sumun$_2$-zi(-da) is well attested in Sargonic (CUSAS 26 175:3; Lagaš) and Ur III sources (OIP 115 187:13, 194:7, 196:6, 327:8; etc.), as is the variant Lu$_2$-^{d}Sumun$_2$-zi(-da) (MVN 9 73:20; MVN 12 64:2; etc.). Related names are Amar-Sumun$_2$-zi(-da) (CTNMC 54 xi 45; Nisaba 13 52:3; etc.), Lu$_2$-^{d}Nin-sumun$_2$-zi (MVN 11 12:2), Nin-sumun$_2$-zi (RTC 404:17), and the priestly name En-Nin-sumun$_2$-zi, found in an inscription of Lipit-Eštar of Isin (Frayne RIME 4 56–58 Lipit-Eštar 6:15). This misunderstanding of a well-known Sumerian name led to further wild speculation. See, e.g., Vidale 2004: 269: "after considering the name Lu-sunzida I would venture to guess that the Indus settled communities—such as those living in the Meluhha village of Lagash—might have referred to themselves as to 'The people of the just gaur,' or something similar."
12. Other Sargonic attestations of this personal name (likely the same person in all instances) are found in three Lagaš tablets (ITT 1 8015; no copy; an ugula Me-luh-ha; ITT 4 8015; no copy; an ugula Me-luh-ha; ZA 74 [1984] 65 A 5446:2). See further CUSAS 26 259 rev. 2'–3', from Ur, which lists a Lu$_2$-mar-za ⌜dumu⌝ Me-luh-ha, "Lu-marza, son of Meluhha."
13. Another important argument against such a possibility is that a "village of the Meluhhans" would be called *E$_2$-duru$_5$-Me-luh-ha(-ke$_4$)-e-ne, as in E$_2$-duru$_5$-Elam-e-ne, U$_3$-Mar-tu-ne, E$_2$-duru$_5$-sipad-e-ne, etc. A good parallel for Eduru-Meluhha is the toponym E$_2$-duru$_5$-lu$_2$-Ma-gan^{ki}, "village of the man of Makkan," which is documented in the Ur III sources from Umma. It is likely that the person after whom this village was named had some connection with Makkan, either by being a native of Makkan or by simply traveling there. But there is no indication that it was a distinctive Makkan enclave. Note well: these data were already cited by Edzard in Parpola et al. 1977: 165.
14. The term giš sum-ma qualifies various types of oil (i$_3$-šah$_2$, i$_3$-giš, and i$_3$ dug$_3$-ga) in the Sargonic sources from Adab (see Molina 2014: 74 commentary to no. 27:2). We assume that this term describes the aromatic varieties of oils, which were created by the addition of aromatics (giš and šim). Hence giš sum-ma means "given/added an aromatic." For this process and the corresponding Ur III expressions, see Brunke and Sallaberger 2010: 52–58.
15. For gir$_3$-gin-na, "trip, expedition," see most recently Molina 2014: 84 commentary to no. 44:7. Though generally restricted to Sargonic sources, this term occasionally appears in Ur III documentation as well. See, e.g., lu$_2$ gir$_3$-gin-na-ke$_4$-ne (CUSAS 16 56 ii 13, iii18; ASJ 2 28 81 ii 6, iii 5; CT 9 38 BM 13657:30).

(2) še-ba 4 guruš ma$_2$ Me-luh-ha, "grain allotments of the workers/men of the ships of Meluhha" (Yang 1986: 327 A 712:10; Adab).

(3) 1 i$_3$ sila$_3$ Da-ti lu$_2$-tukul ma$_2$ Me-luh-ha-ka (BIN 8 298:6–8; origin uncertain, possibly Umma).

(4) 1 udu nu-banda$_3$ ma$_2$ Me-luh-ha, "1 sheep (for) the captain of the Meluhha ships" (CUSAS 20 153:3; Adab).

Unfortunately, these four passages are ambiguous, since they do not (as does the Sargon example) conclusively establish that the ships in question were native Meluhhan vessels. The possibility that these actually were Babylonian ships that were used for commercial ventures to Meluhha cannot be ruled out. Be that as it may, these data attest to direct contacts between Babylonia and Meluhha in Sargonic times. This point is confirmed by the famous Babylonian cylinder seal belonging to a Meluhhan dragoman named Šu-ilišu.[16] Given his *Akkadian* name, the individual in question was a native Babylonian, who, in one way or another, was involved in first-hand contacts with the Meluhhans, either in Meluhha itself or in some location outside of Meluhha that was frequented by the Meluhhan merchants.[17]

A similar datum is a bulla with the impression of a Harappan seal, found in Babylonia.[18] Since such bullae were customarily attached to various forms of merchandise, this object shows that shipments of Meluhhan goods did come to Babylonia, at least occasionally, either directly from Meluhha or via some intermediary place. Unfortunately, neither the provenance nor the specific date of this bulla is known.

In the following Ur III and Isin-Larsa periods, we have neither any mention of Meluhhan boats, nor is there firm evidence of direct contacts between Babylonia and Meluhha. A notable exception is a mention, in a tablet from Urusagrig dating to year Šu-Suen 6, of three Meluhhans: 1 sila$_3$ i$_3$-giš Na-na-za 1 sila$_3$ Sa$_6$-ma-ar ½ sila$_3$ A-li-a-hi dam-a-ni i$_3$-ba lu$_2$ Me-luh-ha^{ki}-me a-ru-a lugal sipad a-dara$_4$-me, "1 liter of sesame oil (for) Nanaza, 1 liter (of sesame oil for) Samar, (and) ½ liter (of sesame oil for) Ali-ahi, his wife; the oil allotment of the Meluhhans, royal donated slaves, the shepherds of bezoars"[19] (Nisaba 15 371:1–7). There is no reason to doubt that the first of these two individuals, whose names are distinctly foreign, did come from Meluhha (or some neighboring region). Importantly, these two personal names are the only evidence available that may pertain to the language of Meluhha. Although there is no way of telling how Nanaza and Samar had ended up in Babylonia, the fact that they were royal slaves suggests that they had been acquired by the crown somewhere in

16. Šu-i$_3$-li$_2$-su eme-bala Me-luh-ha^{ki}, "Šu-ilišu, translator of Meluhha" (Boehmer 1965: no. 1299, fig. 557; Aruz 2003: 413 no. 303).

17. This individual assuredly was not a native Meluhhan, as thought by Wright 2010: 224–25. The idea that this seal depicts "a Meluhhan interpreter sitting on the knee of an Agade ruler" (Crawford 2013: 456) is preposterous. The alleged "ruler" is a goddess, and the "interpreter" is a human child. As is typical of Mesopotamian seals, this image is unrelated to the seal's inscription.

18. Scheil 1925: 55–56; Ratnagar 2004: 259. The bulla shows the imprints of a textile, suggesting that the merchandise associated with it was some type of cloth. The dealer from whom Scheil obtained this sealing claimed that it came from Umma (Scheil 1925: 56), but, as usual in such cases, this information is highly unreliable and therefore useless. Nevertheless, this provenance is widely cited in literature (Ratnagar 2004: 259; Wright 2010: 222; etc.). In addition, a number of Meluhhan seals have been found at Girsu and Kiš (see above, p. 27). But this evidence does not necessarily prove the physical presence of Meluhhans in Babylonia.

19. Technically, a-dara$_4$ is a hybrid of the Bezoar (wild) goat (*Capra aegagrus*) and the domestic goat. The term darah/dara$_4$ may also describe the Ibex (*Capra ibex*) and the Markhor (*Capra falconeri*). See Steinkeller 1995: 50, 59.

the Gulf, probably as part of the Ur III commercial activity in that region. Interestingly, the name of Samar's wife is Akkadian, indicating that she was a Babylonian native. Another remarkable fact about these individuals is that they took care of bezoars. Since the designation "bezoar shepherd" is completely unique, one cannot but suspect that Nanaza and Samar had been "recruited" owing to their familiarity with these exotic animals, which undoubtedly formed part of a royal animal park.

A number of inscriptions from the reign of Gudea of Lagaš, which belong to the very beginning of the Ur III period, talk of various materials (gold, carnelian, and ebony) that Gudea supposedly obtained from Meluhha.[20] Another of Gudea's texts even mentions the boats of Meluhha (together with those of Makkan, Kupin, and Tilmun).[21] It is highly doubtful, however, that these materials had been acquired as a result of direct exchanges between Lagaš and Meluhha. A much more likely possibility is that these particular goods came to Babylonia via the trade with Makkan, which is known to have flourished at that time, as shown by the mentions of garments being exported to Makkan during Gudea's reign and the records of diorite being acquired there for Gudea's statues (see above, p. 54). This conclusion finds support in the fact that the scribes who composed Gudea's inscriptions had very imprecise knowledge of the Gulf geography, treating Makkan and Meluhha—and Tilmun as well—as essentially a single entity. This is demonstrated by the following passage, where the Tilmunite deities Nin-zak and Nin-sikila[22] are mistakenly associated with Makkan and Meluhha, the suppliers of copper and exotic woods (oak, ebony, and mangrove) respectively:

> Ma$_2$-gan Me-luh-ha kur-bi-ta gu$_2$ giš mu-na-ab-gal$_2$ e$_2$ ^{d}Nin-gir$_2$-su-ka du$_3$-de$_3$ Gu$_3$-de$_2$-a uru-ni Gir$_2$-su^{ki}-še$_3$ gu$_2$ mu-na-si-si ^{d}Nin-zag-ga-da a$_2$ mu-da-ag$_2$ urud(a)-da-ni še mah de$_6$-a-gim Gu$_3$-de$_2$-a lu$_2$ e$_2$ du$_3$-a-ra mu-na-ab-us$_2$-e ^{d}Nin-sikil-a-da a$_2$ mu-da-ag$_2$ ^{giš}ha-lu-ub$_2$ gal-gal ^{giš}esi giš-ab-ba-bi ensi$_2$ e$_2$ du$_3$-ra mu-na-ab-us$_2$-e

> The Makkanites and Meluhhites submitted themselves to him (i.e., Ningirsu) from their lands. They assembled together for Gudea, for his city Girsu, in order to build the temple of Ningirsu. He (Ningirsu) placed orders with Nin-zak—and he is sending to Gudea, the builder of the temple, his copper, which is brought in like the great volumes of barley; he placed orders with Nin-sikila; and she is dispatching to the governor, the builder of the temple, big oak trees, ebony, and mangrove wood" (Gudea Cylinder A xv 8–18).[23]

20. kug-sig$_{17}$ sahar-ba kur Me-luh-ha-ta im-ta-e$_{11}$, "(Gudea) brought down gold in its ore from the land of Meluhha" (Statue B vi 38–40); [urud]a-nagga lagab za-gin$_3$-na gug ^{giš}girin Me-luh-ha-da, "along with tin-bronze (Gudea presents) the blocks of lapis lazuli (and) the beads of Meluhhan carnelian" (Cylinder B xiv 13) [for ^{giš}girin, see girin = *girinnum* (*girimmum*), *kirinnum*, "fruit, fruit-shaped bead/pearl"]; gug ^{giš}girin-e Me-luh-ha-ta šu mu-na-peš-e, "one spreads before him the carnelian beads from Meluhha" (Cylinder A xvi 22–23); kur Me-luh-ha⟨-ta⟩ ^{giš}esi im-ta-e$_{11}$, "from the land of Meluhha he brought down ebony" (Statue B vi 26–27); kur Me-luh-ha-t[a?] iši im-ku$_4$-ku$_4$ = *i-na ša-du Me-luh-ha i-ši-ʾa-amʾ ú-še-ri-da*[m], "from the land of Meluhha he brought down ebony" (Wilcke 2011: 40 no. 22 iv 1–2).

21. Gudea Statue D iv 7–13, for which see above, p. 21 n. 59.

22. Nin-zak appears as ^{d}En-sa$_6$-ak in "Enki and Ninhursag" line 271, and as ^{d}In-za-ak in various later sources. See also the writing ^{d}Nin^{in}-za-ak in UET 5 286:9 (OB). Nin-sikil(-la) is put in charge of Tilmun in "Enki and Ninhursag" lines 29–49 and "Enki and the World Order" lines 238–39. In "Enki and Ninhursag" line 274, the same deity, named ^{d}Nin-siki-la/la$_2$, is identified as the "lord of Makkan" (en Ma$_2$-gan-na). She is probably identical was the later Tilmunite deity Meskilak: *Nin-me-sikil-ak > Meskilak. For Nin-zak and Meskilak, see Nashef 1986: 344. Note, however, that Nashef's suggestion (ibid., 344) that Nin-zak and Meskilak were not originally Sumerian deities is unfounded. Both names are undeniably Sumerian. Cf. Marchesi 2014: 51.

23. Elsewhere in Gudea's inscriptions, the ^{giš}ha-lu-ub$_3$ oak is said to come from Kupin. See Statue B vi 45–48: Gu-bi-in^{ki} kur ^{giš}ha-lu-ub$_2$-ta ^{giš}ha-lu-ub$_2$ im-ta-e$_3$. For Kupin, which possibly designates Baluchistan or Makran, see Steinkeller 2014a: 693 n. 8, and discussion above, p. 35 n. 53. Cf. also Cylinder A xii 3–4: sig-ta ^{giš}ha-lu-ub$_3$ giš NE-HA.AN?

Mangrove wood[24] and carnelian are associated with Meluhha also in the early Old Babylonian composition "Enki and Ninhursag" lines 49c–e,[25] where, in addition, the ^{giš}mes-šag$_4$-gan wood is named. The latter item is almost certainly identical with ^{giš}mes-ma$_2$-gan-na, Akk. *musukkannum*, which possibly denotes "sissoo tree."[26] As indicated by its name, this wood was believed to come from Makkan. In the composition "Enki and the World Order" lines 221–22, which also dates to Old Babylonian times, Meluhha is identified as the source of ^{giš}mes kur-ra, "mountain mes wood" fit for royal chairs (^{giš}gu-za). This wood, as well as the mes Me-luh-ha appearing in a tablet from Ur (UET 3 1241:2), probably are alternative designations of ^{giš}mes-ma$_2$-gan-na. Cf. ^{giš}gu-za Ma$_2$-gan$^{(ki)}$, "chair of Makkan (wood)" (UET 3 829:3′; BIN 10 143:2) and various objects made of mes Ma$_2$-gan^{ki} (UET 3 831:3′–4′, 1498 rev. i 21–22).

mu-ra-ta-e$_{11}$-de$_3$, "from the Below (i.e., the south = the Gulf region) oaks, the . . . wood, will come down for you." Kupin is also mentioned in "Curse of Akkade" lines 152–53, where it designates the farthest point of the Akkadian universe: kur Gu$_2$-bi$_2$-na-še$_3$ igi na-an-il$_2$ hur-sag dagal teš$_2$-bi nam-ta-an-si-ig, "(Enlil) looked up (as far as) to the land of Kupin; he *scoured* all the wide mountain ranges (looking for the Gutians)." For a possibility that this exotic toponym (written *Ku-up-pi*) and its ruler *Ra-a-mit/bat-te* are mentioned much later (together with a king of Tilmun named Hunduru) in an inscription of Assurbanipal, see Oppenheim 1954: 17.

24. As indicated by its name, "tree of the sea," giš-ab-ba, Akk. *kušabkum*, unquestionably is "mangrove." This etymology is supported by the equation giš-a-ab-ba = GIŠ *tam-ti* in K.4906:1f. (CAD K 597 under *kušabku*). For the lexical attestations of giš-ab-ba Me-luh-ha, see ibid. lexical section. Ur III sources mention two types of giš-ab-ba: the giš-ab-ba of Meluhha and the local giš-ab-ba, which was harvested in the riverine forests of southern Babylonia (especially in the province of Umma; see Steinkeller 1987a: 92). Interestingly, an Ur III text from Umma (AAS 124:1–2) also mentions 5 giš-a-ab A-ra-li-ta, "5 (logs) of the mangrove from Arali," where Arali/Harali, a half-mythical gold-bearing mountain in the east (Steinkeller 2014a: 702), obviously is used as a substitute for Meluhha. The mangrove forests, which consist primarily of the Grey Mangrove (*Avicenna marina*), are still a characteristic feature of the coastal areas and estuaries of the Persian Gulf, in Iran (the Bushehr, Hormuzgan and Sistan/Baluchistan provinces), Qatar (Al Thakira), and Oman (Shinas, Qurm Park, and Mahout Island) (Zahed et al. 2010; Kamoonpuri 2010). They are also widespread along the shores of the Indian Ocean, in Gujarat and Sundarbans (Wafar and Untawale 2001). There is every reason to think that, in ancient times, the mangrove's reach extended farther north, into the coastal areas of Iraq. Here note that the Grey Mangrove has recently been successfully reintroduced to Kuwait (Almulla et al. 2013). This explains the presence of the mangrove at Umma, which either grew there naturally in saline waters or was raised artificially in plantations (against the objections of Heimpel 2011: 127). In modern times, mangrove wood has been used for furniture, roof beams and other forms of house construction, and ship parts (especially keels) (Bandaranayake 1999: 11–17; Wafar and Untawale 2001: 549–550). The Ur III sources refer to the mangrove of Meluhha being used for dagger sheaths, chairs, and weapons. See gir$_2$ ur$_2$-ra zabar SAL.UŠ-bi giš-ab-ba Me-luh-ha 2-a ga$_2$-ga$_2$-de$_3$, "a bronze side-dagger; it two sheaths made of the mangrove of Meluhha are to be inlaid [with gold]" (UET 3 430:1′–3′); 3 ^{giš}SAL.UŠ gir$_2$-gi-ka dub-ba Me-luh-ha [. . .] ba-a-gar (UET 3 701:3–4); 1 ^{giš}gu-za giš-ab-ba sig$_5$ Me-luh-ha ^{d}Ma-iš-ti$_2$-su, "1 chair made of the fine mangrove of Meluhha, (belonging to) divine Maništušu" (UTI 4 2849:1–2); 1 ^{giš}gu-za munus . . . da?-bi giš-ab-ba Me-luh-ha-kam, "1 lady's chair . . . its sides(?) are of the mangrove of Meluhha" (Nisaba 7 40:7–9); ^{giš}tukul giš-ab-ba Me-luh-ha, "weapon/staff of the mangrove of Meluhha (UET 3 660:3). The local mangrove was employed for chairs (^{giš}gu-za tur giš-ab-ba sag-ba kug-sig$_{17}$ gar-ra; RA 5 86 AO 3367 iii 5, 88 AO 3368 iv 1), sickle handles (šu ^{uruda}še-gur$_{10}$; e.g., MVN 1 106 ii 8′), hoe handles (šu ^{giš}al; e.g., UTI 3 1940:1), posts/poles (^{giš}dim, e.g., TCL 5 6036 i 12′), loops (^{giš}gam-ma; BRM 3 136:1), and bowls (^{giš}sila$_3$ lugal; SANTAG 7 63:1). The length of the mangrove pieces varied from 0.5 m (RA 73 34 47 i 6) up to 3 m (AnOr 7 198:3); they were commonly packed in one-talent bales (gu$_2$; e.g., AAS 128:1). These usages indicate that the giš-ab-ba was a small hardwood, thus supporting the mangrove identification. Since the giš-ab-ba of Meluhha is qualified as "fine" (sig$_5$; "Enki and Ninhursag" lines 49c–e; UTI 4 2849:1–2), it may have represented a higher quality mangrove. We are not aware of any evidence that would lend support to Heimpel's claim (2011: 126–27) that the Babylonian giš-ab-ba might be "Russian olive."

25. kur Me-luh-ha^{ki} ^{na4}gug nig$_2$-al-di kal-la ^{giš}mes-šag$_4$-gan giš-ab-ba sig$_5$-ga ma$_2$-gal-gal ha-mu-ra-ab-sa$_2$.

26. CAD M/2 237–39; Tengberg et al. 2008: 931.

Another product connected with Meluhha is the "big reed" (gi gal), which is mentioned in "Enki and the World Order" lines 223–24: gi-zu gi gal he₂-em gi [. . . he₂-em] ur-sag-e ki me₃-ka ᵍⁱˢtukul [. . .], "your (i.e., of Meluhha) reed indeed is a big reed, it is a [. . .] reed; a warrior [uses it] on the battlefield as [his] weapon." It is highly likely that the reed in question is the same as the "reed of Makkan,"[27] which is named in a group of Ur texts dating to the later part of Ibbi-Suen's reign (years 15–17). According to these sources, the "Makkan reed" was used to produce the shafts of spears and axes.[28] This fits the martial application of gi gal, as described in "Enki and the World Order." A probable identification of gi gal / gi Ma₂-gan^ki is "bamboo,"[29] which is common in the Indus Valley and Baluchistan (though it is conspicuously absent in Oman). As a matter of fact, bamboo is known to be used for spears. A good example here is the Indian *ballam*, a long spear made of bamboo and topped with a large spearhead (P. C. Mehta and S. Mehta 2007: 78–79).

The same confusion between Meluhha and Makkan seems to be responsible for the exceptional mentions of "Meluhhan" copper found in a tablet from Ur (UET 3 368:2) and "Enki and the World Order" lines 219–37. Without any doubt, in either case, the Makkan copper is meant.[30]

To conclude this enumeration of Meluhhan products, one should also mention three animals that were believed to be native to Meluhha: ur-gun₃-a, "spotted 'dog'," am kur-ra, "wild mountain bull," and the bird dar^mušen kur-ra, "mountain dar bird." The first of them is referred to in an inscription of Ibbi-Suen (Frayne RIME 3/2 373–74 Ibbi-Sin 4) that commemorates the fashioning of a "speckled 'dog' of Meluhha," which had been brought to him from Marhaši, apparently as a diplomatic gift. The animal in question is to be identified either as the Arabian Leopard (*Panthera pardus nimr*) or the Cheetah (*Acinonyx jubatus*).[31]

---

27. Cf. gi-zi = ki-i-su = qa-an Ma-ak-kan; gi-zi-hi-a = ṣip-pa-tum = ditto (= qa-an Ma-ak-kan), "reed of Makkan" (MSL 7 68 Hg. 28). For *kīsum*, a type of reed, see CAD K 433 *kīsu* C; for ṣippatum, a type of reed, see CAD Ṣ 203 ṣippatu D.

28. See the following examples: quantities of tin and copper issued to make bronze for eme-gir₂ mu giš-gid₂-da gi Ma₂-gan^ki-še₃, "spearheads for the spears of 'Makkan reed'" (UET 3 493:1–8); 4 giš sag-e₃ giš-gid₂-da gi Ma₂-gan^ki, "4 wooden finials (for) the spears of 'Makkan reed'" (UET 3 803:3–4); dur₁₀-tab-ba [. . .] giš-bi gi Ma₂-gan^ki [. . .] u₃ dur₁₀-tab-ba 3-ta gu₂-la₂-a zabar giš-bi gi Ma₂-gan^ki 2-a a-la₂ sag-e₃-ba ga₂-ga₂-de₃, "the [. . .] double axes, their wood is 'Makkan reed' [. . .], and 2 bronze double axes, each three times . . ., their wood is 'Makkan reed,' their a-la₂ and finials are to be inlaid (with gold?)" (UET 3 363:1′–5′); 1 gi Ma₂-gan^ki gid₂ 7 ⸢kùš⸣ 4 šu-še₃ , "1 'Makkan reed,' its length is 7 cubits (= 3.5 m), (to be used) for 4 handles" (UET 3 859:1); 6 gi Ma₂-⸢gan⸣^ki-a (UET 3 1498 rev. i 19). The word eme-gir₂ appearing in UET 3 493, which usually describes dagger blades, in this instance evidently denotes a spearhead. Cf. 23⅔ ma-na zabar ki-la₂ ^urudagag eme-gir₂ 26-kam (Trouvaille 82:1–2), where eme-gir₂ qualifies gag, itself meaning "spearhead." See also eme-gir₂ as a part of šu-nir, "battle standard" (BPOA 2 2459, etc.). These objects must have been very large, heavy spearheads, shaped like daggers. A possible example of this weapon is the colossal spearhead from Girsu, presented by a Kiš king named Lugal-namnir-sum (Frayne RIME 1 73; Marchesi and Marchetti 2011: 322 fig. 6). There also survives one mention of furniture made of the "Makkan reed": 1 giš-na₂ gi-Ma₂!-gan^ki umbin-gud-bi ᵍⁱˢha-lu-ub₂ kug-sig₁₇ gar-ra, "1 bed of 'Makkan reed'; its 'ox legs' are of oak; it is inlaid with gold" (PDT 1 543:1–3).

29. This identification was considered already by L. Legrain, UET 3 Index Volume, 233 under no. 859. Cf. also Heimpel 1987: 63.

30. Thus, the claim by Begemann et al. 2010: 162 that "epigraphic evidence from Mesopotamia describes Meluhha as having played an important role as the source of its copper" is without any foundation.

31. Steinkeller 1972: 253 and nn. 60–61; D. T. Potts 2002. Evidently, this animal is the same ur-mah gun₃-a, "spotted lion," which is mentioned in a number of texts from Puzriš-Dagan (AUCT 1 381:19; MVN 10 144 v 24; UTI 6 3779:19′), and the pirig-gun₃, "spotted lion/panther," referred to in the inscription of a Sargronic seal (Steinkeller 1987).

The am kur-ra is named uniquely in "Enki and the World Order" lines 225–26: gud-zu gud gal he$_2$-em gud kur-[ra-ka he$_2$-em] gu$_3$-bi gu$_3$ am kur-ra-ka [he$_2$-em], "your (i.e., of Meluhha) oxen indeed are great oxen; they are the oxen of the mountains; their roaring indeed is that of the wild bulls of the mountains." This animal is conceivably identical with am-si, "elephant."[32]

As for dar^{mušen} kur-ra, this particular bird species is mentioned in line 228 of the same composition: dar^{mušen}-dar^{mušen} kur-ra su$_4$ ^{na4}gug [he$_2$-em-la$_2$], "(your) dar birds of the mountains indeed [wear] the 'beards of carnelian.'" It is highly likely that the bird in question is identical with dar^{mušen} Me-luh-ha, figurines of which are mentioned in a number of texts from Ur.[33] Even more important here is the testimony of two economic tablets from Umma, which record disbursements of wheat to feed these birds.[34] This evidence establishes conclusively that the dar Meluhha was introduced to Babylonia in Ur III times.

As considered many years ago by B. Landsberger (1962: 148; 1966: 247–48) and A. Falkenstein (1964: 75), this bird species is likely to be identified as the chicken. This identification rests on the following set of data:

1. The starting point of our investigation must be the fact that the dar Meluhha was thought by the ancients to be a variety of (or at least similar to) the ordinary dar bird, Akkadian *ittidûm*,[35] which almost certainly is the Black Francolin (*Francolinus francolinus*), also known as the Black Partridge, whose primary color is black. The dar Meluhha also was black or dark, as indicated by its Akkadian name *ṣulāmum*, "the black one" (from *ṣalāmum*, "to be black").[36]

2. The term dar Meluhha is limited to Ur III sources, and the lexical attestations cited earlier. Due to the fact that, by the beginning of the second millennium, the designation Meluhha had become largely meaningless, in the later periods the bird in question apparently came to be known as dar-lugal^{mušen}, Akkadian *tarlugallum*, "royal/kingly dar."[37] The dar-lugal, which is documented since Old Babylonian times,[38] assuredly is "chicken, rooster," because of the Syriac loanword *tarnāglā* (*tarngōl(ā)* in Aramaic and Hebrew), "rooster." It is tempting to think the designation lugal, "royal, kingly," has its origin in the chicken's comb or crest, which resembles a crown.

3. This suggestion finds support in the passage from "Enki and the World Order" cited earlier, where the "dar birds of the mountains" are said to have "carnelian beards" (su$_6$ ^{na4}gug). As

---

32. Note that the composition "Curse of Akkade" lines 21–22 names "big elephants" (am-si mah) among the exotic animals that were presented to Sargon as gifts, apparently by the land of Marhaši. The other animals mentioned there are monkeys and ab$_2$-za-za, probably "water buffalos." For ab$_2$-za-za, see below.

33. UET 3 757:5, 761:3, 764:4, 768:7, 770:5.

34. 6 dar^{mušen} Me-luh-a 6 gin$_2$ gig-ta gig-bi 0.3.3 6 sila$_3$ ki ka-guru$_7$ kišib Šag$_4$-kug-ge, "6 dar Meluhha birds, each (receiving) 6 shekels of wheat; their (total) wheat is 216 liters; received by Šag-kuge from the granary superintendent" (MVN 16 1141:1–4; ŠS 5/-); 0.1.0 gig šag$_4$-gal dar^{mušen} . . . 1.2.4 8 sila$_3$ gig šag$_4$-gal ⸢dar⸣ Me-luh⟨-ha⟩, "60 liters of wheat, the feed of the dar (Meluhha) birds . . . 468 liters of wheat, the feed of the dar Meluhha birds" (YOS 4 313:17, 32; ŠS 2/-).

35. See CAD I/J 304 under *ittidû*; Veldhuis 2004: 234–35. The dar/*ittidûm* is described as "speckled" or "colorful": dar^{mušen} = ba-ra-ma-nu-um (MEE 4 302 EV 912); *aššum* MUŠEN *burrumtu* NU ZU DAR.MUŠEN MU.NI (CT 39 5:55 + CT 41 22:14). As noted by Veldhuis (op. cit.), this "is certainly an apt description for the black francolin."

36. [d]ar-me-luh-ha^{mušen} = *ṣu-la-mu* (Hh. XVIII 320 = MSL 8/2 147); dar-me-luh-ha^{mušen} (Veldhuis 2004: 176 085', 189 rev. ii 13', 190 rev. i 04' A). Cf. CAD Ṣ 238 under *ṣulāmu*.

37. See CAD T 237–38.

38. dar-lugal^{mušen} (an OB bird list) (ZA 77 [1987] 123 IM 90646:1); dar-lugal^{mušen} (Veldhuis 2004: 176 083', 189 rev. ii 11', 202 D ii 07'); *ana pāni* [. . .] *u ta-ar-lu-ga-al-lim illik* (AbB 1 86:10).

already suggested by Falkenstein (1964: 75), this "carnelian beard" undoubtedly refers to the bird's red wattle, which is characteristic of the chicken. It is significant that the wattles on the throat or neck otherwise are very rare in birds, thus corroborating the conclusion that the dar Meluhha is "chicken."

4. As for the exact taxonomic identity of the dar Meluhha, the best candidate appears to be the Grey Junglefowl (*Gallus sonneratii*), a wild relative of domestic fowl that is endemic to India (the Deccan Peninsula, extending into Gujarat, Madhya Pradesh, and south Rajasthan). The male has a black cape with ochre spots. It also wears red wattles and combs (consult "Grey junglefowl" in *Wikipedia* online).[39] Both the black color of the Grey Junglefowl and the fact that it is speckled agree with the characteristics of the dar bird (= the Black Francolin) noted earlier.

Yet another animal of possible Meluhhan origin is ab$_2$-za-za (Akkadian *apsasûm*), which is mentioned, together with monkeys (^{ugu}ugu$_4$-bi) and elephants (am-si mah), in the composition "Curse of Akkade" line 21. The passage in question describes various exotic animals that were brought as gifts for Sargon of Akkade. These animals apparently came from the land of Marhaši, which is named in the preceding line. It has been suggested that ab$_2$-za-za is to be identified as the water buffalo (*Bubalus bubalis*), which was native to the Indus Valley (Boehmer 1974; D. T. Potts 1997: 257–59). As demonstrated by the depictions of the water buffalo in Sargonic art, this bovine species had been brought to Babylonia during the Sargonic period. The fact that the attestations of ab$_2$-za-za are exceedingly rare and limited to the Sargonic and Ur III periods (OSP 2 28:2; AnOr 7 154 i 2, 10, 20, iii 7, 17; UET 3 415:2) appears to support this identification. Cf. PSD A/2 174; CAD A/2 193–94. An alternative, though less likely, identification of ab$_2$-za-za would be the zebu (*Bos indicus*), which also was imported to Babylonia at an early date. (See D. T. Potts 1997: 254–57; Matthews 2002.)[40]

39. To the best of our knowledge, no bones of the Grey Junglefowl have been reported from the Harappan sites. Note, however, that Ratnagar (2004: 98) notes that the bones of the Black Francolin have been identified at Ropar (Punjab).

40. To this list of Meluhhan imports one should add sesame (*Sesamum indicum*), a native of India, which, in all likelihood, was imported to Babylonia during the Sargonic period. See Steinkeller 2016b.

Chapter 10

Conclusion

The aim of this study has been to cast new light on some of the major trends in the patterns of interaction between Babylonia and the lands of the Gulf region by combining the evidence of archaeology and texts. During the third millennium BC, societies across Western Asia witnessed unparalleled social transformations, most notably the increasing urbanization and emerging globalization, in a process that was to become instrumental to the later advances of modern society. In this pivotal development in human history, the Persian Gulf played a paramount role as the corridor linking East and West—a function that the Gulf waterway had already performed for several millennia.

Even before the flooding of the Gulf basin at the end of the last glaciation, what was then a major river valley functioned as a principal channel of movement and exchange. However, we are able to study these phenomena only from the sixth millennium BC onward. The first solid evidence stems from the Ubaid period, demonstrating that seafarers from present-day Iraq navigated far down the Gulf. By the end of the fifth millennium BC, almost all interaction had ceased, because climate changes led to greater aridity. This development marked the beginning of a pattern of ever-changing intensity in the interactions between Babylonia, the Gulf, and the more elusive lands beyond.

Focusing on the third millennium BC, this book has presented a comprehensive chronological review and a discussion of the pertinent archaeological and philological evidence. Arguments are presented for a scenario in which by ca. 3000 BC a combination of endemic developments in the Gulf and impulses of globalization emanating from advancing Babylonian urbanism facilitated the social, cultural, and economic changes that eventually gave rise to Tilmun and Makkan. That selected Babylonian products enjoyed high status in the Gulf around 3000 BC is suggested by the conspicuous frequency of Jemdat Nasr vessels from Babylonia, which have been found in graves ranging from Kuwait to the Oman peninsula.

Copper was mined in the mountains of the Oman peninsula and, sometime in the Early Dynastic period, a trading station was established on Umm an-Nar Island. Concurrently, a new cultural formation that derived its name from this eponymous island site materialized in Oman. The Umm an-Nar trading station served as a Makkanite commercial hub that occasionally also linked Tilmunite and Babylonian merchants to the markets of Makkan, Marhaši, and Meluhha. By the time of the appearance of the Umm an-Nar Culture, the influence of the latter regions on Makkan had surpassed that of Babylonia. In Tilmun, trade with Babylonia continued in the Early Dynastic period but now trade links were also established between the kingdom of Marhaši and some Tilmunite chiefdom based at a center on Tarut Island.

A gradual institutionalization of long-distance trade in Babylonia, particularly in the city-state of Lagaš, led to the introduction of ships of larger capacity with longer ranges. As a consequence, following the Early Dynastic period, the Tilmun center on Tarut Island could no longer effectively exploit its midway position. Probably already under Sargon, in order to exclude the involvement of middlemen and thus to minimize transaction costs, Babylonian commercial sea ventures began to bypass Tarut, obtaining copper directly from the merchants based in Makkan. Economically, Tilmun continued, at least to some extent, to be connected with Babylonia and Makkan, and the relations established with Marhaši during the Early Dynastic period probably endured as well. In Makkan, copper production apparently increased in the Sargonic period, and the interactions with southeastern Iranian communities and the Indus world intensified. Archaeological and textual evidence of trade between Sargonic Babylonia and Makkan is limited but probably only because this contact was confined to a few commercial outposts, the locations of which have escaped discovery.

The control of east–west trade routes was the major motivation behind Sargon's empire-building schemes. That the Gulf route was the main target of his strategy is made apparent by the prominence given in Sargon's inscriptions to the conquest of the seaport of Gu'abba and the control of the ships of Tilmun, Makkan, and Meluhha. The nature and the extent of direct interactions between the Babylonians and the people from Meluhha remain elusive. The data in hand suggest that these contacts were rather rare.

Coinciding with the collapse of the Sargonic Empire and the commercial highway it had established between the Mediterranean and the Indian Ocean, the polity of Tilmun witnessed a conspicuous reorganization. Most importantly, the population of Tilmun migrated to the well-watered Bahrain Island and the adjacent Dammam Dome. Tilmun subsequently assumed the shape of a more distinctive cultural entity and, in the immediate after-effect of these changes, the burial mounds began to display distinct, albeit modest, social hierarchization. Contacts with Babylonia and Makkan continued to be maintained, whereas trade relations with Marhaši came to an end. However, as we argue in this book, apart from the temporary breakdown of trade, another apparent reason for the transition of Tilmunites to sheltered island localities was the concurrent global aridity that sent pastoralists such as the Amorites migrating southeastward, with the resulting push-effects on mainland oasis communities. It was probably at this time or shortly thereafter that Tilmun came under Amorite leadership. On the other hand, Makkan, which may already have been dominated by Amorites earlier, probably flourished in the Sargonic period and, having apparently been unaffected by the Sargonic collapse, continued to prosper during in the post-Sargonic and Ur III periods.

In the subsequent period, Gulf trade was restored through the diplomatic and military efforts of the Ur III empire. It may be conjectured that the volumes of merchandise exported from Babylonia to the Gulf region during that time reached staggering figures. Operating out of the seaport of Gu'abba in the Girsu/Lagaš province, the Babylonian fleet of "big ships" carried an extensive trade in cereals, oils, and textiles in exchange for copper and exotic materials from Makkan, Marhaši, and Meluhha. In order to ensure the smooth running of this trade operation, military personnel were stationed at various strategic locations along the Gulf route. One such commercial and military emplacement existed on Failaka Island, which served as an advance bridgehead for trade expeditions destined for the copper markets in Makkan. It appears that, at this time, merchandise from Marhaši and Meluhha was shipped directly to Makkan, with the merchants of these two more distant lands coming into contact with the Babylonians only sporadically.

The fall of the Ur III dynasty marked the end of state-run commercial ventures in the Gulf. From now on, such trading was done by private merchants who possessed ships with smaller capacities and more limited range of operation. This development once again changed the makeup of the commercial networks that facilitated the Gulf trade. Tilmun could once more exploit her midway position between the great markets of the east and west. Makkan, Marhaši, and Meluhha disappeared from the historical record. Marhaši may have been absorbed by the Šimaški, as the latter had gained control over the Iranian plateau and increasingly began to open up the overland east–west trade routes. Amorite dynasties steadily seized power in Babylonia, and a small but prosperous Tilmun kingdom flourished on the Island of Bahrain. The Amorite Dynasty of Tilmun would eventually cement the economic and political power it amassed as a Gulf trade-intermediary by constructing temples and a grand royal cemetery. Babylonia continued to trade with the Gulf, but many centuries would pass before the intensity of exchanges would return to the level they enjoyed at the end of the third millennium BC, the high point of commercial and cultural contacts between the east and west within that geographical region.

Appendix 1

The Ur III and Isin Texts Bearing on the Gulf Trade

In this appendix, we present the most important economic sources dealing with the commercial exchanges between Babylonia and the Gulf region (Makkan and Tilmun) during the Ur III and Isin-Larsa periods. Texts 1–9 concern Makkan; texts 10–14 deal with Tilmun. This selection is by no means exhaustive. For other relevant sources, see the main part of this book, as well as chaps. 8 and 9 and Appendixes 2 and 3. For textual data bearing on Makkan, see in particular Appendix 2. The sources pertaining to Meluhha are extensively discussed in chap. 9.

Text 1 (UET 3 299). Ur. Šulgi 28/iv.

1) [1?] ⌜x⌝-im kug-sig$_{17}$
2) lugal Ma$_2$-gan^{ki}
3) mu-DU
4) ki Šu-gu-bu-um-ta
5) Inim-gi-na
6) šu ba-ti
7) iti šu-numun-na
8) mu en ^{d}En-ki ba-hun

1) [1?] ⌜. . .⌝ of gold
2) the king of Makkan
3) delivered.
4) From Šu-Kubum
5) Inim-gina
6) received it.
7–8) Date.

The record of a gold object delivered, probably as a gift, by the unnamed king of Makkan. Unfortunately, the name of the object cannot be restored. It appears that it had been received by Šu-kubum, who then passed it on to Inim-gina.

This mention of the king of Makkan is completely unique. See above, pp. 36, 56. The date of the tablet (year Šulgi 28) is significant as well, since it comes ten years after a diplomatic marriage between Šulgi's daughter and the ruler of Marhaši had been concluded (year-formula Šulgi 18), and two years before a similar union with Anšan took place (year-formula Šulgi 30). It is highly likely, therefore, that the gift in question was sent to Ur in connection with Šulgi's diplomatic offensive in the Gulf, which aimed to bring this whole region into the orbit of Babylonia's influence.

It is remarkable that the ruler of Makkan is identified here as "king" (lugal), which is an obvious indication of his (and of Makkan's) political importance. In the Ur III period, the only other foreign ruler explicitly given such a recognition was the king of Mari (Frayne RIME 3/2 86 Ur-Namma 52). Note, however, that the daughters of Šulgi mentioned in the year-formulae Šulgi 18 and 30 were elevated to queenship ((nam-)nin), which implies that their husbands had the status of kings. For the year-formula Šulgi 30, see the variants found in UET 3 300 and NABU 2014:10.

That the date-formula appearing in the present text is Šulgi 28 (rather than Amar-Suen 8) is assured by the tablet's early Ur III script and shape, and its connection with UET III 302 (Šulgi 30/xii), 368 (Šulgi 26/ii), and NABU 2001:7. Showing the same script and shape, the latter sources likewise deal with metals and name the same recipient (Inim-gina). The issuing party acting in the present text (Šu-Kubum) possibly appears also in UET 3 773:3 (Šulgi 34/ix).

Text 2 (MVN 7 407). Girsu/Lagaš. Gudea "15."

1) 240 $^{\text{tug}_2}$bar-dul$_5$
2) 80 $^{\text{tug}_2}$aktum
3) 156 $^{\text{tug}_2}$nig$_2$-lam uš-bar
4) 60 $^{\text{tug}_2}$nig$_2$-lam us$_2$
5) Ma$_2$-gan^{ki}-še$_3$
6) Lugal-inim-dug$_3$-ra
7) sag nig$_2$-gur$_{11}$-ra-ka ba-na-gar
8) zi-ga
9) ^{d}Šara$_2$-i$_3$-šag$_5$
10) mu E$_2$-ba-gara$_2$ ba-du$_3$-a

A record of 536 garments sent to Makkan. The garments were assigned to the account of a certain Lugal-inimdug, who may have been responsible for their transportation. The issuing party was Šara-išag.

Text 3 (ITT 5 6806). Girsu/Lagaš. Undated.

1) 240 $^{\text{tug}_2}$guz-za us$_2$
2) Ma$_2$-gan^{ki}-še$_3$
3) gir$_3$ Lam-lam-ma
4) dumu Lugal-ra
5) 60 $^{\text{tug}_2}$guz-za us$_2$
6) Ad-da-mu
7) dumu sanga ^{d}Nin-gir$_2$-su-ka

8) zi-ga
9) Ba-zi-ge

A record of 300 garments sent to Makkan. The garments came from two different sources. The issuing party was Bazige. On the basis of the attestations of Bazige (see Steinkeller 1988: 48), the tablet dates either to the reign or Gudea or the beginning of Šulgi's reign.

Text 4 (MVN 6 437). Girsu/Lagaš. Undated.

1) 480 ^{tug_2}guz-za
2) Ma$_2$-gan^{ki}-še$_3$
3) gir$_3$ Ur-e$_2$-gal
4) zi-ga
5) Ba-zi-ge

A record of 480 garments sent to Makkan. The garments were supplied by a certain Ur-egal. The issuing party was Bazige. On the basis of the attestations of Bazige (see Steinkeller 1988: 48), the tablet dates either to the reign or Gudea or the beginning of Šulgi's reign.

Text 5 (UET 3 1511). Ur. Ibbi-Suen 2/i.

1) 60 gu$_2$ siki gir$_x$(GI)
2) 10 gu$_2$ ^{u_2}nin$_9$
3) 20 gu$_2$ peš-mu[rgu$_2$]
4) é-kišib-ba-ta
5) 70 ^{tug_2}uš-bar
6) ki Ur-^{d}Šul-gi-ta
7) 6.0.0 i$_3$-giš dug$_3$-ga gur
8) ki Lugal-gaba-ta
9) 180 kuš-[. . .]
10) ki Ur-^{d}Šul-pa-e$_3$-ta
11) e$_2$ ^{d}Nanna-ta
12) nig$_2$-sam$_2$-ma uruda-še$_3$
13) Lu$_2$-^{d}En-lil$_2$-la$_2$
14) šu ba-an-ti
15) gir$_3$ Li-bur-be-li$_2$ l[u$_2$-na]
16) iti-še-sag$_{11}$-kud
17) mu us$_2$-sa ^{d}I-bi$_2$-^{d}Suen lugal
18) kišib Li-bur-be-li$_2$ pisan nig$_2$-sam$_2$-ma
19) ma$_2$-a gar-ra Ma$_2$-gan^{ki}-ka i$_3$-gal$_2$

1) 60 talents (= 3,600 minas) of "Sumerian" wool,
2) 10 talents (= 600 minas) of alfalfa grass,
3) (and) 20 talents (= 1,200 minas) of date palm fronds
4) from the warehouse;

5) 70 "weaver" garments
6) from Ur-Šulgi;
7) 6 bushels of fine (aromatic) sesame oil
8) from Lugal-gaba;
9) 180 leather [. . .]
10) from Ur-Šulpae;
11) (these goods came) from the household of the god Nanna
12) as the merchandise (to buy) copper.
13) Lu-Enlila
14) received it.
15) Via Libur-beli, [his] man.
16–17) Date
18–19) The receipt tablet of Libur-beli has been deposited in the basket (of the records of the expenditures) of the merchandise
20) loaded on the boats of Makkan.

A record of wool, garments, sesame oil, alfalfa grass, date palm fronds, and unknown leather objects (probably hides) shipped to Makkan as merchandise to buy copper. All the materials came from the household of the god Nanna at Ur. The alfalfa grass, date palm fronds, and hides were probably used as packing materials. The recipient was Lu-Enlila, the head of the central "foreign trade" organization, for whom see above, p. 58, and below Texts 6 and 9.

Line 7. For the designation dug_3-ga of various oils, see Brunke and Sallaberger 2010: 52–58, who show that this term refers to the addition of aromatic substances to the oil, which they call the *Aromatisierungsprozess*. In this connection, they discuss the text UET 3 1017 (Šu-Suen 7), which lists aromatic oils of various grades, qualified by the expression giš a-ra_2 n (from 6 to 1), in a descending order. The lowest grade of oil listed there is i_3-giš dug_3-ga i_3 Ma_2-gan^{ki}, which Brunke and Sallaberger (2010: 54) take to mean "'Magan-Öl,' was wohl den Zusatz einer aus Magan stammenden Ölmischung bedeutet." But this cannot be right, since, as shown by the present text, this type of oil was *exported* to Makkan! Therefore, in UET 3 1017 i_3 Ma_2-gan^{ki} means "oil (meant for) Makkan." Interestingly, this export represented the lowest quality of aromatic oil produced in Babylonia.

Text 6 (UET 3 1689). Ur. Ibbi-Suen 4.

1) 300 ⌜tug₂⌝guz-za
2) 300 ᵗᵘᵍ²sag-uš-bar
3) 300 ᵗᵘᵍ²uš-bar
4) ki Ur-ᵈŠul-gi-ra-ta
5) ⅔ gu_2 siki gir_x(GI)
6) e_2-kišib-ba-ta
7) nig_2-sam_2-ma uruda Ma_2-gan^{ki}
8) e_2 ᵈNanna-[ka-ta?]
9) ki Da-a-a sabra-ta
10) Lu_2-ᵈEn-lil_2-la_2

11)   šu ba-an-ti
12)   iti-še-sag₁₁-kud
13)   mu Ibbi-Suen 4 (signs not copied)

1)   330 guza garments,
2)   300 first-class "weaver" garments,
3)   (and) 300 "weaver" garments
4)   from Ur-Šulgira;
5)   40 minas of "Sumerian" wool
6)   from the warehouse;
7)   this is the merchandise (to buy) Makkan copper.
8)   From the household of the god Nanna,
9)   from Daʾaya, the majordomo,
10)   Lu-Enlila
11)   received.

A record of garments and wool sent to Makkan as merchandise to buy copper. The garments and wool came from the household of the god Nanna at Ur. The recipient was Lu-Enlila, the head of the central "foreign trade" organization, for whom see above, p. 58, and below Texts 5 and 9.

As copied, the numbers in lines 1, 2, and 3 are 5×60 (rather than 5×1).

Text 7 (UET 3 1193 + photographs in CDLI P137518). Ur. Date not preserved (probably Ibbi-Suen's reign). Only first two columns are transliterated here).

obv. i   (begining destroyed)
1′)   [. . .] ⌜i₃⌝-giš dug₃-ga
2′)   [ki] Nam-zi-tar-ra dub-sar-ta
3′)   [x] gu₂ siki gir$_x$(GI)
4′)   [ki] ^{d}Nanna-i₃-šag₅ SAHAR-ta
5′)   [x] ^{tug_2}guz-za gin
6′)   [x] ^{tug_2}sag-uš-bar
7′)   [. . .] PA ZI ⌜. . .⌝
       (rest destroyed)
ii   (beginning destroyed)
1′)   [ki] ^{d}Nanna-i₃-šag₅-ta
       (double line)
2′)   kišib Ur-^{d}Nanše
3′)   Ma₂-gan^{ki} gu-la-kam
4′)   60.0.0 še gu[r]
5′)   ki Arad₂-⌜^{d}⌝[Nanna dub-sar zag-10-ta]
6′)   1(or 60) [. . .]
       (rest destroyed)
rev. i   (beginning destroyed)
1′)   103.0.0 še gur

2')   1.2.0 bappir gin gur
3')   [x]+5 ^{tug_2}sag-uš-bar
4')   [k]i Arad$_2$-^{d}Nanna dub-sar-zag-10-ta
5')   [x]+⌜20⌝ še gur
6')   [ki Ur?]-^{d}Nin-giš-zi-da dub-sar-ta
7')   [x] še gur
       (rest destroyed)
ii   (beginning destroyed)
1')   [x] 5⅔ sila$_3$ i$_3$-dug$_3$-ga gur
2')   [ki Nam-zi]-tar-ra dub-sar-ta
3')   [x] ^{tug_2}guz-za gin
4')   [x] ^{tug_2}sag-uš-bar
5')   [ki x-^{d}Šul]-gi-ra dub-sar-ta
6')   [x]+20 ma-na siki gi[r$_x$(GI)]
7')   [ki ^{d}Nanna]-i$_3$-šag$_5$ SAHAR-ta
       (rest destroyed)

A fragmentarily preserved record of the merchandise destined for "Greater Makkan." For a discussion of this designation, see above, p. 34. The sequence of the obverse and reverse is uncertain; provisionally, we follow the editor's description (UET 3 1193). If one follows this solution, the sections of the text that assuredly deal with Makkan are column i and column ii of the obverse, down to the statement: "these are the receipts of Ur-Nanše concerning (lit., of) Greater Makkan" (kišib Ur-^{d}Nanše Ma$_2$-gan^{ki} gu-la-kam, lines 2'–3'). These sections mention perfumed oil, garments, and wool. It is likely that the reverse, which names some of the same issuing parties and mentions, apart from perfumed oil, garments, and wool, also large volumes of barley and a quantity of "ordinary 'beer' bread" (bappir gin), also concerns shipments to Makkan. This possibility is even more likely if the obverse-reverse sequence is reversed.

Text 8 (ITT 2 776). Girsu/Lagaš. Šu-Suen 8/xi.

1)   600.0.0 še gur
2)   gu$_2$ Ma$_2$-gan^{ki}-še$_3$
3)   ki ensi$_2$ Gir$_2$-su^{ki}-ta
4)   Pu$_3$-u$_2$-du
5)   šu ba-ti
6)   kišib Ur-^{gi6}gipar$_x$(KISAL)
7)   dumu Šu-na-ka
8)   i$_3$-dub A-šag$_4$-NI-zi-na
9)   iti-še-sag$_{11}$-kud
10)   mu ^{d}Šu-^{d}Suen lugal Urim$_2^{ki}$-ma-ke$_4$ ma$_2$-gur$_8$ mah ^{d}En-lil$_2$ ^{d}Nin-lil$_2$-ra mu-ne-du$_8$

1)   600 bushels of barley,
2)   the delivery for Makkan,
3)   from the governor of Girsu

4) Pu'udu
5) received.
6) Sealed/received by Ur-gipar,
7) son of Šuna.
8) (The barley came from) the granary of the field NI-zi-na.
9–10) Date.

The head of the central "foreign trade organization" Pu'udu receives 600 bushels of barley as a shipment for Makkan. For Pu'udu, see above, p. 58. The barley was supplied by the governor of Girsu/Lagaš. The person in question can be identified as Aradmu (aka Arad-Nanna), who also held the position of the chancellor (sukkal-mah) of the realm. He also acts as the supplier of barley in Text 9.

Text 9 (TCTI 2 2768, tablet and envelope). Girsu/Lagaš. Ibbi-Suen 3/-.

1) 1,800.0.0 še gur
2) numun gub-ba Ma$_2$-gan-na
3) ki ensi$_2$ Gir$_2$-su^{ki}-ta
4) Lu$_2$-^{d}En-lil$_2$-la$_2$
5) šu ba-ti
6) mu Lu$_2$-^{d}En-lil$_2$-la$_2$-še$_3$
7) kišib Ur-sukal dumu Lugal-m[ug]
8) gur-bi su-su-dam
9) mu Si-mu-ru-um^{ki} ba-hul
    Seal: Ur-kisal / dub-sar / dumu lugal-mug

1) 1,800 bushels of barley,
2) the "seed" designated for Makkan,
3) from the governor of Girsu
4) Lu-Enlila
5) received.
6) In place of Lu-Enlila
7) sealed by Ur-sukal, son of Lugal-mug.
8) The gur (measuring containers) (which came with the barley) are to be returned.
9) Date.
    Seal of Ur-kisal, scribe, son of Lugal-mug.

A record of 1,800 bushels of barley, supplied by the governor of Girsu/Lagaš as a shipment for Makkan. The recipient of the barley was Lu-Enlila, the head of the central "foreign trade" organization, for whom see above, p. 58, and above Texts 5 and 6.

As in Text 8, the supplier of barley can be identified as Aradmu (aka Arad-Nanna), who, apart from having served as the governor of Girsu/Lagaš, also held the position of the chancellor (sukkal-mah) of the realm.

Line 2. As K. Maekawa informs me in a personal communication, the term numun gub-ba occurs also in the Ur III tablet PPAC 5 1285:2, 8, 10 (from Girsu/Lagaš), as well as in the lexical series Proto-Lu line 816 (= MSL 12 63). In PPAC 5 1285, numun gub-ba designates large volumes of dried bitumen (60, 30, and 50 bushels of esir$_2$ had$_2$), which was loaded on individual ships. This suggests that, rather than referring specifically to "seed," numun gub-ba is a generic commercial term for "cargo" or "boat shipment."

Text 10 (UET 3 1507). Ur. Ibbi-Suen 1/vi/14.

1) 10 gu$_2$ siki hi-a gin
2) siki tug$_2$ mu-tag-ta
3) ma$_2$-a gar-ra Dilmun^{ki}-še$_3$
4) Ur-GUR?
5) lu$_2$ ma$_2$-gal-[gal(-ke$_4$)]
6) šu ba-an-ti
7) iti ezen-^{d}Nin-a-zu ud 14-kam
8) mu Ibbi-Suen 1 (signs not copied)
9) [gir$_3$?] ^{d}Nanna-an-d[ul$_2$] dub-sar

1) 10 talents (= 600 minas) of various wool of ordinary quality,
2) the wool left from garment production,
3) was loaded on a boat (traveling) to Tilmun.
4) Ur-GUR(?), the man of "big ships,"
5) received it.
7–8) Date.
9) [Via?] Nanna-andul, the scribe.

A record of wool shipped to Tilmun. The recipient was a "big ship" commander named Ur-GUR(?).

Text 11 (BIN 10 129). Isin. Išbi-Erra "19"/vi/7. Collated.

1) 0.2.3 esir$_2$-e$_2$-a
2) ma$_2$ Dilmun^{ki} gu-la ba-an-gar
3) gir$_3$ Lu$_2$-bala-šag$_5$-ga
4) 0.3.0 esir$_2$-e$_2$-a
5) dag-ši-ru-um
6) ma$_2$ gu-la lugal
7) gir$_3$ Šu-la-num$_2$ ma$_2$-lah$_4$
8) sukkal-mah maškim
9) ki Šu-^{d}Nin-kar-ak-ta
10) ba-zi ud 7-kam
11) iti kin-Inana
12) mu Bad$_3$⟨-^{d}Iš-bi-Er$_3$-ra-⟩ri-im-^{d}En-lil$_2$ ba-du$_3$
Seal: Bu-ku-šum / dub-sar / dumu A-bu-bu

1) 150 liters of refined bitumen
2) were applied to the big ship of Tilmun,

3)   via Lu-balašaga;

4)   180 liters of refined bitumen

5)   (were used for) the repairs of

6)   a large royal ship,

7)   via Šulanum, the sailor.

8)   The chancellor was the requsitioner (of the bitumen)

9)   Issued by Šu-Ninkarak.

10–12) Date.

      Seal of Bukušum, scribe, son of Abubu.

A record of two expenditures of bitumen, for the work on a "Tilmun ship" and the repairs of a royal ship respectively. The recipient of the first expenditure, Lu-balašaga, is identified elsewhere as a lu$_2$-ma$_2$-gal-gal (BIN 10 137:4; spelled ⟨Lu$_2$-⟩bala-šag$_5$-ga; collated), dating to year Išbi-Erra "22"/iv. He receives there bitumen for a ship (gir$_3$ ma$_2$ GIŠGAL/UTU-la^{ki}-še$_3$ ba-an-gar, meaning unclear; cf. ma$_2$ GIŠGAL-la-GA?-še$_3$ in BIN 10 135:5). The same Lu-balašaga probably appears also in BIN 9 263:3 (collated), from Išbi-Erra "22"/ii, where he is qualified simply as ma$_2$, "ship." Because of his title, Lu-balašaga must have been the skipper of the ship in question. Accordingly, the "Tilmun ship" was a native Babylonian vessel that was used to sail to Tilmun.

Text 12 (BIN 9 403 = BIN 9 404). Isin. Išbi-Erra "19"/vi/20. Collated.

1)   1 ^{kuš}dug$_3$-gan tug$_2$

2)   kuš udu-bi 2

3)   2 dug-šagan 0.0.1-ta

4)   kuš udu u$_2$-hab$_2$-bi

5)   ka-tab u$_3$ sagšu-bi-še$_3$

6)   zag-bar-ta

7)   nig$_2$-šu-taka$_4$-a

8)   Dilmun^{ki}-še$_3$

9)   gir$_3$ Lugal-iti-da dam-gar$_3$

10)   ki Šu-^{d}Nin-kar-ak-ta

11)   ba-zi

12)   iti kin-^{d}Inana

13)   mu Bad$_3$-^{d}Iš-bi-Er$_3$-ra-ri-im-^{d}En-lil$_2$ ba-du$_3$

14)   ud 20-kam

1)   1 leather bag for garments,

2)   its sheep skins are two;

3)   2 šagan jars (of the capacity of) 10 liters each,

4)   the red-tanned sheep skins

5)   (used to make) their stoppers and the covers

6)   (came) from the scraps;

7)   (to be used) for the gift of

8) Tilmun.
9) Via Lugal-itida, the merchant.
10–11) Issued by Šu-Ninkarak.
12–14. Date.

The expenditure of a leather bag and two jars, which served as containers for the "gift" sent to Tilmun. The goods in question must have been garments and probably oil. The recipient of the containers was the merchant Lugal-itida, who, it appears, was responsible for the transport of the "gift" to Tilmun. The expenditure was made by Šu-Ninkarak.

Line 1. dug$_3$-gan tug$_2$ denotes a leather bag (Akk. *tukkannum*) for garments. See dug$_3$-gan tug$_2$ 1, "cloth-bag for 1 garment," appearing in an Isin tablet (Ferwerda 1985: no. 18:23). Against Ferwerda 1985: 33, in this context, the numeral 1 does not mean 1 sìla (liter) capacity. Note that in the Umma examples cited by Ferwerda (ibid.) in support of his interpretation, the sign sila$_3$ is specified, as is required by the metrological convention.

Text 13 (BIN 9 391). Isin. Išbi-Erra "27"/iii/24. Collated.

1) 1 ^{kuš}ummud(A.EDEN.L[A$_2$])
2) kuš siki uz$_3$-bi [1?]
3) kaskal Bar-zi-[pa^{ki}-še$_3$]
4) Lu-lu-ba-ni [mašk]im
5) ⌜Puzur$_4$-^{d}En⌝-[lil$_2$ mašk]im
6) 2 dug-šagan [. . .]
7) kuš udu u$_2$-hab$_2$-bi 1 [ka-tab] u$_3$ sa[gšu-še$_3$]
8) 1 gi-gur tug$_2$ [(. . .)]
9) kuš udu-bi 1 [ba-a]-si
10) 20 gi-gur [tug$_2$ ga]l? [x] sila$_3$
11) esir$_2$-⌜e$_2$-a⌝-bi 4 sila$_3$
12) ba-ab-tag
13) kuš udu u$_2$-hab$_2$-bi 5 ka-ba ba-a-si
14) 12 dug 0.0.3-ta ^{giš}hašhur-a ba-an-si
15) kuš udu babbar-bi 2 ka-tab-še$_3$
16) 2 dug 0.0.1-ta
17) kuš udu u$_2$-hab$_2$-bi ⅔ ka-tab
18) bil$_2$-ga u$_3$ ha-al us$_2$-sa
19) 2 kuš A.LUM babbar
20) šim-ku-ru ba-an-si
21) nig$_2$-šu-taka$_4$-a lugal
22) Tilmun^{ki}-še$_3$
23) gir$_3$ Eš$_3$-he$_2$-gal$_2$ lu$_2$ ma$_2$-gal-gal
24) Puzur$_4$-^{d}En-lil$_2$ maškim
25) ki Lu$_2$-^{d}En-ki-ta
26) ba-zi

27) gir$_3$ Bu-ku-šum u$_3$ Lu$_2$-šag$_5$-ga
28) iti sig$_4$-a
29) mu us$_2$-sa Elam šag$_4$ Urim$_2$^{ki}-ma ba-dab$_5$
30) ud 24-kam

1) 1 waterbag,
2) its hairy goat skin is [1?],
3) [for] an expedition to Borsi[ppa],
4) Lullubani was the requsitioner,
5) Puzur-Enlil was the (second) requisitioner;
6) 2 jars [. . .],
7) the red-tanned sheep skin for their [stoppers] and covers is 1,
8) 1 basket for garments [. . .]
9) it was filled in with 1 sheep skin;
10) 20 baskets for large(?) [garments], each of the capacity of [x] liters,
11–12) they were coated with 4 liters of refined bitumen,
13) 5 red-tanned sheep skins were used to fill in their openings;
14) 12 jars of 30 liters capacity (each) were filled with apples,
15) 2 white sheep skins (were used) for their stoppers;
16) 2 jars of 10 liters (capacity) each,
17) ⅔ of a red-tanned sheep skin (was used for their) stoppers,
18) (for) fresh fruits(?) and . . .;
19) 2 long-haired white sheep-skins
20) were filled with the *kukrum* aromatic;
21) (to be used for) the royal gift for
22) Tilmun.
23) Via Eš-hegal, the man of "big ships."
24) Puzur-Enlil was the requsitioner.
25–26) Issued by Lu-Enki.
27) Via Bukušum and Lu-šaga.
28–30) Date.

The tablet records two separate expenditures: a waterbag for an expedition to Borsippa (lines 1–5) and the various containers housing the royal "gift" for Tilmun (lines 6–24). The latter items included 2 jars (probably for oil), 21 baskets for garments, 12 jars for apples, and 2 jars for fresh fruits(?), and 2 skins for the *kukrum* aromatic. The recipient of the "gift" was the man of "big ships" named Eš-hegal, who apparently was responsible for its delivery to Tilmun. The transaction was authorized by Puzur-Enlil. The issuing party was Lu-Enki.

Line 18. The meaning of this line is obscure. The term bil$_2$-ga probably means "fresh fruit." See, especially, ma$_2$ mun-gazi u$_3$ bil$_2$-ga, "ship (loaded with) condiments and fresh fruits" (MVN 3 362:5–6), and the Ur III examples of leather stoppers/wrapping (ka-tab) for bil$_2$/bil$_3$-ga cited in Ferwerda 1985: 44. bil$_2$-ga also appears in the Isin tablet Ferwerda 1985: no. 27:6, which is a listing of various foodstuffs. See further PSD B 153.

Line 20. šim-ku-ru apparently stands for *kukrum*, a type of aromatic. See CAD K 500–501; Steinkeller and Postgate 1992: 79.

Text 14 (BIN 9 405). Isin. Šu-ilišu 2/ii/14. Collated.

1) 1 ^{kuš}dug$_3$-gan tug$_2$
2) kuš udu u$_2$-hab$_2$-bi 2
3) 1 dug-šagan 5 sila$_3$
4) 5 dug-šagan i$_3$-dug$_3$-ga
5) kuš udu babbar-bi 1 ka-tab-še$_3$
6) nig$_2$-šu-taka$_4$ Tilmun^{ki}
7) u$_3$ Mar-tu-ne
   (space)
8) ki ^{d}Iš-bi-Er$_3$-ra-zi-kalam-ma-ta
9) ba-zi
10) iti gud-si-su ud 14-kam
11) mu ^{d}Šu-i$_3$-li$_2$-šu lugal-e ^{giš}šu-nir ^{d}Nanna
12) ud 14-kam

1) 1 leather bag for garments,
2) its red-tanned sheep skins are 2,
3) 1 jar of 5 liters (capacity),
4) 5 jars of fine (aromatic) oil,
5) the white sheep skin for their stoppers is 1;
6) (to be used) for the gift(s) of Tilmun
7) and of the Amorites.
8–9) Issued by Išbi-Erra-zikalama.
10–12) Date.

The expenditure of a leather cloth-bag and six jars, which served as containers for the "gift(s)" sent to Tilmun and the Amorites. The jars were filled with fine oil. It is somewhat unclear if one or more "gifts" are meant. Since the Isin texts routinely record gifts for the Amorites, two unrelated shipments may have been involved: one for Tilmun and another one for the Amorites. Since, however, there was a strong Amorite presence at Tilmun at that time (see above, pp. 54–56, 60–62), a possibility exists that it was in fact a single shipment whose destination was Tilmun. The small quantity of merchandise involved may favor this possibility.

Appendix 2

The Seaworthy Ships of Babylonia, the "Makkan Ships," and the Cylinder Seals of the "Big Ships" Personnel from Failaka and Bahrain

1. Big Ships and Big Ship Captains

In the third-millennium documentation, the ships used to venture into the Gulf are consistently described by the term ma_2-gal-gal, "big ship." This term appears to be a specific designation of the seaworthy ship, as distinct from ma_2, "ship, boat," and ma_2-gur_8, "barge."[1] The earliest attestations of ma_2-gal-gal come from the pre-Sargonic sources from Lagaš,[2] which attest to the existence in that city-state of a military organization attached to "big ships" controlled by an official titled gal-uku_3 ma_2-gal-gal. Two sources (Nikolski 1 12 i 3; 306 i 33; date not preserved in either instance) record, respectively, 43 and 33 (lu_2) ma_2-gal-gal, who remained under the command of a gal-uku_3 named Ur-[d]Nin-mar[ki].[3] The locus of this organization was the seaport of Gu'abba = E-Ninmar (for which see in detail chap. 8). This point is assured by another Lagaš tablet (Nikolski 1 164; Lugalanda 6), where the aforementioned Ur-[d]Nin-mar[ki] sends a number of sheep to E-Nimar (which is Gu'abba's alternative designation). Ur-Ninmar's connection with Gu'abba is additionally indicated by his name, which invokes [d]Nin-mar[ki], Gu'abba's chief deity (see chap. 8).[4]

The connection between the ma_2-gal-gal and sea travel is also made explicit in a Sargonic tablet from Adab that records an expenditure of 3 jars of oil, each having a capacity of 4 liters, to a commander of "big ships" (ugula ma_2-gal-gal) as part of a trip to the sea.[5] Our most extensive evidence on such ships, however, comes from the Ur III documentation. Most importantly, we read there of

1. Zarins (2008: 215) thinks that the so-called "Makkan" ships (for which below) are often labeled ma_2-gur_8, but this is incorrect. The ma_2-gur_8 boats were flat river barges, which would have been completely unsuited for sea travel.

2. But note that the designation lu_2 ma_2-gal-gal, "man of big ship," is documented already in the ED IIIa sources from Šuruppak (modern Fara). See, e.g., WF 62 v 4, 67 ii 7, 68 ii 4, 69 ii 4, etc.

3. In both texts, these individuals are listed together with caulkers (ma_2-GIN_2), barge operators (lú-ma_2-gur_8(-ra)-me), fishermen, carpenters, and reed-workers.

4. Ur-Nimar is likely referred to in two other Lagaš sources, which mention the wife of an unnamed gal-uku_3 ma_2-gal-gal (DP 133 x 3–4; Urukagina 1; TSA 5 rev. ii' 6–7; Urukagina 2).

5. 3 i_3 dug 4 $sila_3$ Ur-[d]Utu ugula ma_2-gal-gal-ʼlaʼ ʼaʼ-ab-$še_3$ [m]u-na-[sum?] (Yang 1986: 395 A 1067:1–5).

104

a whole flotilla of the ma$_2$-gal-gal that belonged to the state organization in charge of foreign trade (see Steinkeller 2013a: 417–18; also above, pp. 57–58). Included among the employees of that organization, which was supervised by the merchant Pu'udu and other members of his family, were eight captains (nu-banda$_3$) of "big ships," as well as six "officers of 60 men (each)," with an estimated number of seamen under Pu'udu's command being at least 360.

"Big ship" captains, designated as nu-banda$_3$ or ugula, are mentioned in many other Ur III sources. Characteristically, all of these references come from Girsu/Lagaš, thus confirming that this province, more specifically, the city of Gu'abba and its region, was the embarkation point for seafaring in the Gulf. One such official was Ur-GAR, a nu-banda$_3$ ma$_2$-gal-gal,[6] who, in year Šulgi 33, is documented to have received barley for a crew numbering 120 men.[7] This expenditure, which was made in Gu'abba on behalf of the crown, may have been connected with the military operations against Anšan, which took place in years Šulgi 33 and 34. As we discussed in chap. 8 (p. 75 n. 22), the campaigns in question involved the transportation of troops on ships between Makkan and Anšan.

Another commander of "big ships" was Šar-ili, a subordinate of the chancellor, who was involved in the transportation of sesame,[8] apparently from the Susiana region.[9] If this indeed was the case, Šar-ili's ships followed the standard route between Babylonia and Susa, which started at Gu'abba, continuing then along the coast to the mouth of the Karun, and over the Karun into the Susiana region (see chap. 8). In another instance (MVN 6 166; Š 34/vii), the same Šar-ili authorized an expenditure of barley allotments for 60 men of "big ships," who transported the "delivery/tribute" of Sabum (situated northest of Susa).[10] It is possible that the delivery in question consisted of sesame as well. The actual recipient of the allotments was Šar-ili's subordinate and a sea captain named Ur-lugal, son of Ur-GAR (likely the same Ur-GAR as the captain of "big ships" discussed earlier).

Among other examples of the designations lu$_2$ ma$_2$-gal-gal and ugula ma$_2$-gal-gal, of special interest are the ones appearing on the cylinder seals found in Failaka and Bahrain, dating to the Ur III and Early Old Babylonian periods, which we discuss at the end of this appendix. A lu$_2$ ma$_2$-gal-gal, named

6. The same individual, here called simply lu$_2$ ma$_2$-gal-gal, presented *ex voto* (a-ru-a) a grinding stone to the temple of Bau (RA 66 27 ii 20–21; Š 47/ii). There survive various other records of votive gifts made by the lu$_2$ ma$_2$-gal-gal. For example, according to MVN 2 176 iv 16–19, a captain of "big ships" and a native of Gu'abba named Lugal-melam was a donor of a certain Zankaka, who, judging from her name, was a foreigner (Za-an-ka-ka a-ru-a Lugal-me-lam$_2$ nu-banda$_3$ ma$_2$-gal-gal Gu$_2$-ab-ba^{ki}-ta).

7. 120 guruš 1.0.0 še gur lugal-ta še-bi 120.0.0 gur lu$_2$ ma$_2$-gal-gal ki Ur-^{d}Lama ka-guru$_7$-ta Ur-GAR dumu Ur-nigar$_x^{gar}$ šu ba-ti zi-ga lugal sanga ^{d}Nin-mar^{ki} maškim; seal of Ur-GAR / nu-banda$_3$ ma$_2$-gal-gal / dumu Ur-nigar$_x^{gar}$ (MVN 6 201:1–8; Š 33/-). The granary superintendent Ur-Lama is otherwise attested as ka-guru$_7$ Gu$_2$-ab-ba^{ki} (ASJ 2 19 56:36; Š 32/-; MVN 7 420:5; Š 34/ix) and ka-guru$_7$ ^{d}Nin-mar^{ki}-ka (MVN 6 216 seal; Š 33/xii).

8. In a number of sources, Šar-ili conscripts men to serve as the crew of "sesame boats" (ma$_2$ še-giš-i$_3$). See TLB 3 145 ii 6–7 (Š 34/v–35/ii) and 146 ii 17–19 (Š 34/v–35/ii), where Šar-ili conscripts 6(?) and 11 men respectively, to serve for 70 days on ships carrying sesame. MVN 7 542 (undated) places the same Šar-ili in charge of 45 sailors, 90 fishermen, 11(?) men of "big ships," and 130 regular conscripts, the crew for an "expedition of sesame (transporting) ship(s)" (gir$_3$ ma$_2$ še-giš-i$_3$-ka). His another attestation is MVN 7 587:7 (Š 32/x), where he authorizes an expenditure of 68 bushels of barley for the men of "big ships."

9. There survive numerous references to the transportation of sesame from the Susiana region, where sesame is known to have been cultivated. See Maekawa 2016.

10. 60 guruš 0.1.0 še-ta še-bi 12.0.0 gur lugal lu$_2$ ma$_2$-gal-gal nig$_2$ gun$_2$-na Sa-bu-um-ma^{ki} zi-zi-me ki Ur-^{d}Lama Ur-lugal ugula šu ba-ti; seal of Ur-lugal / nu-banda$_3$ / dumu Ur-GAR (MVN 6 166:1–7; Š 34/vii). For Ur-Lama, see MVN 6 201:4 cited above, n. 7.

Ur-GUR?, appears in a tablet from Ur dating to year Ibbi-Suen 1 (Appendix 1 Text 10:4–5). Importantly, the tablet in question concerns a shipment of merchandise to Tilmun. Two other lu$_2$ ma$_2$-gal-gal, named Lu-balašaga and Eš-hegal, respectively, appear in the sources from the reign of Išbi-Erra of Isin (Appendix 1 Text 11:3, Text 13:23). These documents also concern trade with Tilmun.

As far as we know, the latest attestation of either term is found in an Ur tablet from the reign of Išme-Dagan of Isin (UET 5 279) that records votive gifts (a-ru-a) that were presented to the temple of Ningal by a lu$_2$ ma$_2$-gal-gal named Awel-Sin. These gifts included, apart from a silver ornament, carnelian beads (na$_4$ ellag$_2$ gug), pearls (na$_4$ igi-ku$_6$), and toggle pins made of ivory (tu-di-da zu$_2$-am-si).[11]

As demonstrated by the archaeological data as well, the age of the "big ships" and the long-distance exploration of the Gulf came to its end sometime in Old Babylonian times. A reflection of this glorious experience is preserved in the Sumerian myth "Enki and Ninhursag." Composed (or at least heavily revised) in the early Old Babylonian period, this composition contains a praise of Tilmun, identifying it as an emporium of the Gulf. There, the land of Meluhha and the city of Ur are implored to direct to Tilmun's shores their "big ships," loaded with their specific exports (ma$_2$-gal-gal ha-mu-ra-ab-sa$_2$, lines 49C, 49O).

2. Ships of Makkan

A number of Ur III sources, all from Girsu,[12] use the term ma$_2$ Ma$_2$-gan, "ship of Makkan." Most of these examples involve the professional designation ma$_2$-GIN$_2$ ma$_2$ Ma$_2$-gan$^{(ki)}$, "caulker of Makkan boats," usually abbreviated as ma$_2$-GIN$_2$ Ma$_2$-gan$^{(ki)}$,[13] which describes a category of workers employed by the Girsu/Lagaš shipyards. The remaining attestations concern an expenditure of bitumen for a "Makkan ship" (MTBM 322), an individual assigned to a "Makkan ship" (MVN 17 131:8), expenditures of foodstuffs intended as offerings (sizkur$_2$) of "Makkan ships" (probably made for the intention of their safe return) (CUSAS 16 115; HLC 2 23 iv 5–10), and a caulking operation conducted on "Makkan ships"[14] (CT 7 31 BM 18390).

Although this term undoubtedly describes a seafaring ship (thus paralleling ma$_2$-gal-gal discussed earlier), there are no grounds to think that the ships so designated were native Makkanite vessels. As we argued in detail earlier (see above, p. 57), with the possible exception of the very beginning of the Ur III period, when Gulf-based ships could have conceivably come to Babylonian shores, we lack any evidence whatsoever of Makkanite merchants visiting Babylonia in Ur III times. We must

---

11. Cf. Oppenheim 1954: 7–8.

12. The only exception here is MVN 16 1472, from Umma, which mentions four foresters who, during a period of 90 days, were cutting (lit., striking) timber for a "Makkan ship" (giš ma$_2$ Ma$_2$-gan-na sig$_3$-ga).

13. As a matter of fact, the full spelling is attested only once, in Fs Pettinato 128: 10:12: 2 men ma$_2$-GIN$_2$ Ma$_2$-gan-⸢na⸣-me.

14. ma$_2$ Ma$_2$-gan du$_8$-de$_3$, "to caulk the 'Makkan ships'" (not "for building (constructing) the Magan ships(s)," as translated by Zarins 2008: 217). Although the text in question lists various other materials (such as timber, reeds, etc.), which must have been intended for ship construction, this phrase refers only to the immediately preceding expenditure of bitumen. The two procedures were thought to be practically identical, as shown by the variation between du$_8$, "to caulk," and dim$_2$ "to fashion, construct," in the formula of year Šu-Suen 2, where ma$_2$-darah-Ab-zu ^{d}En-ki in-dim$_2$ alternates with ma$_2$-darah-Ab-zu ^{d}En-ki ba-ab-du$_8$.

conclude, therefore, that what is understood by this rare designation is a Babylonian ship frequenting the Gu'abba–Makkan route or, more generally, a ship fit to be used on long-distance ventures in the Gulf.[15] Because of the large number of ships of this type that were housed at Gu'abba, there were designated caulkers who specialized in the maintenance of these particular vessels.

3. Boat Construction

Studies of ancient Mesopotamian watercraft suffer from the misconception that the Babylonians lacked timber for boat construction[16]—hence the tendency (still common in the literature) to think, even in the face of voluminous textual data demonstrating the extensive use of wooden vessels, that such watercraft was unsophisticated and rare and therefore of marginal importance, as compared with vessels made of reeds. This view, however, is completely mistaken. As we show in detail in chap. 8, in the Ur III period (and probably even much earlier), there were very extensive tree plantations in southern Babylonia that grew pines (${}^{giš}u_3$-suh$_5$) specifically for the construction of ships and other types of watercraft. Additionally, pine and other timber was obtained from the southern reaches of the Iranian plateau via the sea- and river-route connecting Gu'abba with the Susiana Region.

Ur III and earlier sources contain a wealth of information on the materials used in boat and ship construction. In particular, they mention dozens of terms describing various parts of vessels made of timber. Unfortunately, since these terms usually appear in simple listings, with little if any context about the purpose of individual parts and the mutual relationship between them, it is exceedingly difficult to identify them.[17] This difficulty is compounded by the complete absence of visual representations of Mesopotamian seafaring boats.

Among the vessel parts that can be identified with some confidence are ^{giš}gi-muš, "steering oar," and ^{giš}mi-ri$_2$-za, "punting pole,"[18] neither of which, however, says anything about the vessel construction itself. More informative in this respect is the term ^{giš}girah(ŠU.DIM$_2$).[19] It is characteristic that girah are regularly classified according to the boat's capacity. Thus, we have records of the girah for the vessels of the capacity of 20, 30, 40, 50, 60, 90, and 120 bushels (Sumerian gur), respectively.[20] These data imply that the size of the girah depended on the vessel's overall size. It is possible, therefore, that girah denotes the ribs or frames that were attached to the vessel's keel.[21]

15. For this conclusion, see already Zarins 2008: 222 n. 79; Carter 2012: 367.

16. See, e.g., Johnstone 1980: 181: "Local wood suitable for ship-building is virtually non-existent in Mesopotamia and the Arabian Gulf. Hence the dependence on reed craft or inflated skin rafts."

17. A systematic study of this terminology is yet to be undertaken. The transliterations and translations of the pertinent sources offered recently by Zarins (2008) lack philological expertise and are, therefore, highly unreliable.

18. But even in these two cases some uncertainty remains. Although ^{giš}mi-ri$_2$-za is a loanword from the Akkadian *parissum*, "punting pole," lexical sources explain *parissum* as an equivalent of ^{giš}gi-muš! See gi-muš GIŠ.GI.MUŠ = *pa-ri-s[u]* (Diri II 305 = MSL 15 130–31).

19. For the reading, see gi-ra-ah GIŠ.ŠU.DIM$_2$ = *sú-pi-in i-ti-nim* (Diri Nippur 216 = MSL 15 20–21). For *supinnum*, of uncertain meaning, see CAD S 392.

20. See, e.g., TLB 3 144, which lists the girah for the vessels of 20, 30, 40, and 60 bushel capacity. For the girah of 120-bushel vessels, see ITT 5 10011 iii 3; MVN 2 4:3; TCL 5 6037 iii 12. A girah for the boat of 90 bushels is mentioned in RTC 307 v 1.

21. The length of the girah is occasionally given. See 15 ^{giš}girah sumun gid$_2$-bi ½ nindan 2 kuš$_3$-ta (= 4 m) (ITT 3 6139:2); 30 ^{giš}u$_3$-suh$_5$ pa kud girah ma$_2$ 60.0.0 gur gid$_2$-bi 9 kuš$_3$-ta (= 4.5 m) (ITT 5 6998:1–3).

An exceedingly important datum about Ur III seafaring vessels is that stitching was used in their construction. This ancient method, which involves the binding of planks together with twine, was practiced in the Gulf region in Medieval and more modern times.[22] A positive proof of the application of this method in third-millennium Babylonia is a provided by an Ur III tablet, which records 7 pounds of thread or string made of goat hair (nig$_2$-U.NU-a siki uz$_3$),[23] which was used to tie together the boat parts named ^{giš}me-dim$_2$, $^{(giš)}$ma$_2$-gu$_2$, and a$_2$.[24] Of these, a$_2$ (ma$_2$) apparently describes the boat's "sides." Unfortunately, the exact identities of ^{giš}me-dim$_2$ and $^{(giš)}$ma$_2$-gu$_2$ are uncertain, but it is noteworthy that these two objects are common in the listings of ship parts, where they usually appear next to each other. Of special interest here is TCL 5 5673, where, in three instances, there is one ^{giš}me-dim$_2$ per four $^{(giš)}$ma$_2$-gu$_2$ (in one case, the ratio between them is 1:2).[25] The same source also indicates that there were two ^{giš}me-dim$_2$ per one boat.[26]

Goat hair does in fact often appear among the materials used in boat construction, suggesting again its use in plank stitching. Of special interest here is the earlier-cited text CT 7 31 BM 18390, a tally of the materials entrusted to the governor of Girsu/Lagaš for the construction and maintenance of the "Makkan ships." One of the items listed there is 2,688 pounds of goat hair, a huge amount by any standard. It is probably not by chance that the immediately following entry records an equally impressive 1,695 liters of fish oil. It is highly probable that this oil too was used as part of the stitching process, since a standard procedure in the traditional Omani boat building "is to seal a plank seam with a luting compound composed of fish oil and a resin called *khundrus*" (Vosmer 2011: 127; see also Agius 2002: 80). The use of the stitching method in Ur III times is additionally implicated by the references to goat-hair thread (nig$_2$-U.NU-a) as part of the construction of various vessels, among them "barges" (ma$_2$-gur$_8$) (SAT 2 741:1–3, 5–6; MVN 1 226 ii 19; BPOA 1 1254:1–3; BPOA 7 1604:4–6; Ontario 2 480:1–4; Vicino Oriente 8/1 26:8).

Although, as noted earlier, no images of Babylonian seafaring vessels survive, a good idea of what these ships must have looked like is given by the representations of sea watercraft on Tilmun seals, which date broadly to the Ur III and early Old Babylonian periods (Johnstone 1980: 176–78; Kjaerum 1991; Carter 2012: 368–69). The most common type of boat appearing there has an upright bow and stern and is masted at midships. The stern is characteristically decorated with an animal head. A sail is sometimes shown as well. As observed by Johnstone (1980: 176–77), one of these ships, on a seal from Failaka,[27] shows a remarkable resemblance to the vessel depicted in a manuscript written in Basra in AD 1237 (*Maqamat al-Hariri*; now in Bibliothèque Nationale in Paris). This is the oldest

---

22. See Johnstone 1980: 178–81; Vosmer 2011; Agius 2002; Shaikh, Tripati, and Shinde 2012: 148–57.

23. The nig$_2$-U.NU-a thread was usually made from goat hair (siki uz$_3$) or, less often, poor quality wool (see siki mug in AAICAB 1/1 Ashm. 1924-0675 ii 3 and siki gir$_x$(GI) peš$_x$(ŠU.PEŠ$_5$)-a in MVN 1 226 ii 9–11). Early OB texts from Isin also mention, often together with the goat-hair thread, nig$_2$-U.NU-a zi/ze$_2$-ba-tum (BIN 9 139 143:1, etc.), which possibly was made from the wool of sheep's tail (UNT 60 and 122). Cf. Van de Mieroop 1987: 148.

24. 7 ma-na nig$_2$-U.NU-a siki uz$_3$ ^{giš}me-dim$_2$ ma$_2$-gu$_2$ u$_3$ a$_2$ ma$_2$ ba-ra-keš$_2$ (Nisaba 15 461:1–2).

25. The ratio of 1 ^{giš}me-dim$_2$ per 2 $^{(giš)}$ma$_2$-gu$_2$ is found also in SANTAG 6 68:10–11).

26. A close connection between these two ship parts is further indicated by the examples, where they are listed as a single item. See 86 ^{giš}me-dim$_2$ ma$_2$-gu$_2$ (BPOA 7 1992:6); 18 ^{giš}me-dim$_2$ ma$_2$-gu$_2$ (TUT 121 rev. v 3′); cf. also UET 3 1459:2. It should also be noted that $^{(giš)}$ma$_2$-gu$_2$ may alternatively appear together with ^{giš}eme-sig, which plausibly describes a type of plank. See 80 ^{giš}eme-sig 6 ^{giš}ma$_2$-gu$_2$ (PDT 2 1312:12–13); 4 ^{giš}eme-sig ma$_2$-gu$_2$ (MVN 2 3 iv 18, v 8, 23).

27. Kjaerum 1983: catalogue 351 = Carter 2012: 369 fig. 19.9 no. 6.

representation of a Perso-Arab ship on the open sea. The vessel is said to have traveled from Basra to Oman.

4. The Cylinder Seals Owned by the Personnel of "Big Ships" from Failaka and Bahrain

As shown by the earlier discussion, the professional designations "captain of big ships" (ugula / nu-banda₃ lu₂ ma₂-gal-gal) and "man of the big ships" (lu₂ ma₂-gal-gal) are rare in cuneiform sources. Only one impression of a seal belonging to such a professional survives and there are no actual cylinder seals. Therefore, the fact that three seals of this nature have been found in Failaka, Kuwait, and Bahrain is significant, coming as a somewhat unexpected demonstration of these individuals' presence in Tilmun.[28] Of these three seals, one remains unpublished (no. 1), while the other two have only been discussed briefly in the literature (nos. 2 and 3). Dating to the Ur III or the Isin/Larsa period, these seals show in each case the so-called "presentation scene" and mention, in their inscriptions, individuals bearing typical Sumerian names.

Seal 1 (fig. 12:1)[29]

Provenance: Saar mound cemetery, mound 177, season 1984, central chamber, excavated by Dr. Muhammad Najjar. The burial mound was 12 m in diameter, with a ring wall of 5 or 6 courses preserved to a height of 0.76 m. The central chamber was 2.7 m long, 1.5 m wide, and T-shaped, with two alcoves. The chamber was oriented to the northwest. According to the excavation report, the central chamber, which had been looted, also contained the base of a jar and a cylindrical shell bead. The seal was broken when found.

The pottery from the tomb, which would help to date the interment, could not be located in the Bahrain National Museum. However, judging from the type of burial mound as well as its location in the Saar Mound Cemetery, it can confidently be dated to the Isin-Larsa period, ca. 2000–1800 BC. Collectively, the size of the burial mound and the lengths of the T-shaped chamber demonstrate that the interred individual belonged to the economic elite of Tilmun society. Consequently, the most probable, but obviously conjectural, scenario is that the individual buried in mound 177 was a wealthy Tilmunite who was involved in trade with Babylonia. It was conceivably as a result of those contacts that this person came into the possession of the seal in question.

Description: The material was recorded in the inventory as ivory. However, the cool, soft, yellowish seal is more likely made of some type of mineral or shell. The quality of the carving on the heavily

---

28. Yet another Ur III cylinder seal has recently been discovered on Failaka Island, at the Ur III settlement on Tell F6 (Pittman 2016: 160 fig. 752; Eidem 2016: 162). It belonged to a scribe named Lu-Ninšubur, son of Albanidug, a nu-banda₃. Since the title nu-banda₃ when appearing without any further qualification, usually means "colonel," it is likely that Lu-Ninšubur's father (and possibly Lu-Ninšubur as well) was a member of the military, perhaps even a captain of "big ships" (i.e., nu-banda₃ ma₂-gal-gal).

29. This seal has not been published previously and is on permanent display (2012) in the Bahrain National Museum. In 1994, Dr. Jesper Eidem recorded the inscription on this and other seals in the collection of the Bahrain National Museum at the request of Mr. Khalid Al-Sindi and Dr. Flemming Højlund. We kindly thank Khalid Al-Sindi, Dr. Eidem, and Dr. Højlund for bringing our attention to this seal. We also thank the director of the National Museum, Mr. Fouad al Noor, for his permission to publish it.

worn seal is mediocre, with notably crude feature such as the claw-like hands. The seal has a slightly concave profile and measures 36 mm in height and 20 mm in diameter. Judging from the motif, the seal dates to the Ur III period.

The seal displays the classic "presentation scene": a goddess or god is seated on a two-niched throne with a concave seat, which rests on a double-lined dais. The deity wears a horned headdress and what appears to be a flounced robe. The deity's crudely carved open right hand is stretched out in a welcoming gesture toward an approaching minor goddess (the Lamma). A small pole separates the seated deity from the Lamma. Between the two deities, a crescent is depicted. The Lamma leads a profane worshiper by her right hand and raises the left hand in a greeting toward the enthroned deity. The Lamma wears a pleated robe and a horned headdress. A large crack in the seal has erased the right hand of the minor goddess and large parts of the worshiper, who wears a fringed robe and is followed by an inscribed panel of three columns.

Seal inscription:

1)	Šeš-kal-la	Šeš-kala,
2)	dumu Ur-^dNanše	son of Ur-Nanše,
3)	ugula ma₂-gal-gal	the captain of big ships.

Seal 2 (fig. 12:2)[30]

Provenance: Al-Maqsha Cemetery, grave 27a, season 1991–92. The context in which the seal was found is a rock-cut tomb covered by large capstones (without the covering burial mound typical of Bahrain/Tilmun). It was found within a larger cemetery of similar tombs 1.6 km south of the fortified Bronze Age town (city of Tilmun) at Qalaʾat al Bahrain. The cemetery had developed around a large, isolated Late Type burial mound (2050–1800 BC). However, the majority of the rock-cut tombs date to the so-called Late Dilmun period (1000/700 BC). The grave in which the seal was found contained several individuals and numerous ceramic vessels, which were found among the bones strewn across the chamber floor. The pottery, which may provide a more narrow date for grave 27a, could not be located at the Bahrain National Museum. The seal was possibly interred in a burial during the early second millennium BC, recovered during subsequent looting or reuse, possibly to be reinterred in a tomb during the first millennium BC.

Description: The seal is made of hematite and has a slightly concave profile. It is finely cut and measures 26 mm in height and 10 mm in diameter (André-Salvini 1999: 91). Judging from the style of the carvings and the motif, the seal dates to the Ur III period.

The seal shows an elaborate variant of the "presentation scene." The enthroned deity wears a horned crown/headdress and flounced robe and is identified as male by a long beard. The god rests on a two-niched throne resembling a temple, which is placed on a double baseline, with traces of horizontal lines indicating a niched podium, dais, or platform. The open right hand of the deity is stretched out in a welcome gesture toward the approaching Lamma. The Lamma, who originally led a male worshiper (who was later erased by the addition of an inscription), stands in front of the enthroned deity, with her left hand raised in a greeting gesture. The Lamma wears a horned head-

---

30. For an excellent photo of the seal and a modern impression thereof, see André-Salvini 1999: 91 fig. 80.

dress and a flounced robe. Her right arm is cut off at the elbow by the inscribed panel. Two objects are found in the space between the goddess and seated god: a standard topped with the solar disk and lunar crescent, and an elegant vessel on a tall stand. Two rampant antithetical lions stand back-to-back, each holding a staff and mirroring one another in a symmetrical composition that is topped by a bird of prey with open claws. The staff held by the lion on the right and the animal's paws were erased when the seal was recut to accommodate a three-line inscription, which is a later addition. It is clear that the original composition also included a human worshiper, who also was erased and replaced by the inscription.

1.

2.

Seal inscription:

1)   Dug₄-ga   Duga,
2)   lu₂ ma₂-gal-gal   the man of big ships,
3)   dumu Ab-ba-gu-la   son of Abba-gula.

Seal 3 (fig. 12:3)

Provenance: The seal was discovered at the Al-Khidr Settlement, Failaka Island, Kuwait.[31] The site is a small Tilmunite settlement located on the northwestern coast of Failaka Island. The excavators have not provided information regarding the date of the context in which the seal was found. However, a recent examination of the more than 71 Dilmun Type seals found at the site shows that they include many seals carved in Dilmun style II (personal communication of Aiysha

3.

Fig. 12. Drawings of seals 1–3 as seen in modern impressions.

Abu-Laban), which after the recent excavations in Tell F6 on Failaka can be dated to around 1800 BC (personal communication of F. Højlund). It remains a distinct possibility that the seal was either traded or lost by its owner during his visit to Failaka Island some time during the late Ur III or Isin-Larsa period.

Description: The slightly concave seal is made of a dark green grey-spotted steatite. The coarsely cut seal is 39 mm high and 19 mm in diameter. Judging from the style of its carving, the seal probably belongs to the Isin-Larsa period.

31. Barta et al. 2008. The context information is provided by David-Cuny and Azpeitia (2012: 32–33), who claim that the seal came from "trench RM, square L:5 at Elevation 6.51." This clearly is a mistake, since this data derives from the contextual system developed by Poul Kjaerum (Moesgaard Museum) for his post-excavation analysis of the Danish campaigns at Tell F3 and F6. Trench RM, square L:5 at Elevation 6.51, represents the find-spot of an unknown object in Tell F3 and is completely unrelated to the cylinder seal in question and the al-Khidr excavations more generally.

The seal displays a classic but somewhat compressed "presentation scene." A god is seated on a single-niched throne. The god wears a horned headdress and robe. A crudely carved open right hand is stretched out in a welcoming gesture toward an approaching Lamma. A lunar crescent topped with a stellar disk appears between the two deities. The Lamma leads a bald, clean-shaven worshiper by her right hand and raises the left hand in a greeting gesture toward the enthroned deity. The Lamma wears a fringed robe and a horned headdress. The worshiper is also wearing a fringed robe and raises his right hand in a greeting gesture. Hereafter follows an inscribed three-column panel.

Seal inscription:[32]

1)	Eš$_3$-gi-na	Eš-gina,
2)	lu$_2$ ma$_2$-gal-gal	the man of big ships,
3)	dumu Ur-ab-ba	son of Ur-abba.

32. An earlier translation was offered by Barta et al. 2008: 124 fig. 11.

Appendix 3

The Babylonian Burial Jar
in the Gulf Countries

In this appendix, we digress to comment on the custom of interring in graves in Tilmun and Makkan of a particular functional category of small-sized Babylonian pottery vessels, which attests to a long-lasting exotic consumer habit in the Gulf during the third and early second millennia BC. Under the relevant chronological sections of this study, we have already paid brief attention to each of these import types, which date to the Jemdat Nasr/Early Dynastic I, Late Sargonic–Ur III, and Isin-Larsa periods, respectively. Although the styles and types of these containers invariably changed across the millennium, striking dimensional and functional similarities can be discerned that encourage further inquiry. These similarities suggest the enduring presence of an elusive but no doubt luxurious substance that was exported from Babylonia to the Gulf region throughout the third and well into the early second millennium BC.

The earliest evidence of this practice are the small and characteristically painted Babylonian "Jemdat Nasr style" vessels (see above, p. 11), which were habitually included in Hafit Type tombs in Makkan between 3000–2700 BC (fig. 2: nos. 3–10) and in contemporary burials in Tilmun (fig. 2: nos. 1–2). The typical specimens found in the Gulf vary from 0.24 to 0.9 liter in volume and display only minor variations (see fig. 2, p. 13).

The fact that the same vessel type also frequently occurs in the contemporary Babylonian grave kit[1] reflects the importance of the specific contents for which these vessels initially were intended. Although the original, but now often faded, bi-chrome decoration found on these vessels obviously rendered them attractive to Gulf populations, their special status must primarily have been predicated on the contents with which they were traded along the Gulf.

In the archaeological record dating to the Late Sargonic and Ur III periods, we are again faced with a situation where a single Babylonian vessel-type exclusively was selected for burials. This time the situation is reversed, and the evidence is now strongest from Tilmun (fig. 6: nos. 1–7) and less substantial for Makkan.[2] Typically, these pointy-based vessels are of an exceedingly standardized volume ranging from 0.21 to 0.35 liters (see fig. 6, pp. 42–43). As in the case of the small "Jemdat Nasr style" vessels, this vessel type also held a most prominent position in the funerary assemblage

---

1. E.g. Woolley 1956: pl. 26 a, d and e; pl. 57 JN. 38–40.
2. For the four examples from Makkan, see Laursen 2011: fig. 5 with references.

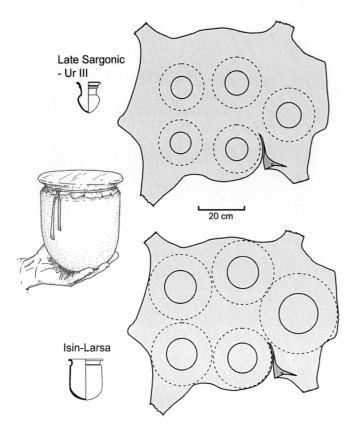

Late Sargonic - Ur III

20 cm

Isin-Larsa

Fig. 13. Templates for 5 leather stoppers for our two vessel types compared against the skin of small (Gotland) sheep. Pencil drawing by Sara Heil Jensen.

of Babylonia[3] and was employed as a "fine ware" vessel as far north as Tell Arbid and Tell Mozan in Syria.[4] It is noteworthy that this type's distribution in the Gulf matches the range of the "Makkan trade" in the Ur III period.[5]

In the early second millennium BC, a novel type of Babylonian vessel replaces the previous types in graves in Tilmun (fig. 6: nos. 8–14). These round-based vessels range from 0.83 to 2.0 liters in volume and, although these capacities exceed those of the two previous vessel types, their function appears to be analogous.

The archaeological evidence allows us to conclude that the numbers in which each of the three vessel types originally arrived in the Gulf should be counted in the thousands.

There is good reason to suspect that all of these vessels served as receptacles for the same Babylonian substance. First, all of the enumerated types share important morphological attributes, including the presence of a distinctly marked shoulder, a short vertical neck, and a heavily everted rim. The shared functional solution generally suggests that these containers were specifically designed to be sealed with a string-fastened skin or cloth cover (fig. 13). The general standardization of the vessels' sizes suggests some form of semi-institutionalized exchange (fig. 14). The assumption that their contents were highly prized is corroborated by the prominent/exclusive status these vessels enjoyed in the burial assemblages of the Gulf communities. This, and the relatively small volume of all three types, indicates that all of them functioned as containers of a relatively high-value semi-liquid substance.

Although the substantial archaeological evidence for these three types is not fully published, the available sample is sufficiently representative to determine that the three chronologically successive types were shipped in average volumes of ca. 0.7 liter, 0.4 liter, and 1.1 liter, respectively.[6] However, the data sets for each of the three types also contain examples that are abnormally large, which makes them distinctive among the otherwise uniform assemblage. The extra-large examples possibly represent more prestigious vessels that were sent as diplomatic gifts to the higher echelons of Tilmun and Makkan societies.

3. For example, Boehmer et al. 1995: tables 5/a, 9/c, 16/b, 17/e; Woolley 1934: pl. 254, type 44a.
4. For Tell Arbid, see Koliński 2012: fig. 9a; for Tell Mozan, see Dohmann-Pfälzner and Pfälzner 2000.
5. For a map, see Laursen 2011: fig. 9.
6. The extremely large outliers discussed below are not included in the average values.

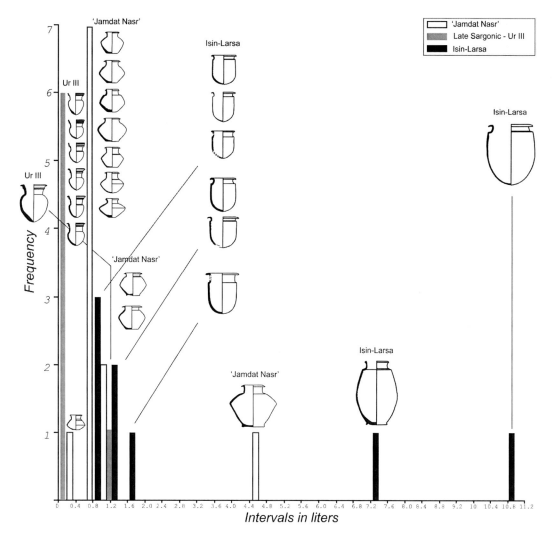

Fig. 14. Histogram showing the volume of "Jemdat Nasr style" vessels and the volumes of two standardized Babylonian import vessels found in burial mounds in Tilmun (Bahrain).

The earliest possible example of this practice is the unusually large "Jemdat Nasr style" vessel found in a Hafit type tomb (see fig. 2: no. 14), which, with its volume of 4.45 liters, is six times larger than the standard import. A possible example of Late Sargonic or Ur III period international gift exchange is the remarkably large vessel from a burial mound in Bahrain (fig. 6: no. 7 and fig. 14), with a volume of 1.2 liters, which is three times the size of its contemporary import.[7] Finally, the most convincing example of international gift exchange is the 10.8-liter vessel of the Isin-Larsa type from an unknown burial mound in Bahrain (fig. 5: no. 14 and fig. 13). Importantly, this vessel is significantly larger than any specimen of the types known from Babylonia. While the exact provenance

7. Fragments of two similarly large size vessels of this type are reported from the Makkan site of Tell Abraq and Kalba. See Laursen 2011: 134–37 and fig. 5 with references.

of this vessel is unknown, a 7.21-liter Babylonian import vessel of a related type came from a large "aristocratic" burial mound just east of the Royal Mounds of Aʾali (fig. 6: nos. 15 and fig. 14).[8]

Although the archaeological data do not suggest any candidate for our hypothesized article of trade, there survive several textual references to jars with oil that were sent as gifts or goods to Tilmun. An early example of this comes from the Early Dynastic city-state of Lagaš, where merchants or envoys brought perfumed oils as gifts to Tilmun (see chap. 3, p. 22). Also, a Sargonic text from Adab mentions a big-ship commander as a recipient of oil in 3 jars of 4-liter capacity intended for an expedition to the sea (Tilmun?) (see p. 104 n. 5).

Information regarding the identity of the substance traded in our jars is also suggested by an Isin tablet dated to ca. 1984 BC (Appendix 1 Text 14; Šu-ilišu 2/ii/14). This text contains a list of packing materials issued for a shipment of goods/gifts destined for "Tilmun and the Amorites." According to lines 4–5, the goods in question included five jars of fine (aromatic) oil, for which one white sheepskin was expended as well, in order to fabricate their jar stoppers/lid. Since one sheepskin was deemed sufficient to make stoppers for all five jars, it follows that the jars or their openings must have been relatively small. In practice, we must envision that the sheep-skin was cut into five circular pieces, each of a size sufficient to cover the vessel's mouth and allow for its fastening around the vessel neck (see drawing, fig. 13). The skins would then, probably in a soaked condition, be strapped over the vessel with a string and left to dry and shrink into position, thereby tightly sealing the vessel's mouth.

Given the date of the text in question, it is instructive to compare its information against our two late-vessel types. The sizes of the mouth and neck of the two types are slightly different but, as illustrated in fig. 6: no. 7 for both types, pieces sufficient for five jar stoppers can easily be cut from a small- to medium-size sheep-skin.[9]

Comparable exchanges are attested in other Isin texts. One of them (Appendix 1, Text 12), dated to year Išbi-Erra "19", mentions two jars of 10-liter capacity each and one sheep-skin for their jar stoppers in connection with gifts (probably also oil) for Tilmun. In another text (Appendix 1, Text 13), dated eight years later, we again hear of two jars of 10-liter capacity (possibly for oil) as part of a larger consignment. In this instance, it is specifically stated that the jars were part of *royal* gifts for Tilmun. These two accounts, which in each case involved a shipment to Tilmun of 10-liter capacity jars, seem to match our 10.8 liter Babylonian vessel from Bahrain (fig. 6: no. 14) exceedingly closely.

One of the best examples of royal gift-exchange involving Tilmun is found in the correspondence between king Shamshi-Addu and his son Yasmah-Addu, which forms part of the Mari archives. The letter in question mentions a gift of three liters of aromatic oil (cypress oil?), which, on Shamshi-Addu's instructions, Yasmah-Addu was supposed to send to the king of Tilmun in a reinforced *kisikkum* jar.[10] For reasons unclear to us, in the end, Yasmah-Addu sent only two liters of

8. The vessel was found in 1982 by Bahraini excavator Muhammad Saleha in a Big Aʾali mound by Road 3401; it had been badly destroyed by bulldozers. See Laursen in preparation a.

9. Narrow-mouth vessels for oil transport comparable to the classic amphoras are not readily identifiable in the south Babylonian pottery assemblage, with the possible exception of the type fig. 2: no. 15 from the Early Dynastic period. This is possibly because Babylonian oil and lard products generally were intentionally concentrated and made more viscous than, for instance, olive oil.

10. Instructions to send a *kisikkum* jar for the king of Tilmun are given in A.2761 (Groneberg 1992: nos. 6, 76–77, 80); an expenditure of two liters of cypress oil for the king of Timun is mentioned in Charpin 1984: 92 no. 61.

oil to its intended recipient. Nevertheless, this transaction makes it clear that, in Tilmun, quality oil was in high demand.

The oil products exported to the Gulf from Babylonia, as recorded in texts, consisted of aromatic oil,[11] fine sesame oil,[12] and aromatic lard.[13] One may conjecture that the contents of the burial jars excavated in Tilmun and Makkan were of a similar nature.

11. Appendix 1, Text 14:4 (p. 103).
12. Appendix 1, Text 5:7 and note (p. 95).
13. See p. 82 under (1).

Bibliographic Abbreviations

Abbreviations used are those of the *Assyrian Dictionary of the Oriental Institute of the University of Chicago* (Chicago, 1956–2010) and/or CDLI: Cuneiform Digital Library Initiative [cdli.ucla.edu], "Abbreviations for Assyriology," with the following additions:

BDTNS   Database of Neo-Sumerian Texts, Centro de Ciencias Humanas y Sociales, Consejo Superior de Investigaciones Cientificas, Madrid, Spain [bdtns.filol.csic.es].

MTBM   F. D'Agostino and L. Verderame, "Umma Messenger Texts in the British Museum, Part Three," *Rivista degli Studi Orientali* 76, Suppl. no. 2 (Rome, 2003).

Titles of Sumerian literary compositions are those used by ETCSL: The Electronic Corpus of Sumerian Literature, Oriental Institute, University of Oxford [etcsl.orinst.ac.uk].

Bibliography

Abdi, Kamyar
   2000   Review of Timothy F. Potts, *Mesopotamia and the East: An Archaeological and Historical Study of Foreign Relations 3400–2000 BC*. *Journal of Near Eastern Studies* 59: 277–84.

Agius, Dionisius A.
   2002   *In the Wake of the Dhow: The Arabian Gulf and Oman*. Reading, UK: Ithaca.

Algaze, Guillermo
   1989   "The Uruk Expansion: Cross-cultural Exchange in Early Mesopotamian Civilization." *Current Anthropology* 30: 571–608.

   1993   *The Uruk World System: The Dynamics of Expansion of Early Mesopotamian Civilization*. Chicago: The University of Chicago Press.

   2008   *Ancient Mesopotamia at the Dawn of Civilization: The Evolution of an Urban Landscape*. Chicago: The University of Chicago Press.

Allotte de la Fuÿe, François-Maurice
   1920   *Documents présargoniques, fascicule supplementaire*. Paris: E. Leroux.

Almulla, Laila, Narayana Bhat, Binson Thomas, Lekha Rajesh, Sasni Ali, and Preetha George
   2013   "Assessment of Existing Mangrove Plantation along Kuwait Coastline." *Biodiversity Journal* 4: 111–116.

Al-Sadeqi, Waleed
  2013   "The Ancient Beads of Bahrain: A Study of Ornaments from the Dilmun and Tylos Era." Unpublished PhD dissertation, Department of Archaeology, Durham University.
Al-Tikriti, Waleed
  1985   "The Archaeological Investigations on Ghanada Island: Further Evidence for the Coastal Umm an-Nar Culture." *Archaeology in the United Arab Emirates* 4: 9–19.
Amiet, Pierre
  1975   "A Cylinder Seal Impression Found at Umm an-Nar." *East and West* 25: 425–426.
  1986   *L'âge des échanges inter-iraniens: 3500–1700 avant J.-C.* Notes et documents des musées de France 11. Paris: Ministère de la culture et de la communication.
  1988   *Les cités oubliées de l'Indus: archéologie du Pakistan.* Paris: Musée Guimet.
Andersen, H. Hellmuth, and Flemming Højlund
  2003   *The Barbar Temples.* Jutland Archaeological Society publications 48. Højbjerg: Jutland Archaeological Society.
Andersson, Ann
  2016   "Beads." Pp. 176–98 in F. Højlund and A. Abu-Laban (eds.), *Tell F6 on Failaka Island: Kuwaiti-Danish Excavations 2008–2012.* Jutland Archaeological Society Publications 92. Aarhus: Kuwaiti National Council for Culture, Arts and Letters / Jutland Archaeological Society and Moesgaard Museum.
André-Salvini, Béatrice
  1999   "Cylindrical Seal with Inscription and Showing a Scene of Presentation to a Deity." P. 91 in P. Lombard (ed.), *Bahrain, the Civilization of the Two Seas, from Dilmun to Tylos.* Paris: Institut du Monde Arabe.
Aruz, Joan, ed.
  2000   *Art of The First Cities: The Third Millennium B.C. from the Mediterranean to the Indus.* New York: The Metropolitan Museum of Art, New York.
Avanzini, Alessandra, Alexia Pavan, and Michele D. Esposti
  2012   *Oman, the Land of Sindbad the Sailor.* Exhibition catalogue, 6 June–7 July 2012, Museo di San Matteo, Pisa. Pisa: University of Pisa.
Azzarà, Valentina M.
  2009   "Domestic Architecture at the Early Bronze Age Sites HD-6 and RJ-2 (Ja'alan, Sultanate of Oman)." *Proceedings of the Seminar for Arabian Studies* 39: 1–16.
Bandaranayake, Wickramasinghe M.
  1999   *Economic, Traditional and Medicinal Uses of Mangroves.* AIMS Report no. 28. Townsville: Australian Institute of Marine Science.
Barta, Peter, Lucia Benediková, Mária Hajnalová, Zora Miklíková, Tereza Belanová, and A. H. Shehab
  2008   "Al-Khidr on Failaka Island: Preliminary Results of the Fieldworks at a Dilmun Culture Settlement in Kuwait." *Türkiye Bilimler Akademisi Arkeoloji Dergisi / Turkish Academy of Sciences Journal of Archaeology* 11: 121–34.
Beech, Mark J.
  2004   *In the Land of the Ichthyophagi: Modeling Fish Exploitation in the Arabian Gulf and Gulf of Oman from the 5th Millennium BC to the Late Islamic Period.* BAR International Series 1217. Oxford: Archaeopress.
Begemann, F., A. Hauptmann, S. Schmitt-Strecker, and G. Weisgerber
  2010   "Lead Isotope and Chemical Signature of Copper from Oman and its Occurrence in Mesopotamia and Sites on the Arabian Gulf Coast." *Arabian Archaeology and Epigraphy* 21: 135–69.
Bernhardt, E. C., B. P. Horton, and J. D. Stanley
  2012   "Nile Delta Vegetation Response to Holocene Climate Variability." *Geology* 40/7: 615–18.

Bibby, T. G.
    1971   ". . . According to the Standard of Dilmun." *Kuml 1970*: 345–53.
    1973   *Preliminary Survey in East Arabia 1968*. Aarhus: Jutland Archaeological Society.
    1986   "Origins of the Dilmun Civilization." Pp. 109–15 in H. Al Khalifa and M. Rice (eds.), *Bahrain Though the Ages: The Archaeology*. London: KPI.
Bisht, R. S.
    2014   "How Harappans Honoured Death at Dholavira." Pp. 265–318 in N. N. Rao (ed.), *Sindhu-Sarasvati Civilization: New Perspectives. A Volume in Memory of Dr. Shikaripur Ranganatha Rao*. New Delhi: D.K. Printworld.
    forthcoming   *Excavation at Dholavira (1989–90 to 2004–2005)*.
Black, Jeremy A., and Farouk N. H. Al-Rawi
    1987   "A Contribution to the Study of Akkadian Bird Names." *Zeitschrift für Assyriologie* 77: 117–26.
Black, Jeremy A., and Anthony Green
    1992   *Gods, Demons and Symbols of Ancient Mesopotamia*. Austin: University of Texas Press.
Boehmer, Rainer M.
    1965   *Die Entwicklung der Glyptik während der Akkad-Zeit*. Untersuchungen zur Assyriologie und vorder-asiatischen Archäologie 4. Berlin: De Gruyter.
    1974   "Das Auftreten des Wasserbüffels in Mesopotamien in historischer Zeit und seine sumerische Bezeichnung." *Zeitschrift für Assyriologie* 64: 1–19.
Brunke, Hagan, and Walther Sallaberger
    2010   "Aromata für Duftöl." Pp. 41–74 in A. Kleinerman and J. M. Sasson (eds.), *Why Should Someone Who Knows Something Conceal It? Cuneiform Studies in Honor of David I. Owen on His 70th Birthday*. Bethesda, MD: CDL.
Brunswig, Robert H., Asko Parpola, and Daniel T. Potts
    1983   "New Indus Related Seals from the Near East." Pp. 101–15 in D. T. Potts (ed.), *Dilmun*. Berliner Beiträge zum Vorderen Orient 2. Berlin: Dietrich Reimer.
Buccellati, Giorgio
    1966   *The Amorites of the Ur III Period*. Naples: Instituto Orientale di Napoli.
Burkholder, Grace
    1984   *An Arabian Collection: Artifacts from the Eastern Province*. Boulder City, NV: GB Publications.
Carter, Robert
    2010   "Boat-Related Finds." Pp. 89–104 in R. Carter and H. Crawford (eds.), *Maritime Interactions in the Arabian Neolithic: Evidence from H3, As-Sabiyah, an Ubaid-Related Site in Kuwait*. Leiden: Brill.
    2012   "Watercraft." Pp. 346–72 in vol. 1 of D. T. Potts (ed.), *A Companion to the Archaeology of the Ancient Near East*. Chichester, West Sussex: Wiley-Blackwell.
    2013   "The Sumerians and the Gulf." Pp. 579–99 in Harriet Crawford (ed.), *The Sumerian World*. London: Routledge.
Carter, Robert, and Harriet Crawford
    2010a   "Introduction." Pp. 1–8 in R. Carter and H. Crawford (eds.), *Maritime Interactions in the Arabian Neolithic: Evidence from H3, As-Sabiyah, an Ubaid-Related Site in Kuwait*. Leiden: Brill.
    2010b   "Conclusion." Pp. 203–12 in R. Carter and H. Crawford (eds.), *Maritime Interactions in the Arabian Neolithic: Evidence from H3, As-Sabiyah, an Ubaid-Related Site in Kuwait*. Leiden: Brill.
Casanova, Michèle
    2003   "Alabaster and Calcite Vessels." In H. H. Andersen and F. Højlund (eds.), *The Barbar Temples*, Volume 1. Jutland Archaeological Society Publications 48. Højbjerg: Jutland Archaeological Society.

Cavigneaux, Antoine, and Béatrice André-Salvini
  Forthcoming   "Cuneiform Tablets from QaPat. Dilmun and the Sealand at the Dawn of the Kassite Era."
             In P. Lombard and Kh. Al-Sindi (eds.), *Twenty Years of Bahrain Archaeology, 1986–2006*. Actes du
             colloque international de Manama, 9–12 décembre 2007. Bahrain: Ministry of Culture.

Charpin, Dominique
  1984   "Nouveaux documents du bureau de Phuile à Pépoque assyrienne." *M.A.R.I.* 3: 83–126. Paris: Édi-
             tions Recherche sur les Civilisations.

Ciarla, R.
  1979   "The Manufacture of Alabaster Vessels at Shahr-I Sokhta and Mundigak in the 3rd Mill. BC. A
             Problem of Cultural Identity." Pp. 319–35 in G. Gnoli and A. V. Rossi (eds.), *Iranica*. Seminario di
             studi asiatici, series minor 10. Naples: Istituto universitario orientale.

Cleuziou, Serge
  1989   "Excavations at Hili 8: A Preliminary Report on the 4th to 7th Campaigns." *Archaeology of the
             United Arab Emirates* 5: 61–87.
  1994   "Black boats of Magan." Pp. 745–61 in A. Parpola and P. Koskikallio (eds.), *South Asian Archaeol-
             ogy, 1993: Proceedings of the Twelfth International Conference of the European Association of South
             Asian Archaeologists Held in Helsinki University, 5–9 July 1993*. Annales Academiae Scientiarum
             Fennicae B271. Helsinki: Suomalainen Tiedeakatemia.
  1996   "The Emergence of Oases and Towns in Eastern and Southern Arabia." Pp. 159–65 in G. Afanas'ev,
             S. Cleuziou, J. R. Lukacs, and M. Tosi (eds.), *The Prehistory of Asia and Oceania, XIII International
             Congress of Prehistoric and Protohistoric Sciences, Forlì, Italia, 8–14 sept. 1996*. Series Colloquia 16.
             Forlì: A.B.A.C.O. Edizioni.
  2007   *In the Shadow of the Ancestors: The Prehistoric Foundation of the Early Arabian Civilization in Oman*.
             Sultanate of Oman: Ministry of Heritage and Culture.

Cleuziou, Serge, and Sophie Méry
  2002   "In-Between the Great Powers: The Bronze Age Oman Peninsula." Pp. 273–316 in S. Cleziou,
             M. Tosi, and J. Zarins (eds.), *Essays on the Late Prehistory of the Arabian Peninsula*. Series Orientale
             Roma XCIII. Rome: Istituto Italiano per l'Africa e l'Oriente.

Cleuziou, Serge, and Maurizio Tosi
  1989   "The Southeastern Frontier of the Ancient Near East." Pp. 15–48 in K. Frifelt and P. Sørensen
             (eds.), *South Asian Archaeology 1985: Papers from the Eighth International Conference of South Asian
             Archaeologists in Western Europe, held at Moesgaard Museum, Denmark, 1–5 July 1985*. Bath: Curzon.

Collins, Paul
  2003   "The Island of Tarut." Pp. 323–24 in Joan Aruz (ed.), *Art of the First Cities: The Third Millennium
             B.C. from the Mediterranean to the Indus*. New Haven: Yale University Press.

Collon, Dominique
  1987   *First Impressions: Cylinder Seals in the Ancient Near East*. Avon: The Bath Press.
  1996   "Mesopotamia and the Indus: The Evidence of the Seals." Pp. 209–26 in J. Reade (ed.), *The Indian
             Ocean in Antiquity*. London: Kegan Paul.

Cornwall, P. B.
  1946   "Ancient Arabia: Explorations in Hasa, 1940–41." *The Geographical Journal* 107: 28–50.
  1952   "Two Letters from Dilmun." *Journal of Cuneiform Studies* 6: 137–45.

Crassard, Rémy, and Phillip Drechsler
  2013   "Towards New Paradigms: Multiple Pathways for the Arabian Neolithic." *Arabian Archaeology and
             Epigraphy* 24: 3–8.

Crawford, Harriet
  1998   *Dilmun and its Gulf Neighbours*. Cambridge: Cambridge University Press.

2013   "Trade in the Sumerian World." Pp. 447–61 in H. Crawford (ed.), *The Sumerian World*. London: Routledge.

Crawford, Harriet, and Khalid Al-Sindi
1996   "A 'Hut Pot' in the National Museum, Bahrain." *Arabian Archaeology and Epigraphy* 7: 140–42.

Cripps, Eric L.
2010   *Sargonic and Presargonic Texts in The World Museum Liverpool*. BAR International Series 2135. Oxford: Archeopress.

Cros, Gaston
1910   *Nouvelles Fouilles de Tello, Mission française de Chaldée*. Paris: Leroux.

Cullen, H. M., P. B. de Menocal, S. Hemming, G. Hemming, F. H. Brown, T. Guilderson, and F. Sirocko
2000   "Climate Change and the Collapse of the Akkadian Empire: Evidence from the Deep Sea." *Geology*: 28: 379–82.

Cuttler, Richard
2013   "Considering Marine Transgressions as a Mechanism for Enforced Migration and Littoral Gulf Ubaid Phenomenon." *Arabian Archaeology and Epigraphy* 24: 37–43.

Dales, George F.
1962   "Harappan Outposts on the Makran Coast." *Antiquity* 26: 86–92.

Dales, George F., and Jonathan M. Kenoyer
1986   *Excavations at Mohenjo Daro, Pakistan: The Pottery*, University Museum Monograph 53. Philadelphia: The University Museum of the University of Pennsylvania.

David, Hélène
1996   "Styles and Evolution: Soft Stone Vessels During the Bronze Age in the Oman Peninsula." *Proceedings of the Seminar for Arabian Studies* 26: 31–46.

David-Cuny, Hélène, and Johanne Azpeitia
2012   "Catalogue." Pp. 29–109 in J. Azpeitia, H. David-Cuny and S. A. H. Shehab (eds.), *Failaka Seals Catalogue. Vol 1: Al-Khidr*. Kuwait City: National Council for Culture Arts and Letters.

David-Cuny, Hélène, and Carl Phillips
2008   "A Unique Stone Vessel from a Third Millennium Tomb in Kalba." Pp. 118–23 in E. Olijdam and R. H. Spoor (eds.), *Intercultural Relations between South and Southwest Asia: Studies in Commemoration of E.C.L. During Caspers (1934–1996)*. Society for Arabian Studies Monographs 7. BAR International Series 1826. Oxford: Archaeopress.

Deadman, William, and Derek Kennet
2015   "Hafit Tombs and the Development of Early Bronze Age Social Hierarchy in al-Batinah, Oman." *Proceedings of the Seminar for Arabian Studies* 45: 49–56.

De Cardi, Beatrice
1968   "Excavation at Bampūr, S. E. Iran: A Brief Report." *Iran* 6: 135–55.

Delaporte, Louis
1920   *Musée du Louvre, Catalogue des cylindres orientaux, cachets et pierres gravées de style orientale I: Fouilles et Missions*. Paris: Hachette.

Demange, Françoise
2003   "Cylinder Seal of Shu-ilishu, Interpreter for Meluhha." Pp. 415 no. 303 in J. Aruz (ed.), *Art of the First Cities: The Third Millennium B.C. from the Mediterranean to the Indus*. New York: The Metropolitan Museum of Art, New York.

Dixit, Yama, David A. Hodell, and Cameron A. Petrie
2014   "Abrupt Weakening of the Summer Monsoon in Northwest India ~4100 yr Ago." *Geology* 42: 339–42.

Dohmann-Pfälzner, Heike, and Peter Pfälzner
   2000   *Ausgrabungen der Deutschen Orient-Gesellschaft in der Zentralen Oberstadt von Tall Mozan/Urkeš: Bericht über die in Kooperation mit dem IIMAS durchgeführte Kampagne 1999.* Mitteilungen der Deutschen Orient-Gesellschaft zu Berlin 132. Berlin: Deutsche Orient-Gesellschaft.

Drechsler, Philipp
   2012   "The Arabian Peninsula." Pp. 485–500 in D. T. Potts (ed.), *A Companion to the Archaeology of the Ancient Near East.* Chichester, West Sussex: Wiley-Blackwell.

During-Caspers, Elisabeth C. L.
   1973   "Harappan Trade in the Arabian Gulf in the Third Millennium BC." *Proceedings of the Seminar for Arabian Studies* 3: 3–20.

Edzard, Dietz O.
   1997   *Gudea and His Dynasty.* The Royal Inscriptions of Mesopotamia, Early Periods 3/1. Toronto: University of Toronto Press.

Eidem, Jesper
   1994   "Cuneiform Inscriptions." Pp. 301–2 in F. Højlund and H. Hellmuth Andersen (eds.), *Qalaʾat al-Bahrain. The Northern City Wall and the Islamic Fortress.* Højbjerg: Jutland Archaeological Society.
   2016   "Cuneiform Inscriptions." Pp. 162–63 in F. Højlund and A. Abu-Laban (eds.), *Tell F6 on Failaka Island: Kuwaiti-Danish Excavations 2008–2012.* Jutland Archaeological Society Publications 92. Aarhus: Kuwaiti National Council for Culture, Arts and Letters / Jutland Archaeological Society and Moesgaard Museum.

Eidem, Jesper, and Flemming Højlund
   1993   "Trade or Diplomacy? Assyria and Dilmun in the Eighteenth Century BC." *World Archaeology* 24: 441–48.
   1997   "Assyria and Dilmun Revisited." Pp. 25–31 in H. Waetzoldt and H. Hauptmann (eds.), *Assyrien im Wandel der Zeiten: XXXIXe Rencontre assyriologique internationale, Heidelberg, 6.–10. Juli 1992.* Heidelberger Studien zum Alten Orient 6. Heidelberg: Heidelberger Orientverlag.

Englund, Robert
   1983   "Dilmun in the Archaic Uruk Corpus." Pp. 35–37 in D. T. Potts (ed.), *Dilmun: New Studies in the Archaeology and Early History of Bahrain.* Berliner Beiträge zum Vorderen Orient 2. Berlin: Dietrich Reimer.

Falkenstein, Adam
   1964   "Sumerische religiöse Texte. 5. Enki und die Weltordnung." *Zeitschrift für Assyriologie* 56: 44–113.

Ferwerda, G. T.
   1985   *A Contribution to the Early Isin Craft Archive.* TLB/SLB 5. Leiden: Nederlands Instituut voor het Nabije Oosten.

Foster, Benjamin R.
   1982   *Umma in the Sargonic Period.* Memoirs of the Connecticut Academy of Arts and Sciences 20. Hamden CT: Archon.
   1997   "A Sumerian Merchant's Account of the Dilmun Trade." *Acta Sumerologica* 19: 53–62.

Frachetti, Michael D.
   2008   *Pastoralist Landscapes and Social Interaction in Bronze Age Eurasia.* Berkeley: University of California Press.

Franke, Ute
   2011   "Zwischen Euphrat und Indus: die Arabische Halbinsel von 3500–1700 v. Chr." Pp. 72–82 in U. Franke and J. Gierlichs (eds.), *Roads of Arabia. Archäologische Schätze aus Saudi-Arabien.* Tübingen: Ernst Wasmuth.

Frayne, Douglas R.
    1990   *Old Babylonian Period (2003–1595 BC)*. The Royal Inscriptions of Mesopotamia, Early Periods 4. Toronto: University of Toronto Press.
    1993   *Sargonic and Gutian Periods (2334–2113 BC)*. The Royal Inscriptions of Mesopotamia, Early Periods 2. Toronto: University of Toronto Press.
    1997   *Ur III Period (2112–2004 BC)*. The Royal Inscriptions of Mesopotamia, Early Periods 3/2. Toronto: University of Toronto Press.
    2008   *Presargonic Period (2700–2350 BC)*. The Royal Inscriptions of Mesopotamia, Early Periods 1. Toronto: University of Toronto Press)

Frenez, Dennes
    forthcoming   "Ancient Oman and the Indus Civilization External Trade." To appear in the 2nd English edition of S. Cleuziou and M. Tosi (eds.), *In the Shadow of the Ancestors: The Prehistoric Foundation of the Early Arabian Civilization in Oman*. Sultanate of Oman: Ministry of Heritage and Culture.

Frifelt, Karen
    1971   "Jamdat Nasr Graves in the Oman." *Kuml* 19: 355–83.
    1980   "'Jemdet Nasr Graves' on the Oman Peninsula." Pp. 273–80 in B. Alster (ed.), *Death in Mesopotamia. Papers read at the XXVIe Rencontre Assyriologique Internationale*. Copenhagen Studies in Assyriology 8. Copenhagen: Akademisk.
    1991   *The Island of Umm an-Nar. Volume 1: Third Millennium Graves*. Jutland Archaeological Society Publications 26:1. Aarhus: Aarhus University Press.
    1995   *The Island of Umm an-Nar. Volume 2: The Third Millennium Settlement*. Jutland Archaeological Society Publications 26:2. Aarhus: Aarhus University Press.

Gagnaison, Cyril, Pascal Barrier and Sophie Méry
    2004   "Extractions de calcaires éocènes à l'Age du Bronze et architecture funéraire à Hili (Emirat d'Abou Dhabi." *Revue d'Archéométrie* 28: 97–108.

Gibson, McGuire
    1976   "The Nippur Expedition." Pp. 22–29 in *The Oriental Institute of the University of Chicago Annual Reports 1975/76*. Chicago: The Oriental Institute of the University of Chicago.

Glassner, Jean-Jacques
    1996a   "The Bronze Age Complex Societies of Eastern Arabia: a Survey of the Cuneiform Sources." Pp. 155–58 in G. Afanas'ev, S. Cleuziou, J. R. Lukacs, and M. Tosi (eds.), *The Prehistory of Asia and Oceania, XIII International Congress of Prehistoric and Protohistoric Sciences, Forlì, Italia, 8–14 Sept. 1996*. Series Colloquia 16. Forlì: A.B.A.C.O. Edizioni.
    1996b   "Dilmun, Magan, and Meluhha: Some Observations on the Language, Toponymy, Anthroponymy and Theonymy." Pp. 235–50 in J. Reade (ed.), *The Indian Ocean in Antiquity*. London: Kegan Paul.
    2002   "Dilmun et Magan: Le peuplement, l'organisation politique, la question des Amorrites et la place de l'écriture. Point de vue de l'assyriologue." Pp. 337–81 in S. Cleuziou, M. Tosi, and J. Zarins (eds.), *Essays on the Late Prehistory of the Arabian Peninsula*. Rome: Istituto Italiano per l'Africa e l'Oriente.

Glennie, K. W.
    2001   "Evolution of the Emirates' Land Surface: An Introduction." Pp. 9–27 in P. Hellyer and I. al-Abed (eds.), *United Arab Emirates. A New Perspective*. London: Trident.

Golding, Marny
    1974   "Evidence for Pre-Seleucid Occupation of Eastern Arabia." *Proceedings of the Seminar for Arabian Studies* 4: 19–32.

Gouin, P.
    1991   "Râpes, jarres et faisselles: la production et l'exportation des produits laitiers dans l'Indus du 3 millénaire." *Paléorient* 16/2: 37–54.

Grave, P., D. T. Potts, N. Yassi, W. Reade, and G. Bailey
    1996   "Elemental Characterisation of Barbar Ceramics from Tell Abraq." *Arabian Archaeology and Epigraphy* 7: 177–87.
Green, M. W.
    1984   "Early Sumerian Tax Collectors." *Journal of Cuneiform Studies* 36: 93–95.
Gregoricka, L. A.
    2014   "Human Response to Climate Change during the Umm an-Nar/Wadi Suq Transition in the United Arab Emirates." *International Journal of Osteoarchaeology* doi: 10.1002/oa.2409
Groneberg, Brigitte
    1992   "Mari et le Golfe Arabico-Persique." Pp. 69–80 in J.-M. Durand (ed.), *Florilegium Marianum. Recueil d'études en l'honneur de Michel Fleury*. Mémoires de N.A.B.U. 1. Paris: SEPOA.
Hallo, William W., and Briggs Buchanan
    1965   "A 'Persian Gulf' Seal on an Old Babylonian Mercantile Agreement." Pp. 199–209 in H. G. Güterbock and T. Jacobsen (eds.), *Studies in Honor of Benno Landsberger on His Seventy-Fifth Birthday, April 21, 1965*. Assyriological Studies 16. Chicago: The University of Chicago Press.
Hauptmann, Andreas
    1985   *5000 Jahre Kupfer in Oman, Bd. 1: Die Entwicklung der Kupfermetallurgie vom 3. Jahrtausend bis zur Neuzeit, Der Anschnitt*. Beiheft 4. Bochum: Die Vereinigung der Freunde von Kunst und Kultur in Bergbau.
Heimpel, Wolfgang
    1987   "Das Untere Meer." *Zeitschrift für Assyriologie* 77: 22–99.
    2011   "Twenty-Eight Trees Growing in Sumer." Pp. 75–152 in D. I. Owen (ed.), *Garšana Studies*. Cornell University Studies in Assyriology and Sumerology 6. Bethesda, MD: CDL.
Heinemeier, Jan, and Flemming Højlund
    2016   "Radiocarbon Chronology." Pp. 239–50 in F. Højlund and A. Abu-Laban (eds.), *Tell F6 on Failaka Island: Kuwaiti-Danish Excavations 2008–2012*. Jutland Archaeological Society Publications 92. Aarhus: Kuwaiti National Council for Culture, Arts and Letters / Jutland Archaeological Society and Moesgaard Museum.
Hilton, Anna
    2016   "Stone vessels." Pp. 164–75 in F. Højlund and A. Abu-Laban (eds.), *Tell F6 on Failaka Island: Kuwaiti-Danish Excavations 2008–2012*. Jutland Archaeological Society Publications 92. Aarhus: Kuwaiti National Council for Culture, Arts and Letters / Jutland Archaeological Society and Moesgaard Museum.
Højlund, Flemming
    1987   *Failaka/Dilmun: The Second Millennium Settlements. The Bronze Age Pottery*. Højbjerg: Jutland Archaeological Society.
    1989a   "The Formation of the Dilmun State and the Amorite Tribes." *Proceedings of the Seminar for Arabian Studies* 19: 45–59.
    1989b   "Dilmun and the Sealand." *Northern Akkad Project Reports* 2: 9–12.
    1994   "Pottery from the Pre-Barbar and Barbar Periods (I–II)." Pp. 73–178 in F. Højlund and H. H. Andersen (eds.), *Qala'at al-Bahrain. The Northern City Wall and the Islamic Fortress*. Aarhus: Jutland Archaeological Society.
    1999   "Qal'at al-Bahrain in the Bronze Age." Pp. 73–76 in P. Lombard and K. al-Sindi (eds.), *Bahrain: the Civilisation of the Two Seas*. Ghent: Institute du Monde Arabe.
    2007   *The Burial Mounds of Bahrain — Social Complexity in Early Dilmun*. Aarhus: Jutland Archaeological Society.
    2012   "The Dilmun Temple on Failaka, Kuwait." *Arabian Archaeology and Epigraphy* 23: 165–73.

2013a   "Dilmun: Beyond the Southern Frontier of Mesopotamia." Pp. 541–47 in S. Bergerbrant and S. Sabatini (eds.), *Counterpoint: Essays in Archaeology and Heritage Studies in Honour of Professor Kristian Kristiansen*. BAR International Series 2508. Oxford: Archaeopress.

2013b   "The Stone Quarry on Jiddah Island, Bahrain." *Arabian Archaeology and Epigraphy* 24: 174–76.

2016   "Pottery." Pp. 93–128 in F. Højlund and A. Abu-Laban (eds.), *Tell F6 on Failaka Island: Kuwaiti-Danish Excavations 2008–2012*. Jutland Archaeological Society Publications 92. Aarhus: Kuwaiti National Council for Culture, Arts and Letters / Jutland Archaeological Society and Moesgaard Museum.

Forthcoming   "Transformations of the Dilmun State, c. 2050–1600 BC." Paper presented at the conference *Twenty Years of Bahrain Archaeology (1986–2006) 9th–13th December 2007, Bahrain*. To appear in the proceedings of the conference.

Højlund, Flemming, and Aiysha Abu-Laban

2016   *Tell F6 on Failaka Island — Kuwaiti-Danish Excavations 2008–2012*. Jutland Archaeological Society Publications 92. Aarhus: Kuwaiti National Council for Culture, Arts and Letters / Jutland Archaeological Society and Moesgaard Museum.

Højlund, Flemming, and H. Hellmuth Andersen

1994   *Qala'at al-Bahrain — The Northern City Wall and the Islamic Fortress*. Højbjerg: Jutland Archaeological Society.

1997   *Qala'at al-Bahrain — The Central Monumental Buildings*. Højbjerg: Jutland Archaeological Society.

Højlund, Flemming, Anna S. Hilton, Christian Juel, Nanna Kirkeby, Steffen T. Laursen, and Lars E. Nielsen

2008   "Late Third-Millennium Elite Burials in Bahrain." *Arabian Archaeology and Epigraphy* 19: 143–154.

Hunger, Hermann

2009   "How Uncertain Is the Mesopotamian Chronology?" Pp. 145–52 in D. A. Warburton (ed.), *Time's Up! — Dating the Minoan Eruption of Santorini: Acts of the Minoan Eruption Chronology Workshop*, Monographs of the Danish Institute at Athens 10. Aarhus: Aarhus University Press.

Ippolitoni-Strika, Fiorella

1986   "The Tarut Statue as a Peripheral Contribution to the Knowledge of Early Mesopotamian Plastic Art." Pp. 311–24 in H. A. Al Khalifa and M. Rice (eds.), *Bahrain Though the Ages: The Archaeology*. London: KPI.

Jacobsen, Thorkild

1953   "On the Textile Industry at Ur under Ibbi-Sîn." Pp. 172–87 in *Studia Orientalia Ioanni Pedersen . . . dedicata*. Copenhagen: E. Munksgaard.

Johnstone, Paul

1980   *The Sea-Craft of Prehistory*. London: Routledge & Kegan Paul.

Kamoonpuri, Hasan

2010   "Mangrove Forests Add to Scenic Beauty; Promote Fishery, Forestry." *Oman Daily Observer*, Friday 15, October 2010.

Kenoyer, Jonathan M.

1998   *Ancient Cities of the Indus Valley Civilization*. Karachi: American Institute of Pakistan Studies.

2008   "Indus and Mesopotamian Trade Networks: New Insights from Shell and Carnelian Artifacts." Pp. 19–28 in E. Olijdam and R. H. Spoor (eds.), *Intercultural Relations between South and Southwest Asia: Studies in Commemoration of E.C.L. During Caspers (1934–1996)*. Society for Arabian Studies Monographs 7. BAR International Series 1826. Oxford: Archaeopress.

Kjærum, Poul

1980   "Seals of the 'Dilmun Type' from Failaka, Kuwait." *Proceedings of the Seminars for Arabian Studies* 10: 45–54.

1983   *Failaka/Dilmun. The Second Millennium Settlements, vol. 1: The Stamp and Cylinder Seals: Plates and Catalogue Descriptions.* Jutland Archaeological Society Publications 17. Aarhus: Jysk arkæologisk selskab.

1991   "The Ships of Dilmun." *FOLK – Journal of the Danish Ethnographic Society* 33: 137–47.

1994   "Stamp-seals, Seal Impressions and Seal Blanks." Pp. 319–50 in F. Højlund and H. H. Andersen (eds.), *Qala'at al-Bahrain — The Northern City Wall and the Islamic Fortress.* Aarhus: Jutland Archaeological Society.

Kohl, Philip L.

1978   "The Balance of Trade in Southwestern Asia in the Mid-Third Millennium B.C. *Current Anthropology* 19: 463–92

1979   "The 'World-Economy' of West Asia in the Third Millennium BC." In M. Tosi (ed.), *South Asian Archaeology 1977: Papers from the Fourth International Conference of the Association of South Asian Archaeologists in Western Europe Held in the Istituto Universitario Orientale, Naples.* Naples: Istituto Universitario Orientale.

1986   "The Lands of Dilmun: Changing Cultural and Economic Relations during the Third to Early Second Millennia B.C." Pp. 367–75 in H. A. Al Khalifa and M. Rice (eds.), *Bahrain through the Ages: The Archaeology.* London: KPI.

2001   "Reflections on the Production of Chlorite at Tepe Yahya: 25 Years Later." Pp. 209–30 in C. C. Lamberg-Karlovsky and D. T. Potts (eds.), *Excavations at Tepe Yahya, Iran 1967–1975: The Third Millennium,* American Schools of Prehistoric Research Bulletin 45. Cambridge MA: Peabody Museum of Archaeology and Ethnology, Harvard University.

2006   "The Materiality of History: Reflections on the Strengths of the Archaeological Record." Pp. 327–38 in N. Yoffee and B. L. Crowell (eds.), *Excavating Asian History: Interdisciplinary Studies in Archaeology and History.* Tuscon: University of Arizona Press.

Koliński, Robert

2012   "Generation Counts at Tell Arbid, Sector P." Pp. 109–28 in H. Weiss (ed.), *Seven Generations since the Fall of Akkad.* Studia Chaburensia 3. Wiesbaden: Harrassowitz.

Læssøe, Jørgen

1958   "A Cuneiform Inscription from the Island of Bahrain." *Kuml* 1957: 164–66.

Lamberg-Karlovsky, C. C.

1970   *Excavations at Tepe Yahya 1967–69. Progress Report 1.* American School of Prehistoric Research Bulletin 27. Cambridge MA: Peabody Museum of Archaeology and Ethnology, Harvard University.

Landsberger, Benno

1954   "Assyrische Königsliste und 'Dunkles Zeitalter'." *Journal of Cuneiform Studies* 8: 47–73.

1962   *The Fauna of Ancient Mesopotamia, Second Part,* MSL VIII/2. Rome: Pontificium Institutum Biblicum.

1966   "Einige unerkannt gebliebene oder verkannte Nomina im Akkadischen." *Die Welt des Orients* 3: 246–68.

Langdon, Stephen

1931   "A New Factor in the Problem of Sumerian Origins." *Journal of the Royal Asiatic Society* 63: 593–96.

Laursen, Steffen T.

2008   "Early Dilmun and Its Rulers: New Evidence of the Burial Mounds of the Elite and the Development of Social Complexity, c. 2200–1750 BC." *Arabian Archaeology and Epigraphy* 19: 156–67.

2009   "The Decline of Magan and the Rise of Dilmun: Umm an-Nar Ceramics from the Burial Mounds of Bahrain, c. 2250–2000 BC." *Arabian Archaeology and Epigraphy* 20: 134–55.

2010a   "The Westward Transmission of Indus Valley Sealing Technology: Origin and Development of the 'Gulf Type' Seal and Other Administrative Technologies in Early Dilmun, c. 2100–2000 BC." *Arabian Archaeology and Epigraphy* 21: 96–134.

2010b   "Rapid Urbanization and Cultural Heritage Management in Bahrain: Reconstructing the Original Distribution of Bronze Age Burial Mounds from a 1959 Aerial Photograph Archive." Pp. 207–14 in D. C. Cowley, R. A. Standring, and M. J. Abicht (eds.), *Landscapes Through the Lens – Aerial Photographs and Historic Environment.* Oxford: Oxbow.

2010c   "The Emergence of Mound Cemeteries in Early Dilmun: New Evidence of a Proto-Cemetery and its Genesis, c. 2050–2000 BC." Pp. 115–39 in L. Weeks (ed.), *Death and Burial in Arabia and Beyond: Multidisciplinary Perspectives,* Society for Arabian Studies Monographs 10. BAR International Series 2107. Oxford: Archaeopress.

2011   "Mesopotamian Ceramics from the Burial Mounds of Bahrain, c. 2250–1750 BC." *Arabian Archaeology and Epigraphy* 22: 32–47.

2013   "A Late Fourth- to Early Third-millennium Grave from Bahrain, c. 3100–2600 BC." *Arabian Archaeology and Epigraphy* 24: 125–33.

Forthcoming   "Reconstructing the World's Largest Mound Cemetery and Its 'Living' Population. Airphotographic Survey of the Burial Mounds of Bahrain with Estimates of the Average Size of the Population in Early Dilmun, c.2250–1800 BC." Paper submitted for publication in P. Lombard and K. Al-Sindi (eds.), *Proceedings of the Conference "20 Years of Bahrain Archaeology, 1986–2006."*

In preparation a   *The 'Royal' Mounds of A'ali, Bahrain: The Emergence of Kingship in Early Dilmun.*

In preparation b   "Seals and Sealing Technology in the Dilmun Culture: The Post Harappan Life of the Indus Valley Sealing Tradition." Accepted for publication in G. Jamison and M. Ameri (eds.), *Small Windows: New Approaches to the Study of Seals and Sealing as Tools of Identity, Political Organization and Administration in the Ancient World.* Cambridge: Cambridge University Press.

Laursen, Steffen T., and K. L. Johansen
2007   "The Potential of Aerial Photographs in Future Studies of Mound Cemeteries." Pp. 137–48 in F. Højlund (ed.), *The Burial Mounds of Bahrain – Social Complexity in Early Dilmun.* Højbjerg: Jutland Archaeological Society.

Leemans, W. F.
1960   *Foreign Trade in the Old Babylonian Period, as Revealed by the Texts from Southern Mesopotamia.* Leiden: Brill.

Lombard, Pierre
2014   *Qal'at al-Bahrain Site Museum.* Manama, Kingdom of Bahrain: Ministry of Culture.

Lowe, Anthony
1986   "Bronze Age Burial Mounds on Bahrain." *Iraq* 48: 73–84.

Mackay, E. J. H.
1925   "Sumerian Connections with Ancient India." *Journal of the Royal Asiatic Society* 11: 697–701.

Maekawa, Kazuya
2016   "Susa and Girsu-Lagaš in the Ur III Period." Pp. 53–91 in K. Maekawa (ed.), *Ancient Iran: New Perspectives from Archaeology and Cuneiform Studies. Proceedings of the International Colloquium Held at the Center for Eurasian Cultural Studies, Kyoto University, December 6–7, 2014.* Ancient Text Studies in the National Museum, vol. 2. Kyoto.

Maekawa, Kazuya, and Wakaha Mori
2011   "Dilmun, Magan and Meluhha in Early Mesopotamian History: 2500–1600 BC." Pp. 245–69 in T. Osada and M. Witzel (eds.), *Cultural Relations between the Indus and the Iranian Plateau during the Third Millenium BCE: Indus Project, Research Institute for Humanities and Nature, June 7–8, 2008.* Harvard Oriental Series, Opera minora 7. Cambridge MA: Department of South Asian Studies, Harvard University.

Maigret, Alessandro de
1980   "Riconsiderazioni sul system ponderal di Ebla." *Oriens Antiquus* 19: 161–69.

Makowski, Maciej
2013   "Tumulus Grave SQM 49 (As-Sabbiya, Kuwait. Preliminary Report on the Investigations in 2009–2010." Pp. 518–27 in I. Zych (ed.), *Polish Archaeology in the Mediterranean XXII. Annual reports of the Polish Centre of Mediterranean Archaeology, University of Warsaw.* Warsaw: University of Warsaw Press.

Marchesi, Gianni
2011   "Goods from the Queen of Tilmun." Pp. 189–99 in G. Barjamovic, J. L. Dahl, U. S. Koch, W. Sommerfeld, and J. G. Westenholz (eds.), *Akkade is King: A Collection of Papers by Friends and Colleagues Presented to Aage Westenholz on the Occasion of His 70th birthday 15th of May 2009.* PIHANS CXVIII. Leiden: Nederlands Instituut voor het Nabije Oosten.
2014a   "Tilmun (Dilmun). A. Philologisch. Name of a Country and a City in the Gulf Region." *Reallexikon der Assyriologie und vorderasiatischen Archäologie* 14/1–2: 52–54. Berlin: De Gruyter.
2014b   "From Sumerian Grammar to Tilmun's Taxes: Interpreting é GÚ kar-ra kalam-ma-ka in the *Enki and Ninsikila* Myth." *Kaskal* 11: 47–56.
Forthcoming   "Inscriptions from the Royal Mounds of Aꞌali (Bahrain) and Related Texts."

Marchesi, Gianni, and Nicolò Marchetti
2011   *Royal Statuary of Early Dynastic Mesopotamia,* Mesopotamian Civilizations 14. Winona Lake, IN: Eisenbrauns.

Masry, Abdullah H.
1974   *Prehistory in Northeastern Arabian: The Problem of Interregional Interaction.* Miami: Field Research Projects.

Matthews, Roger
2002   "Zebu: Harbingers of Doom in Bronze Age Western Asia?." *Antiquity* 76: 438–46.

McCown, Donald E., and Richard C. Haines
1967   *Nippur I, Temple of Enlil, Scribal Quarter, and Soundings,* Oriental Institute Publications 78. Chicago: The University of Chicago Press.

Mehta, Prakash, and Sonu Mehta
2007   *Cultural Heritage of Indian Tribes.* New Delhi: Discovery Publishing House.

Méry, Sophie
1996   "Ceramic Patterns of Exchange Across the Arabian Sea and the Persian Gulf in the Early Bronze Age." Pp. 167–79 in G. Afanas'ev, S. Cleuziou, J. R. Lukacs, and M. Tosi (eds.), *The Prehistory of Asia and Oceania, XIII International Congress of Prehistoric and Protohistoric Sciences, Forlì, Italia, 8–14 sept. 1996.* Series Colloquia 16. Forlì: A.B.A.C.O. Edizioni.
2000   *Les céramiques d'Oman et l'Asie moyenne : une archéologie des échanges à l'Age du Bronze.* Monographie du CRA 23. Paris: CNRS.
2013   "The First Oases in Eastern Arabia: Society and Craft Technology, in the 3rd Millennium BC at Hili, United Arab Emirates." *Revue d'ethnoécologie* 4: 2–17.

Méry, Sophie, and J. M. Blackman
2004   "Socio-economic Patterns of a Ceramic Container: the Harappan Black Slipped Jar." Pp. 226–36 in C. Jarrige and V. Lefévre (eds.), *South Asian Archaeology 2001, vol. I: Prehistory.* Paris: Recherche sur les Civilizations.

Michalowski, Piotr
1988   "Magan and Meluhha Once Again." *Journal of Cuneiform Studies* 40: 156–64.

Millard, A. R.
1973   "Cypriot Copper in Babylonia, c. 1745 B.C." *Journal of Cuneiform Studies* 25: 211–14.

Molina, Manuel J.
2014   *Sargonic Tablets in the Real Academia de la Historia. The Carl L. Lippmann Collection.* Madrid: Real Academia de la Historia.

Mortensen, Peder
  1970   "On the Date of the Temples at Barbar in Bahrain." *Kuml* 1970: 393–98.
Mutin, Benjamin
  2012   "Cultural Dynamics in Southern Middle-Asia in the Fifth and Fourth Millennia BC: A Recon-
         struction Based on Ceramic Tradition." *Paléorient* 38: 159–84.
Mynors, H. S.
  1983   "An Analysis of Mesopotamian Ceramics Using Petrographic and Neutron Activations Analysis."
         Pp. 377–87 in *Proceedings of the 22nd Symposium of Archaeometry.* Bradford: University of Bradford.
Nashef, Khaled
  1986   "The Deities of Dilmun." Pp. 340–66 in H. A. Al Khalifa and M. Rice (eds.), *Bahrain through the
         Ages: The Archaeology.* London: KPI.
Oates, Joan, T. E. Davidson, D. Kamilli, and H. McKerrel
  1977   "Seafaring Merchants of Ur?" *Antiquity* 51: 221–34.
Oppenheim, Leo A.
  1954   "The Seafaring Merchants of Ur." *Journal of the American Oriental Society* 74: 6–17.
Parker, Adrian G.
  2009   "Developing a Framework for Hominin Dispersal over the Last 350 ka." Pp. 39–49 in M. D. Petra-
         glia and J. I. Rose (eds.), *The Evolution of Human Populations in Arabia: Paleoenvironments, Prehistory
         and Genetics.* Dordrecht: Springer.
Parker, Adrian G., and Andrew S. Goudie
  2008   "Geomorphological and Palaeoenvironmental Investigations in the Southeastern Arabian Gulf
         Region and the Implications for the Archaeology of the Region." *Geomorphology* 101: 458–70.
Parker, Adrian G., A. S. Goudie, S. Stokes, K. White, M. Hodson, M. Manning, and D. Kenneth
  2006   "A Record of Holocene Climate Change from Lake Geochemical Analysis in South-Eastern Ara-
         bia." *Quaternary Research* 66: 465–76.
Parpola, Asko
  1994   "Harappan Inscriptions." Pp. 304–15 in F. Højlund and H. H. Andersen (eds.), *Qala'at al-Bahrain
         — The Northern City Wall and the Islamic Fortress.* Aarhus: Jutland Archaeological Society.
Parpola, Simo, Asko Parpola, and Robert H. Brunswig, Jr.
  1977   "The Meluhha Village: Evidence of Acculturation of Harappan Traders in Late Third Millennium
         Mesopotamia?" *Journal of the Economic and Social History of the Orient* 20: 129–65.
Pettinato, Giovanni
  1981   *The Archives of Ebla: An Empire Inscribed in Clay.* New York: Doubleday.
Peyronel, Luca
  2006   "Sailing the Lower Sea: The Oldest Roots of the Lands of Dilmun and Magan." Pp. 445–87 in
         F. Baffi, R. Dolce, S. Mazzoni, and F. Pinnock (eds.), *Ina Kibrat Erbetti: Studi di archaeologia orientale
         dedicati a Paolo Matthiae.* Roma: Università La Sapienza.
  2008   "Some Thoughts on Iconographic Relations between the Arabian Gulf and Syria-Mesopotamia
         during the Middle Bronze Age." Pp. 236–52 in E. Olijdam and R. H. Spoor (eds.), *Intercultural
         Relations between South and Southwest Asia. Studies in Commemoration of E.C.L. During Caspers
         (1934–1996).* Society for Arabian Studies Monographs 7. BAR International Series 1826. Oxford:
         Archaeopress.
Pézard, Maurice
  1914   *Mission à Bender-Bouchir,* Publications de la Mission archéologique de Perse 15. Paris: E. Leroux.
Piesinger, Constance M.
  1983   *Legacy of Dilmun: The Roots of Ancient Maritime Trade in Eastern Coastal Arabia in the 4th/3rd Millen-
         nium B.C.* Unpublished PhD dissertation, University of Wisconsin-Madison.

Pittman, Holly
  2016   "Mesopotamian Cylinder Seals." Pp. 157–61 in F. Højlund and A. Abu-Laban (eds.), *Tell F6 on Failaka Island: Kuwaiti-Danish Excavations 2008–2012.* Jutland Archaeological Society Publications 92. Aarhus: Kuwaiti National Council for Culture, Arts and Letters / Jutland Archaeological Society and Moesgaard Museum.

Pomponio, Francesco
  1980   "AO 7754 ed il sistema ponderale di Ebla" *Oriens Antiquus* 29: 171–86.

Possehl, George L., Christopher P. Thornton, and Charlot M. Cable
  2009   "Bat 2009: A Report from the American Team." Unpublished research report to the Oman Ministry of Heritage and Culture.

Potter, Lawrence G.
  2014a   "Introduction." Pp. 1–20 in L. G. Potter (ed.), *The Persian Gulf in Modern Times: People, Ports, and History.* New York: Palgrave Macmillan.
  2014b   "The Rise and Fall of Port Cities in the Persian Gulf." Pp. 131–52 in L. G. Potter (ed.), *The Persian Gulf in Modern Times: People, Ports, and History.* New York: Palgrave Macmillan.

Potts, Daniel T.
  1983   "Dilmun: Where and When?" *Dilmun: Journal of the Bahrain Historical and Archaeological Society* 11: 15–19.
  1986a   "Ǧamdat Naṣr Period or Regional Style?" Pp. 121–70 in U. Finkbeiner and W. Röllig (eds.), *Papers Given at a Symposium Held in Tübingen, November 1983.* Wiesbaden: Ludwig Reichert.
  1986b   "The Booty of Magan." *Oriens Antiquus* 25: 271–85.
  1986c   "Nippur and Dilmun in the 14th Century B.C." *Proceedings of the Seminar for Arabian Studies* 1985: 169–74.
  1989   *Miscellanea Hasaitica.* Copenhagen: University of Copenhagen, Museum Tusculanum Press.
  1990a   *The Arabian Gulf in Antiquity.* Oxford: Clarendon.
  1990b   *A Prehistoric Mound in the Emirate of Umm al-Quiwain, U.A.E.: Excavations at Tell Abraq in 1989.* Copenhagen: Munksgaard.
  1991   *Further Excavations at Tell Abraq, The 1990 Season.* Copenhagen: Munksgaard.
  1993   "Rethinking Some Aspects of Trade in the Arabian Gulf." *World Archaeology* 24: 423–40.
  1995   "Watercraft of the Lower Sea." Pp. 559–71 in U. Finkbeiner, R. Dittmann, and H. Hauptmann (eds.), *Beiträge zur Kulturgeschichte Vorderasiens: Festschrift für Rainer Michael Boehmer.* Mainz: Phillip von Zabern.
  1997   *Mesopotamian Civilization: The Material Foundations.* Ithaca, NY: Cornell University Press.
  2000   *Ancient Magan — The Secrets of Tell Abraq.* London: Trident.
  2002   "Total Prestation in Marhashi-Ur Relations." *Iranica Antiqua* 37: 343–53.
  2005   "In the Beginning: Marhashi and the Origins of Magan's Ceramic Industry in the Third Millennium BC." *Arabian Archaeology and Epigraphy* 16: 67–78.
  2014   *Nomadism in Iran: From Antiquity to the Modern Era.* Oxford: Oxford University Press.

Potts, Timothy F.
  1989   "Foreign Stone Vessels of the Late Third Millennium B.C. from Southern Mesopotamia: Their Origins and Mechanisms of Exchange." *Iraq* 51: 123–64.
  1994   *Mesopotamia and the East: An Archaeological and Historical Study of Foreign Relations c. 3400–2000 B.C.* Monograph 37. Oxford: Oxford University Committee for Archaeology.

Rao, Shri R.
  1963   "A 'Persian Gulf' Seal from Lothal." *Antiquity* 37: 96–99.

Rashid, Subhi A.
  1972   "Eine frühdynastische Statue von der Insel Tarut im Persischen Golf." Pp. 159–66 in D. O. Edzard (ed.), *Gesellschaftsklassen im Alten Zweistromland und in den Angrenzenden Gebieten, XVIII Rencontre*

assyriologique internationale, München, 29. Juni bis 3. Juli 1970. Bayerische Akademie der Wissenshaften, Phil.-Hist. Klasse, Abhandlungen N.F. 75. Munich: Verlag der Bayerischen Akademie der Wissenschaften.

Ratnagar, Shereen
2004   *Trading Encounters: From the Euphrates to the Indus in the Bronze Age.* 2nd ed. Oxford: Oxford University Press.

Reade, Julian
1995   "Magan and Meluhha Merchants at Ur?" Pp. 597–600 in U. Finkbeiner, R. Dittmann, and H. Hauptmann (eds.), *Beiträge zur Kulturgeschichte Vorderasiens: Festschrift für Rainer Michael Boehmer.* Mainz: Philipp von Zabern.
2008   "The Indus-Mesopotamia Relationship Reconsidered." Pp. 12–18 in E. Olijdam and R. H. Spoor (eds.), *Intercultural Relations between South and Southwest Asia: Studies in Commemoration of E.C.L. During Caspers (1934–1996).* Society for Arabian Studies Monographs 7. BAR International Series 1826. Oxford: Archaeopress.

Reiche, Andrzej
2013   "Tumulus Graves SQM 30 in As-Sabbiya – Mugheira. Northern Kuwait. A Report on the 2007–2008 Investigations." Pp. 528–41 in I. Zych (ed.), *Polish Archaeology in the Mediterranean XXII. Annual Reports of the Polish Centre of Mediterranean Archaeology, University of Warsaw.* Warsaw: University of Warsaw Press.

Risso, Patricia
1986   *Oman & Muscat: An Early Modern History.* London: Croom Helm.

Rose, Jeffrey I.
2010   "New Light on Human Prehistory in the Arabo-Persian Gulf Oasis." *Current Anthropology* 51: 849–83.

Roaf, Michel
1976   "Excavations at al-Markh, Bahrain." *Proceedings of the Seminar for Arabian Studies* 6: 144–60.
1982   "Weights on the Dilmun Standard." *Iraq* 44: 137–41.

Rutkowski, Łukasz
2013   "Tumuli Graves and Desert Wells in the As-Sabbiya Preliminary Excavation Report on the Spring Season in 2010." Pp. 493–517 in I. Zych (ed.), *Polish Archaeology in the Mediterranean XXII. Annual Reports of the Polish Centre of Mediterranean Archaeology, University of Warsaw.* Warsaw: University of Warsaw Press.

Salvatori, Sandro
2008   "A New Cylinder Seal from Ancient Margiana: Cultural Exchange and Syncretism in a 'World Wide Trade System' at the End of the Third Millennium BC." Pp. 111–18 in S. Salvatori and M. Tosi (eds.), *The Bronze Age and Early Iron Age in the Margiana Lowlands.* BAR International Series 1806. Oxford: Archaeopress.

Sarzec, Ernest de, and Léon A. Heuzey
1884–1912   *Découvertes en Chaldée.* Paris: E. Leroux.

Scheil, Vincent
1913   *Textes élamites-sémitiques, cinquième série.* Mémoires de la Mission archéologique de Susiane 14. Paris: E. Leroux.
1925   "Un nouveau sceau hindou pseudo-sumérien." *Revue d'assyriologie* 22: 55–56.

Schiettecatte, Jérémie, et al.
2014   *Preliminary Report: Third Season of the Saudi French Mission in al-Kharj, Province of Riyadh. 24 October–29 November 2013.* Unpublished report.

Selz, Gebhard
1995   *Untersuchungen zur Götterwelt des altsumerischen Stadtstaates von Lagaš.* Occasional Publications of the Samuel Noah Kramer Fund 13. Philadelphia: The University of Pennsylvania Museum.

Shaikh, Zeeshan A., Sila Tripati, and Vasant Shinde
  2012   "Study of Sewn Plank Built Boats in Goa." *International Journal of Nautical Archaeology* 41: 148–57.
Steible, Horst
  1991   *Die neusumerischen Bau- und Weihinschriften I–II.* Freiburger Altorientalische Studien 9. Stuttgart: Franz Steiner.
Steinkeller, Piotr
  1982   "The Question of Marhaši: A Contribution to the Historical Geography of Iran in the Third Millennium B.C." *Zeitschrift für Assyriologie* 72: 237–65.
  1987a   "The Foresters of Umma: Toward a Definition of Ur III Labor." Pp. 73–115 in M. A. Powell (ed.), *Labor in the Ancient Near East.* American Oriental Series 68. New Haven CT: American Oriental Society.
  1987b   "The Stone pirig-gùn." *Zeitschrift für Assyriologie* 77: 92–95.
  1988   "The Date of Gudea and His Dynasty." *Journal of Cuneiform Studies* 40: 47–53.
  1995   "Sheep and Goat Terminology in Ur III sources from Drehem." *Bulletin on Sumerian Agriculture* 8: 49–56.
  1999   "On Rulers, Priests and Sacred Marriage: Tracing the Evolution of Early Sumerian Kingship." Pp. 103–37 in K. Watanabe (ed.), *Priests and Officials in the Ancient Near East, Papers of the Second Colloquium on the Ancient Near East: The City and Its Life.* Heidelberg: C. Winter.
  2003   "Archival Practices at Babylonia in the Third Millennium." Pp. 37–58 in M. Brosius (ed.), *Ancient Archives and Archival Traditions: Concepts of Record-keeping in the Ancient World.* Oxford Studies in Ancient Documents 1. Oxford: Oxford University Press.
  2006   "City and Countryside in Third Millennium Southern Babylonia." Pp. 185–211 in Elizabeth C. Stone (ed.), *Settlement and Society: Essays Dedicated to Robert McCormick Adams.* Los Angeles: Cotsen Institute of Archaeology, University of California.
  2007   "New Light on Šimaški and Its Rulers." *Zeitschrift für Assyriologie* 97: 215–32.
  2010   "On the Location of the Towns of Ur-Zababa and Dimat-Enlil and on the Course of the Arḫatum." Pp. 369–82 in J. C. Fincke (ed.), *Festschrift for Gernot Wilhelm.* Dresden: ISLET.
  2012   "New Light on Marhaši and its Contacts with Makkan and Babylonia." Pp. 261–74 in J. Giraud and G. Gernez (eds.), *Aux marges de l'archéologie: Hommage à Serge Cleuziou.* Travaux de la Maison René-Ginouvès 16. Paris: De Boccard.
  2013a   "Trade Routes and Commercial Networks in the Persian Gulf during the Third Millennium BC." Pp. 413–31 in C. Faizee (ed.), *Collection of Papers Presented at the Third International Biennial Conference of the Persian Gulf (History, Culture, and Civilization.* Tehran: University of Tehran Press.
  2013b   "Puzur-Inšušinak at Susa: A Pivotal Episode of Early Elamite History Reconsidered." Pp. 293–317 in K. De Graef and J. Tavernier (eds.), *Susa and Elam: Archaeological, Philological, Historical and Geographical Perspective: Proceedings of the International Congress Held at Ghent University, December 14–17, 2009.* Mémoires de la Délégation en Perse 58. Leiden: Brill.
  2014   "Marhaši and Beyond: The Jiroft Civilization in a Historical Perspective." Pp. 691–707 in C. C. Lamberg-Karlovsky and B. Genito (eds.), *"My Life is Like a Summer Rose": Marizio Tosi e l'Archaeologia Come Mode di Vivere. Papers in Honour of Maurizio Tosi for his 70th Birthday.* BAR International Series 2690. Oxford: Archaeopress.
  2015   "The Gutian Period in Chronological Perspective." Pp. 281–88 in W. Sallaberger and I. Schrakamp (eds.), *Arcane III. History and Philology.* Turnhout: Brepols.
  2016a   "The Role of Iran in the Inter-Regional Exchange of Metals: Tin, Copper, Silver and Gold in the Second Half of the Third Millennium BC." Pp. 127–50 in K. Maekawa (ed.), *Ancient Iran: New Perspectives from Archaeology and Cuneiform Studies. Proceedings of the International Colloquium Held at the Center for Eurasian Cultural Studies, Kyoto University, December 6–7, 2014.* Ancient Text Studies in the National Museum, vol. 2. Kyoto.

2016b   "Economic Growth in Early Mesopotamia: General Considerations and Some Specific Examples."
Unpublished paper read at the workshop "Economic Growth in Antiquity," Excellence Cluster
Topoi, Freie Universität Berlin, November 18–21, 2016.

Steinkeller, Piotr, and J. N. Postgate
1992   *Third Millennium Legal and Administrative Texts in the Iraq Museum, Baghdad.* Mesopotamian Civilizations 4. Winona Lake, IN: Eisenbrauns.

Teller, J. T., K. W. Glennie, N. Lancaster, and A. K Singhvi
2000   "Calcareous Dunes of the United Arab Emirates and Noah's Flood: The Postglacial Reflooding of
the Persian (Arabian) Gulf." *Quarternary International* 68–71 (2000): 297–308.

Tengberg, M., D. T. Potts, and H.-P. Francfort
2008   "The Golden Leaves of Ur." *Antiquity* 82: 925–36.

Thureau-Dangin, François
1925   "Sceaux de Tello et sceaux de Harappa." *Revue d'Assyriologie* 22: 99–101.

Uerpmann, Hans-Peter, and Margarethe Uerpmann
2008   "Trading Mesopotamian Sheep to the Lower Gulf and Beyond?." in E. Olijdam and R. H. Spoor
(eds.), *Intercultural Relations between South and Southwest Asia: Studies in Commemoration of E.C.L.
During Caspers (1934–1996)*, Society for Arabian Studies Monographs 7, BAR International Series
1826. Oxford: Archaeopress): 72–77.

Uerpmann, Margarethe
2003   "The Dark Millennium: Remarks on the Final Stone Age in the Emirates and Oman." Pp. 73–84
in D. T. Potts, H. A. Naboodah, and P. Hellyer (eds.), *Archaeology of the United Arab Emirates: Proceedings of the First International Conference on the Archaeology of the United Arab Emirates.* London:
Trident.

Van De Mieroop, Marc
1987   *Crafts in the Early Isin Period: A Study of the Isin Craft Archive from the Reigns of Išbi-Erra and Šū-ilišu.*
Orientalia Lovaniensia Analecta 24. Leuven: Departement Oriëntalistiek.

Van de Velde, Thomas
2016   "Bitumen Provenience." Pp. 214–20 in F. Højlund and A. Abu-Laban (eds.), *Tell F6 on Failaka Island: Kuwaiti-Danish Excavations 2008–2012.* Jutland Archaeological Society Publications 92. Aarhus: Kuwaiti National Council for Culture, Arts and Letters / Jutland Archaeological Society and
Moesgaard Museum.

Van de Velde, Thomas, Mike De Vrieze, Pieter Surmont, Samuel Bodé, and Philipp Drechsler
2015   "A Geochemical Study on the Bitumen from Dosariyah (Saudi-Arabia): Tracking Neolithic-period
Bitumen in the Persian Gulf." *Journal of Archaeological Science* 57: 248–56.

Vasoughi, Mohammad B.
2009   "The Kings of Hormuz: From the Beginning until the Arrival of the Portuguese." Pp. 89–104 in
L. G. Potter (ed.), *The Persian Gulf in History.* New York: Palgrave Macmillan.

Veldhuis, Niek
2001   "A Multiple Month Account from the Gu'abba Rest House." *Zeitschrift für Assyriologie* 91: 85–109.
2004   *Religion, Literature, and Scholarship: The Sumerian Composition Nanše and the Birds, with a Catalogue
of Sumerian Bird Names.* Cuneiform Monographs 22. Leiden: Brill.

Vermaak, Petrus S.
2008   "Guabba, the Meluhhan Village in Mesopotamia." *Journal for Semitics* 17/2: 454–71.

Vidale, Massimo
2004   "Growing in a Foreign World: For a History of the 'Meluhha Village' in Mesopotamia in the 3rd
Millennium BC." Pp. 261–80 in A. Panaino and A. Piras (eds.), *Proceedings of the Fourth Annual
Symposium of the Assyrian and Babylonian Intellectual Heritage Project.* Melammu Symposia 4. Milan:
Università di Bologna and ISIAO.

Vogt, Burkhard
  1998   "State, Problems and Perspectives of Second Millennium B.C. Funerary Studies in the Emirate of
          Ras al-Khaimah." Pp. 273–90 in C. S. Phillips, D. T. Potts, and S. Searight (eds.), *Arabia and Its
          Neighbours: Essays on Prehistorical and Historical Developments Presented in Honor of Beatrice de Cardi*,
          Abiel 2. Turnhout: Brepols.

Vosmer, Tom
  2008   "Shipping in the Bronze Age: How Large was a 60-gur Ship?" Pp. 230–35 in E. Olijdam and R. H.
          Spoor (eds.), *Intercultural Relations between South and Southwest Asia: Studies in Commemoration of
          E.C.L. During Caspers (1934–1996)*. Society for Arabian Studies Monographs 7. BAR Interna-
          tional Series 1826. Oxford: Archaeopress.
  2011   "The Jewel of Muscat: Reconstructing a Ninth-Century Sewn-Plank Boat." Pp. 121–35 in R. Krahl,
          J. Guy, J. K. Wilson, and J. Raby (eds.), *Shipwrecked: Tang Treasures and Monsoon Winds*. Washing-
          ton DC: Smithsonian Books.

Waetzoldt, Hartmut
  1972   *Untersuchungen zur neusumerischen Textilindustrie*. Studi Economici e Tecnologici 1. Rome: Centro
          per le antichità e la storia dell'arte del Vicino Oriente.

Wafar, Sayeeda, and A. G. Untawale
  2001   "Mangroves." Pp. 539–62 in R. Sen Gupta and E. Desa (eds.), *The Indian Ocean — A Perspective*,
          vol. 2. Lisse: A.A. Balkema.

Weeks, Lloyd R.
  2003   *Early Metallurgy of the Persian Gulf: Technology, Trade, and the Bronze Age World*. American School
          of Prehistoric Research Monograph Series 2. Leiden: Brill.
  2007   "Coals to Newcastle, Copper to Magan? Isotopic Analyses and the Persian Gulf Metals Trade." Pp.
          89–96 in S. LaNiece, D. Hook, and P. T. Craddock (eds.), *Metals and Mines: Studies in Archaeometal-
          lurgy*. London: Archetype.

Weisgerber, Gerd
  1981   "Mehr als Kupfer in Oman. Ergebnisse der Expedition 1981." *Der Anschnitt* 33: 174–263.

Weiss, Harvey
  2012   "Quantifying Collapse: The Late Third Millennium Khabur Plains." Pp. 1–24 in H. Weiss (ed.),
          Seven Generations Since the Fall of Akkad. Studia Chaburensia 3. Wiesbaden: Harrassowitz.

Weiss, Harvey, M. A. Courty, W. Wetterstrom, R. Meadow, F. Guichard, L. Senior, and A. Curnow
  1993   "The Genesis and Collapse of North Mesopotamian Civilization." *Science* vol. 261 no. 5124:
          995–1004.

Wilcke, Claus
  2011   "Eine Weihinschrift Gudeas von Lagaš mit altbabylonischen Übersetzung." Pp. 29–47 in A. R.
          George (ed.), *Cuneiform Royal Inscriptions and Related Texts in the Schøyen Collection*. Cornell Uni-
          versity Studies in Assyriology and Sumerology 17. Bethesda, MD: CDL.

Wilkinson, J. C.
  1973   "Arab-Persian Relationships in the Sasanid Oman." Pp. 40–51 in *Proceedings of the Sixth Seminar for
          Arabian Studies Held at the Institute of Archaeology, London, 27th and 28th September 1972*. London:
          Archaeopress.

Williamson, Andrew
  1973   "Hurmuz and the Trade of the Gulf in the 14th and 15th Centuries A.D." Pp. 52–68 in *Proceedings
          of the Sixth Seminar for Arabian Studies Held at the Institute of Archaeology, London, 27th and 28th
          September 1972*. London: Seminar for Arabian Studies.

Wright, Henry T.
   1981   "The Southern Margins of Sumer: Archaeological Survey of the Area of Eridu and Ur." Pp. 295–345 in R. McC. Adams, *Heartland of Cities: Surveys of Ancient Settlement and Land Use on the Central Floodplain of the Euphrates.* Chicago: The University of Chicago Press.

Wright, Rita P.
   2010   *The Ancient Indus: Urbanism, Economy, and Society.* Cambridge: Cambridge University Press.
   2016   "Konar Sandal South, Nindowari, and Lakhan Jo Daro: Beyond the Limits of a Known World." Pp. 25–35 in V. Widorn, U. Franke, and P. Latschenberger (eds.)., *Contextualizing Material Culture in South and Central Asia in Pre-Modern Times, South Asian Archaeology and Art.* Turnhout: Brepols.

Yang, Zhi
   1986   "A Study of the Sargonic Archive from Adab." Unpublished Ph.D. dissertation, University of Chicago.

Yule, Paul, and Ingeborg Guba
   2001   "Did the Ancient Mesopotamian Royal Stone Originate in Oman?" *Adumatu* 4 (2001): 41–52.

Zahed, Mohammad Ali, Fatemeh Rouhani, Soraya Mohajeri, Farshid Bateni, and Leila Mohajeri
   2010   "An Overview of Iranian Mangrove Ecosystems, Northern Part of the Persian Gulf and Oman Sea." *Acta Ecologica Sinica* 30: 240–44.

Zarins, Juris
   1978   "Steatite Vessels in the Riyadh Museum." *Atlal: The Journal of Saudi Arabian Archaeology* 2: 65–94.
   1986   "MAR-TU and the Land of Dilmun." Pp. 233–50 in H. A. Al Khalifa and M. Rice (eds.), *Bahrain Though the Ages: The Archaeology.* London: KPI.
   1989   "Eastern Saudi Arabia and External Relations: Selected Ceramic, Steatite and Textual Evidence — 3500–1900 B.C." Pp. 74–103 in K. Frifelt and P. Sørensen (eds.), *South Asian Archaeology 1985: Papers from the Eighth International Conference of South Asian Archaeologists in Western Europe, Held at Moesgaard Museum, Denmark, 1–5 July 1985,* Scandinavian Institute of Asian Studies, Occasional Papers 4. London: Curzon.
   2008   "Magan Shipbuilders at the Ur III Lagash State Dockyard (2062–2025 B.C.)." Pp. 209–29 in E. Olijdam and R. H. Spoor (eds.), *Intercultural Relations between South and Southwest Asia: Studies in Commemoration of E.C.L. During Caspers (1934–1996),* Society for Arabian Studies Monographs 7, BAR International Series 1826. Oxford: Archaeopress.

Zarins, Juris, Ali S. Mughannum, and Mahmoud Kamal
   1984   "Excavations at the Dhahran South – The Tumuli Field (208–92) 1403 A.H. 1983. A Preliminary Report." *Atlal: The Journal of Saudi Arabian Archaeology* 8: 25–54.

Ziegler, N.
   2008   "Tilmuniter im Königreich Samsî-Addus." Pp. 253–59 in E. Olijdam and R. H. Spoor (eds.), *Intercultural Relations between South and Southwest Asia: Studies in Commemoration of E.C.L. During Caspers (1934–1996).* Society for Arabian Studies Monographs 7. BAR International Series 1826. Oxford: Archaeopress.

Ziolkowski, Michele C.
   2001   "The Soft Stone Vessels from Sharm, Fujairah, United Arab Emirates." *Arabian Archaeology and Epigraphy* 12: 10–86.

Index